AN INTRODUCTION TO COURT INTERPRETING

Theory & Practice

Elena M. de Jongh

UNIVERSITY PRESS OF AMERICA

Lanham • New York • London

University Press of America®, Inc.
4720 Boston Way
Lanham, Maryland 20706

3 Henrietta Street
London WC2E 8LU England

Printed in the United States of America
British Cataloging in Publication Information Available

Typesetting: FIU Publications

Library of Congress Cataloging-in-Publication Data

De Jongh, Elena M.
An introduction to court interpreting : theory and practice /
Elena M. de Jongh.
p. cm.
Includes bibliographical references and index.
1. Courts—United States—Translating services. I. Title.
KF8725.D4 1992 347.73'01—dc20 92-243 CIP
[347.3071]

ISBN 0–8191–8610–4 (cloth : alk.paper)
ISBN 0–8191–8611–2 (pbk. : alk. paper)

The paper used in this publication meets the minimum requirements of American National Standard for Information Sciences—Permanence of Paper for Printed Library Materials, ANSI Z39.48–1984.

To my sons,

William and Edward

The opportunity to be heard must be tailored to the capabilities and circumstances of those who are to be heard.

Mr. Justice William J. Brennan, *Goldberg v. Kelly*

CONTENTS

CHAPTER 3: Defining the Terms

CHAPTER 4: Language and Culture

CHAPTER 5: Interpreting Nonstandard Language

CHAPTER 6: Interpreting in Court

CHAPTER 7: Court Interpreting as a Profession

PART II

PRACTICE

LIST OF TABLES

ACKNOWLEDGMENTS

I wish to acknowledge the support provided by the Florida Endowment Fund for Higher Education through a McKnight Junior Faculty Development Fellowship, by a Summer Research Grant from the Office of the Provost at Florida International University, and by a Small Grants Award from the Southern Regional Education Board.

I am indebted to many friends and colleagues for their help and encouragement, most particularly, to Julian C. Lee who carefully read the manuscript and whose valuable comments improved the text. My appreciation is likewise extended to John Jensen who made important suggestions to an early draft of the manuscript, and to fellow federally certified court interpreters who contributed to this project in various ways. Among them, María Juana Cazabon and Nelson Durán, both of whom reviewed portions of the book. I wish to express my appreciation to Faith Mesnekoff, Esq., Assistant Federal Public Defender, for her careful review of the sections in which legal proceedings are described.

I would also like to thank Tanya Saunders-Hamilton of the Center for Multilingual and Multicultural Studies at Florida International University for the valuable support rendered in the preparation of the manuscript. Special thanks go to Sandra Burnham and Irene Tomassini of the United States District Court for the Southern District of Florida, who facilitated access to audio tapes and court transcripts of trials as well as foreign language documents. To my parents, for their help and support, I extend my sincere appreciation.

PREFACE

This work presents an up-to-date treatment of the principal issues pertaining to court interpreting in the United States. It provides a synthesis of information regarding court interpreting, based upon a variety of published and unpublished sources, many of them obscure or otherwise difficult to access. The approach is by necessity interdisciplinary, dealing with languages in contact, bilingualism, dialectal varieties of language, the interpreting process, and legal issues.

It is beyond the scope of the book, however, to provide detailed treatment of any one of these areas of inquiry (e.g., bilingualism). Instead, I refer the reader to the work of researchers in these various fields. My principal concern is the dissemination of information that will contribute to the preparation of court interpreters. Thus, when I refer to the linguistic consequences of languages in contact, I am primarily concerned with the effect of phenomena such as code-switching on the activity of interpreting in court.

The book is divided into two principal sections. The first part consists of seven chapters. In chapter 1, a brief history of court interpreting in the United States is preceded by an overview of the state and federal court systems. Key legislation affecting the use of foreign language and sign language interpreters in the courts is reviewed, as is the constitutional basis for such legislative measures. It should be noted that although interpreters for the hearing impaired are regularly used in courtrooms across the United States, this book focuses on foreign language interpretation. In particular, the emphasis is on Spanish/English court interpretation, for at the present time, Spanish is the language most in demand in state and federal courts. Chapter 2 addresses theoretical aspects of the interpreting process. The role of extralinguistic knowledge in the interpreter's comprehension of the message is summarized. Language processing, simultaneous listening and speaking, and the importance of memory in consecutive interpretation are also discussed. In chapter 3, the different modes of interpretation are defined and their use in courtroom proceedings is explained. Special features of each mode (e.g, note-taking for consecutive interpretation) are considered. Chapter 4 examines the interdependency between language and culture and the implications of that relationship in court interpreting. In chapter 5, the interpretation of nonstandard language is investigated. The effects of languages in contact and the linguistic and cultural challenges faced by court interpreters in bilingual communities throughout the United States are explored. Chapter 6 deals with the role of the interpreter in various court proceedings (from apprehension through sentencing), and chapter 7 focuses on court interpreting as an emerging profession.

Part II of this book consists of four main sections. The materials contained in each section have been adapted for the practice of the various modes of interpretation used in court settings. Section 1 contains legal documents and other texts for sight translation; section 2 contains dialogues and other materials for consecutive interpretation; section 3 consists of the transcript of a pretrial detention hearing for consecutive and simultaneous interpretation; and section 4 includes texts for simultaneous interpretation practice: an opening statement by a defense attorney, excerpts from the transcript of a criminal trial, and a judge's instructions to the jury.

Several supplementary exercises are included in Part II as an aid to instructors. All of the materials are taken from actual legal cases and are therefore representative of the language interpreters encounter in courtrooms in the United States. All names, dates, locations, addresses, and case numbers have been changed to protect the anonymity of all parties involved in these legal proceedings. Parts I and II complement one another. For instance, the discussion of nonstandard language (chapter 4) is documented in Part II with depositions, letters, and dialogues drawn from court cases. I have intentionally structured the book as two independent units. My purpose in so doing is to allow for maximum flexibility in the use of the text. Instructors are encouraged to integrate the two components by combining theory with practice in the following manner: in the initial stage of instruction Part I is emphasized and interpretation exercises are introduced. The amount of practice is increased gradually, while proportionately reducing the time spent on readings and class discussion.

The present book is intended to be a useful resource for all persons interested in court interpreting and in issues regarding language and the law. It is specifically designed for use in courses in the growing field of court interpreting, but it may also be used in other interpretation courses. Although Spanish/English interpretation is emphasized, the general concepts presented are applicable to court interpreting in general, and the materials may be easily adapted to other foreign languages used in courtrooms in the United States.

An Introduction to Court Interpreting combines scholarly material with authentic texts derived from actual courtroom situations. Thus, the reader will occasionally find practical suggestions for interpreters along with more academic material. I have relied on the work of researchers and scholars in the field of translation and interpretation studies. Nonetheless, the book contains examples, observations, and material derived from my own research and work in the courts.

I have sought to avoid sexist language. For that reason, throughout this book I use the masculine form as a generic term, unless otherwise indicated; *he*, *him*, *himself*, and *his* refer to a person, regardless of gender.

INTRODUCTION

It is generally agreed that there are approximately 4,000 languages in the world. The number of speakers of a particular language varies greatly, however. Mandarin is the mother tongue of approximately 771 million northern Chinese, for instance, whereas Hopi is spoken by fewer than ten thousand individuals.[1] The 771 million Mandarin speakers constitute roughly fifteen percent of the world's population, while English is the native language of approximately eight percent of the population of our planet. It is also estimated that one-half of the world's population, or approximately two and a half billion people, speaks but eight languages: Mandarin Chinese, English, Hindi, Spanish, Russian, Arabic, Bengali, and Portuguese,[2] and that less than one percent of the world's inhabitants are able to communicate in more than three languages.[3]

Naturally, language communities are not closed entities; communication can take place among those expressing themselves in different languages through one of the following methods: 1) by drawing on linguistic competence which allows one of the speakers to express himself in the language of the other, or in a third language understood by both or; 2) by using the services of an interpreter (if oral communication is involved) or of a translator (if the words to be translated are written).

Regardless of the many contexts in which interpreters work—diplomatic, medical, conference, business, or legal—all interpreters have a common role in communication situations: the elimination of linguistic and cultural barriers. Interpreters play a vital role in the exchange of information, since without them there could be little, if any, communication. Because the linguistic skills and cultural knowledge of interpreters will affect the accuracy of communication, they have a direct impact on the interaction(s).

Interpreters and translators have always played a crucial role in human communication. They are able to penetrate the linguistic and cultural barriers that are born of the multiplicity of languages and the ever-increasing need of human beings to communicate with one another. Today, interpreters and translators continue to be indispensable in the world community, because despite the technological and scientific advances that have increased contact among nations, cultural and linguistic heterogeneity persists, and language barriers—the biblical Tower of Babel—still remain.

Interpretation and translation are rapidly growing fields, providing opportunities for those language students that are suitably prepared and trained. In the 1987 *Career Handbook* of the American Association of Teachers of Spanish and Portuguese (AATSP), Ruth Bennett noted that although the professions of translator and interpreter are the most demanding with regard to language skills, and in spite of an increasing need for them, their importance has not been "fully recognized by business and even by our government. Too often companies make use of any member of the firm who has some language background, however scanty. Our embassies and consulates abroad do not operate as efficiently as they should because their personnel lack necessary language skills."[4] Even within the State Department's career Foreign Service, advanced language skills are in short supply. Senator Paul Simon, a persistent advocate of the need for training in foreign languages, has pointed out that only six of the sixty-six hostages taken at the U.S. Embassy in Teheran in 1979 spoke any Farsi, the dominant language of Iran. Quoting former hostage Morehead Kennedy, Simon stated that the price of ignorance was that "we were speaking to the elite in English; we didn't know what was going on in the streets of Teheran."[5]

In common parlance, the terms interpretation and translation are often used interchangeably. Their meanings, however, are very different. Translation deals with the written word and interpretation, which is the focus of this book, allows two or more persons who do not speak the same language to communicate orally. Interpreters listen to a source language speaker, process the information, and convey it in a target language to the listener(s).

With the increase in international trade, commerce, travel and migration, interpreting is becoming commonplace and indispensable. Although popularly associated with the United Nations, interpretation is by no means limited to the international diplomatic arena, and interpreters are critically necessary in a variety of other settings. The judicial system in particular has been affected dramatically by the influx of large numbers of non-English-speaking immigrants into the United States during the past few decades.

The changing ethnic composition of the country, together with the passage of legislation such as the Court Interpreters Act of 1978 which protects the constitutional rights of non-English-speakers, have led to a significant increase in the need for translation and interpretation services (Tables 1.2, 1.4, 5.1). With the projected substantial increase in growth in the immigrant (particularly the Spanish-speaking) population of the United States into the next century and beyond, as well as the anticipated passage of additional legislation requiring the use of certified court interpreters, it is clear that the demand for qualified, competent interpreters will continue to increase, that court interpreting will become an even more attractive vocation for persons with a facility for languages, and that more universities will add courses in court interpretation to their curricula in order to meet the needs of our society. Lack of instructional materials, however, is a serious obstacle faced by those interested in this rapidly growing field. In the related field of translation, "more universities around the world are adding courses to their curriculum, however, the textbooks available for such courses are few."[6] *An Introduction to Court Interpreting* is intended to help fill this void.

This book is structured to reflect the belief held by many scholars in the field of translation and interpretation (Nida & Taber 1969; Roberts 1988) and shared by me, that theory and practice are inseparable, and that students of interpretation and translation should be provided not only with skills (practice) but also with the body of knowledge (theory) that pertains to the process of translation and interpretation and to the profession. Additionally, students need to be informed concerning the nature of the profession itself. This book is an outgrowth of my experiences both in the classroom, where I have taught interpreting for over half a decade, and as a federally certified court interpreter for Spanish/English proceedings since 1985.

PART I

THEORY

Chapter 1

A BRIEF HISTORY OF COURT INTERPRETING IN UNITED STATES COURTS

Accurate interpretation is of paramount importance if the constitutional right to due process is to be meaningful for all people.

–Congressional Committee on the Judiciary,
Report 100-590 (1988)

Introduction

The role of interpretation has always existed, because as long as human beings have possessed the ability to speak, intermediaries have been necessary to facilitate communication from one language and culture to another. In modern times, due to the establishment of international organizations as well as increases in international trade, travel, and migration, interpretation has become a profession increasingly practiced by specialists.

Today, in the United States, foreign language and sign language interpreters are regularly used in federal, state, and municipal court proceedings. This chapter places in historical context the purpose and practice of using foreign language interpreters in the legal setting. The key legislation affecting the use of interpreters in the federal courts of the United States is reviewed and the basis for such legislative initiatives is addressed. This summary of the history of court interpreting is preceded by a brief overview of two kinds of courts –federal and state– in which interpreters are regularly utilized.

In contrast to the development of the interpreting profession in Europe, where the need for highly specialized training has long been appreciated, in the United States court interpreters are generally viewed as individuals who perform this task simply because they possess some degree of bilingualism. In Europe the need for translation and interpretation (T/I) training resulted from the linguistic demands made during World War I by non-French speaking nations as they entered the multilingual international arena. Prior to that time, important international meetings had been held exclusively in French. According to Jean Herbert, "during the First World War, the fact that some of the topmost ranking negotiators from the U.S.A. and the United Kingdom were not sufficiently conversant with French made it necessary to resort to interpreters."[1] As noted by Arjona and Benmaman, the first generation of European interpreters and translators were individuals of exceptional intellectual, cultural, and academic backgrounds. The stakes were high, and a high level of performance became –from the beginning– the norm for the profession.[2]

The practice of *consecutive interpretation,* a method by which an interpreter conveys the target language message (L_B) in a sequential manner after the source language speaker (L_A), was "recognized as a profession in its own right at the post World War I peace talks in Paris, and then at the League of Nations."[3] *Simultaneous interpretation,* the method that requires that an interpreter listen and speak at the same time, had been used sparingly between the two world wars. This method or mode of interpreting received worldwide attention after World War II ended, at the Nuremberg Trial, generally considered the greatest criminal trial in modern history. Due to linguistic difficulties, these trials could not have been conducted without the use of simultaneous interpretation. In 1946, the mode was introduced in the United Nations and replaced the consecutive interpretation system except in a few special cases. It is widely accepted among professional court interpreters that the trials at Nuremberg represents the birth of their profession.

Nuremberg

The Nuremberg Trial dramatized the right of defendants to have all proceedings interpreted into their native language. In 1945, at the

Palace of Justice in Nuremberg, Germany, twenty-one high-ranking leaders of the defeated Third Reich were brought to trial before a tribunal of the victorious Allied powers: Britain, France, Russia, and the United States. Nazi officers stood before an international tribunal to answer charges never before brought against the military: crimes against humanity. It was the first trial in history for crimes against the peace of the world. Clearly, in such an international scenario involving four different languages, interpretation was necessary. Thus, teams of interpreters in glass-enclosed booths used specially designed electronic equipment to simultaneously interpret into four languages everything that was spoken in the courtroom. As a master check on the interpreting system, all testimony was tape recorded. After 217 days of trial, the transcribed proceedings totalled over four million words, amounting to 16,000 pages.[4]

Not until 1978, however, did the federal government of the United States recognize that qualified interpreters are critically necessary in the judicial system to protect the constitutional rights of non-English speakers or those with limited proficiency in English. In that year, Public Law 95-539 was enacted. This law, known as the Court Interpreters Act of 1978, is pivotal in the use of court interpreters in courtrooms in the United States. Its impact has also been felt in the state and municipal courts, for although the jurisdiction of the law is limited to the federal courts, the law has stimulated similar measures in courts of lower level jurisdiction.

Federal and State Courts

In the United States, the federal government and fifty state governments all make and enforce law. These two major court systems are wholly distinct bodies in the sense that they are created under different basic authorities: the respective federal and state constitutions. Although it is beyond the scope of this book to describe the complex judicial system of the United States, some general remarks regarding the state and federal courts will set the stage for this introduction to the role of interpreters in our court system.[5]

The character, jurisdiction and complexity of state courts vary considerably from state to state, and although the terminology and structure among the state courts differ significantly, a discernible structural pattern exists. Abraham explains that the base consists of "a system of justices of the peace and trial courts, with the pyramid gradually winding its way upward through a more or less elaborate appellate system, culminating in a supreme court (not invariably termed 'Supreme Court')."[6] According to *Black's Law Dictionary,* city and county courts may or may not be part of the state system of courts, depending upon the jurisdiction. State law refers to laws of a state or ordinances of a city or town, all as distinguished from federal law which is the supreme law of the land under Article VI of the Constitution of the United States. However, in matters which are not necessarily governed by federal law, the federal courts will look to state law and be governed by it.[7] The cases tried in state courts include robberies, murder, rape, traffic violations, broken contracts, and family disputes.

Different designations are used to refer to the different types of courts ordinarily found in the fifty states. The most common names for the *municipal court,* for instance, include traffic court, city court, night court, general district court, and police court. But regardless of what it may be called, the municipal court is almost always a court of original jurisdiction, and normally also the first court of record in the judicial hierarchy of the state. The municipal court is a city court that administers the law within the city and these courts usually have exclusive jurisdiction (the power to hear and determine cases) over violations of city ordinances. They may also have jurisdiction over criminal cases arising within the city and over certain minor civil cases. They are thus inferior courts of limited jurisdiction.[8]

The geographical jurisdiction of the *county court* as its name indicates, is limited to the level of that subdivision of the state. A county is the largest territorial division for local government in a state. The powers and importance of the county vary from state to state and even within the given state. In Louisiana, the equivalent unit is called a parish. The powers and jurisdiction of county courts are governed by state constitutions or statutes. For instance, some exist mainly for judicial administration, some have only criminal jurisdiction, or only civil, or both.[9] There are, of course, courts of appeals at the state level, which receive and adjudicate appeals on major questions emanating from the courts below.

A *civil action* is a lawsuit that is brought to enforce, redress, or protect private rights, rather than a court action involving the government trying to punish a crime. Civil cases involve a claim by one party that another party failed to carry out a legal duty, such as the duty not to harm others through carelessness, the duty to honor the terms of a contract, or duties identified in laws passed by the legislature. In general, they are noncriminal lawsuits and a party can be a person or a corporation.

In criminal cases, someone is accused of committing an action which is harmful to society as a whole, not just to another person. A *criminal action* is the procedure by which a person accused of a crime –whether in state of federal court– is brought to trial and either found guilty and sentenced or not guilty. It is a suit or cause instituted to punish an infraction of the criminal laws.

State and federal courts are authorized to hear different kinds of cases. There are no federal common law crimes although many federal statutes have incorporated the elements of common law crimes. Most federal crimes are codified in Titles 18 and 21 of the United States Code (U.S.C.), although other code titles also include specific crimes which are prosecuted in federal court (e.g., tax evasion and interstate kidnapping). The cases heard by federal courts may involve the Constitution, laws passed by Congress, cases in which the United States is a party, cases involving foreign diplomats, cases based on state laws that involve parties from different states, and some special kinds of cases, such as incidents at sea and bankruptcy cases. Obviously, federal courts do not have the same jurisdiction as state courts and federal court jurisdiction is limited to the kinds of cases listed in the U.S. Constitution (Article III, Section 2). Owing to the heterogeneity of the state, county, and municipal courts, and in the interest of clarity and uniformity, the sections of this book which describe court proceedings focus on those which take place in the federal system (see, in particular, chapter 6).

Although complex, the federal system is in many ways considerably less confusing and varied than the state system, which is necessarily heterogeneous. In this section, the three chief federal constitutional courts are mentioned, one of which –the United States District Court– is of predominant interest in relation to court interpreting, as will become apparent in the sections that follow.

Article III of the Constitution of the United States calls for the creation of a Supreme Court and whatever other federal courts Congress considers necessary. In addition to the U.S. Supreme Court, there are U.S. District Courts, U.S. Claims Courts, and U.S. Circuit Courts of Appeals. Congress has divided the country into federal judicial districts, each with its own district court. The ninety-four U.S. District Courts, "the workhorses of the federal judiciary,"[10] comprise the trial courts of the federal system. In January 1985, there were 575 district court judges. The districts have been grouped by Congress into twelve regional circuits (there is also a thirteenth "federal" circuit covering the entire country), each with a court of appeals.

U.S. district court cases may be appealed to the U.S. Court of Appeals, which will review the case to see if the U.S. district judge applied the law correctly. The courts of appeals also review cases decided by some federal agencies, such as the National Labor Relations Board. Cases from the court of appeals in each circuit and from the state supreme courts can be appealed to the United States Supreme Court in Washington DC, the most famous federal court. However, the Supreme Court does not have to hear the cases that are brought to it and, in fact, hears only a small percentage of the cases it is asked to review.

Many federal court cases are civil cases, such as equal employment opportunity claims. Federal courts handle an average of 275,000 civil cases annually. Statistics for the Southern District of Florida, the federal district with the heaviest criminal caseload in the United States, indicate that the number of civil cases filed annually far exceeds that of criminal cases. In 1990, for example, 1,398 criminal cases and 4,449 civil cases were filed in the district.[11] Most crimes concern matters that the Constitution leaves to the states, and federal criminal laws generally deal with crimes such as the importation of illegal drugs into the United States, bank robberies in which the deposits are insured by a federal agency, the printing of counterfeit U.S. currency, and money laundering.

Right to an Interpreter

Portions of the Sixth and Fourteenth Amendments to the Constitution of the United States are frequently quoted in federal as well as state cases as justification for appointment of court interpreters. The Sixth Amendment, which is the major federal source of the right to an interpreter, states, in pertinent part:

> In all criminal prosecutions, the accused shall enjoy the right to . . . be informed of the nature and cause of the accusation; to be confronted with the witnesses against him; to have compulsory process for obtaining witnesses in his favor, and to have the Assistance of Counsel for his Defense.

The states are bound to obey the dictates of the Sixth Amendment due to its incorporation by the Fourteenth Amendment with its due process and equal protection clauses. Section I states, in pertinent part:

> No state shall make or enforce any law which shall abridge the privileges or immunities of citizens of the United States; nor shall any state deprive any person of life, liberty or property, without due process of law; nor deny to any person within its jurisdiction the equal protection of the laws.

The Fifth Amendment also has a bearing on the right to a court interpreter. It states, in pertinent part:

> No person . . . shall be compelled in any criminal case to be a witness against himself, nor be deprived of life, liberty, or property, without due process of law . . . .

Without a doubt, the inability to understand what is transpiring in a court of law prevents individuals from fully contributing to their own defense. Pousada has pointed out that the refusal to grant the appointment of an interpreter to a non-English-speaking individual "can be viewed as a denial of both due process and equal protection."[12] For this reason, courts are increasingly recognizing the need for qualified interpreters to aid non-English-speakers during courtroom proceedings. The year 1978 is considered a landmark year for the profession of interpreting, because on October 28 President Carter signed into law the Court Interpreters Act (Public Law 95-539).

Court Interpreting Prior to 1978

Before examining the Court Interpreters Act of 1978 and the current state of court interpretation services in the United States, it will be useful to review the provisions that governed the use of interpreters in the federal courts prior to the enactment of this law. These provisions are: Rule 28(b) of the Federal Rules of Criminal Procedure; Rule 604 of the Federal Rules of Evidence; the Criminal Justice Act of 1964; and Rule 43(f) of the Federal Rules of Civil Procedure.

Two of the most pertinent provisions are Rule 28(b) of the Federal Rules of Criminal Procedure and Rule 604 of the Federal Rules of Evidence. Rule 28(b) states that the court may appoint an interpreter of its own selection and may fix the reasonable compensation of such interpreter, and that such compensation shall be paid out of funds provided by law or by the government, as the court may direct. However, as Schweda-Nicholson has established, two key problems arise from the wording of Rule 28(b). First, Rule 28(b) allows the provision of an interpreter to be at the discretion of the court. As a result, even if the defendant has no knowledge of the English language at all, appointment of an interpreter is not mandatory. Second, Rule 28(b) provides for an interpreter of the court's own selection. Since the overwhelming majority of judges are monolingual English-speakers, a primary consideration in this regard is the competence of a trial judge to determine whether an interpreter of the court's own selection is qualified to perform the job. Undoubtedly, the court is "in no position to assess the competence of a person called to serve as an interpreter."[13]

Prior to 1978, many federal judges appointed Spanish/English interpreters strictly on an *ad hoc* basis. Bailiffs, secretaries who work in the courthouse, relatives of the defendants, spectators in the courtroom, and even defense attorneys, have been called on by the court to provide interpretation services. Clearly, the provision for interpreters under Rule 28(b) was inadequate because it left the critical decision of whether to appoint an interpreter entirely to the discretion of the court, and the court is generally not qualified to determine the foreign language and interpretation skills of a person designated as an interpreter.

Rule 604 of the Federal Rules of Evidence also applies to interpreters working in the federal courts. It states that an interpreter is subject to the provisions of those rules relating to qualification as an expert, and requires the administration of an oath or affirmation that he will make a true translation. Such qualification as an expert witness in an indication that the federal district courts regard interpreting as a specialized activity which requires special knowledge. Furthermore, as any other expert witness, the interpreter is subject to having his interpretation challenged to safeguard the constitutional as well as statutory rights of all parties.

In the history of court interpreting in the United States, there have been cases in which "the courts have blatantly ignored the lack of both communicative and receptive competence in English on the part of the defendant."[14] There are several cases which deal with the right to an interpreter. Because they are relevant to the development of court interpreting legislation, in this section I make reference to several such cases. In Díaz v. State, 491 S.W.2d 166 (Tex. Crim. App. 173), for example, an interpreter was not appointed to assist the defendant during his testimony. On appeal, Díaz noted that his request for an interpreter had been denied by the judge even though the trial record demonstrated that Díaz had minimal knowledge of English. Notwithstanding these problems, Díaz's appeal for a new trial was denied.

Perhaps the most frequently cited case was a precedent-setting decision handed down in 1970 by the U.S. Court of Appeals for the Second Circuit. With that decision, in the case of U.S. ex rel. Negrón v. New York, 434 Fed. 386 (2d Cir. 1970), the Second Circuit granted a *habeas corpus* petition stating that an indigent defendant who has extreme English comprehension and communication problems is entitled to the services of an interpreter as a constitutional right. Habeas corpus is a legal device used to request that a judicial body review reasons for a person's confinement and the conditions of confinement. This case involved the murder trial of a twenty-three-year-old Spanish-speaking migrant worker who was not provided the services of an interpreter, even though an interpreter was necessary in order to translate the testimony of two Spanish-speaking witnesses for the court. The English testimony of some twelve other witnesses was not interpreted for Negrón, although his own testimony had to be given through an interpreter. Negrón was convicted of second-degree murder and sentenced to twenty years. Eventually, the federal district court granted a writ of habeas corpus on the grounds of a denial of constitutional rights. The court concluded that Negrón had been denied due process and the Second Circuit Court of Appeals affirmed the writ. A writ of habeas corpus is a judicial order requesting that a person detaining another produce the "body" (corpus) of the prisoner and give reasons for his or her capture and detention.

In U.S. v. Tapia, 631 F.2d 1207 (1980), the defendant was convicted in the Southern District of Texas, of conspiracy and of transporting aliens. The Court of Appeals held that: 1) when the defendant was arraigned through an interpreter, the district court, on its own motion, should have inquired whether failure to have an interpreter with the defendant throughout the proceedings inhibited his comprehension of the proceedings and his communication with counsel; 2) waiver of right to an interpreter is a decision to be made by the defendant, not by counsel or the court; and 3) the defendant testified at trial through an interpreter. The testimony of other witnesses was not interpreted for him and he contended that this made the trial fundamentally unfair because he was unable to effectively assist his counsel in cross-examination of those witnesses whose testimony he was unable to understand. The court of appeals held that if the court below determined after a hearing that the defendant was inhibited by being unable to understand "to such an extent as to have made the trial fundamentally unfair, he should grant him a new trial."[15]

In R & D Sod Farms v. Vestal, 432 So. 2d 622 (1983), a worker's compensation claimant was unable to communicate in English. His brother, who claimed to be able to understand him, interpreted. There was no showing on the record that the brother was qualified to interpret nor was he sworn to do so. Therefore, the court held that such testimony could not be the basis for an award of benefits. In another such case, Monte v. State of Florida, 443 S. 2d 339 (1983), in Hillsborough County, the defendant pleaded guilty through an interpreter, to second degree murder. The appellate court affirmed the conviction, but ordered a resentencing because the court failed to provide an interpreter at sentencing. The court pointed out that the interpreter merely responded "yes" or "no" to the Court's requests made to the interpreter. Also, the interpreter's reply that Monte "understands the charge" when the judge asked Monte if he understood that he had a right to a trial and that when he pleaded guilty he would be waiving that right, "lends support to Monte's arguments that the translation was not adequate and therefore the plea not valid."[16]

In the 1960s, the civil rights movement addressed the rights of minorities and also focused greater attention on the rights of persons who do not understand court proceedings because of limited ability in the English language. Consequently, the right to have interpreters available in the federal judicial system also received greater attention. By 1977, over forty states and the federal government had rules, procedures or decisions that affected witnesses who had a limited understanding of the English language. However, in many cases, the interpretation was done by persons whose ability as interpreters could not be measured. Eventually, the need to provide *qualified* interpreters in the federal courts became a major concern.

Several bills dealing with court interpreting services were introduced in the early 1970s in the U.S. Congress. Although they never became law, H.R. 4096, H.R. 2243, and the Bilingual Courts Act, can be considered precursors of the Court Interpreters Act of 1978. Of these three legislative initiatives, the Bilingual Courts Act is most relevant to our discussion because this bill, if passed by Congress, would have required the federal judiciary to certify interpreters and use them in the federal district courts. Moreover, it would have allowed the tape recording of court proceedings in which interpreters were used. This would have made it possible to compare the original foreign language testimony with the official (interpreted) English-language court record.[17]

During a Senate hearing on 10 October 1973, regarding the Bilingual Courts Act, concern about the inadequate provisions of Rule 28(b), the Criminal Justice Act of 1964, and Rule 43(f) was noted. The bill was sponsored by Senator John Tunney of California, who testified that the current statutes pointed in the right direction, but did not offer a sufficiently strong mandate to the courts for the appointment of interpreters. More importantly, the existing provisions were lacking in guidance on how the federal courts were to establish the machinery to effectuate the policies that were enunciated. Senator Tunney also stated that although new, stricter legislation would represent "significant additional cost" it would also represent "significant additional justice."[18] The bill, though never enacted, set the stage for Public Law 95-539. Thus, in the United States, until 1978, non-English speakers who were accused and tried in a United States district courtroom did not have the protection of a law that guaranteed that they would be provided with a qualified interpreter who would enable them to understand what was taking place in court.

Court Interpreters Act of 1978

The Court Interpreters Act provided a framework for appointing interpreters in the United States courts and addressed the shortcomings of Rule 28(b), the Criminal Justice Act of 1964, and Rule 43(f) of the Federal Rules of Civil Procedure. It likewise addressed sign language interpretation. The act, signed into law by former President Carter, provided for interpretation services in all criminal and civil actions in the federal district courts where the United States is plaintiff. Due to its importance for court interpreting in the United States, the entire text of this law (and subsequent amendments) is included in Appendix 5. In this chapter, relevant sections of the legislation are cited.

The 1978 Act represents the acknowledgment by the Congress of the United States that court interpreting is a highly specialized profession and not simply a function that any bilingual person might perform. It also marks the beginning of certification of court interpreters to serve the linguistic needs of persons who do not speak English. The legislation requires that:

> The presiding judicial officer, with the assistance of the Director of the Administrative Office of the United States Courts, shall utilize the services of the most available certified interpreter, or when no certified interpreter is reasonably available, as determined by the presiding judicial officer, the services of an otherwise competent interpreter, in any criminal or civil action initiated by the United States in a United States district court (including a petition for a writ of habeas corpus initiated in the name of the United States by a relator), if the presiding judicial officer determines on such officer's own motion or on the motion of a party that such party (including a defendant in a criminal case), or a witness who may present testimony in such action —
>
> (1) speaks only or primarily a language other than the English language; or
>
> (2) suffers from a hearing impairment (whether or not suffering also from a speech impairment) so as to inhibit such party's comprehension of the proceedings or communication with counsel or the presiding judicial officer, or so as to inhibit such witness' comprehension of questions and the presentation of such testimony.[19]

The Court Interpreters Act of 1978 also required the Director of the Administrative Office of the United States Courts to initiate a program for the certification of federal court interpreters. Consequently, the Administrative Office, in conjunction with a team of experts, developed rigorous standards and a certification procedure (written and oral) which would identify those individuals capable of handling the complex criminal and civil proceedings conducted before the United States district courts. At this writing, 388 persons have been certified out of 9,579 individuals who have taken the written exam since the program was initiated in 1980.[20] Candidates must pass the written portion of the test before they may take the oral portion. To date, 2,146 persons have taken the oral portion of the examination. The federal court certification examination is discussed in greater detail in chapter 7.

On several occasions, bills to amend the Court Interpreters Act of 1978 were introduced in the United States Congress. For example, in November 1985, sponsors of a bill presented in the U.S. Senate wrote that failure to provide competent interpretation services to non-English speaking persons and the hearing-impaired in federal judiciary proceedings:

> could, under certain circumstances, constitute a denial of rights secured by the Fifth and Sixth Amendments to the Constitution of the United States because such individuals may__
>
> (A) be deprived of life, liberty, or property without due process of law;
>
> (B) be unable to confront adverse witnesses due to a lack of comprehension;
>
> (C) fail to comprehend the rulings and pronouncements of the court or the documentary evidence introduced in such proceedings.[21]

This bill sought to require certification of interpreters based on the results of criterion-based performance examinations in at least all of the following languages: Spanish, Italian, Chinese, Japanese, French (Creole), Korean, Portuguese, Arabic, and American Sign Language. It also addressed the need for regulations establishing criteria based on interpreter education, training, required performance, and experience, for the selection of otherwise qualified interpreters of languages for which no interpreters have been certified by the Director of the Administrative Office of the United States Courts.[22]

Federal Court Interpreters Advisory Board

In 1986, an eleven member Federal Court Interpreters Advisory Board (FCIAB) was established by the Chief Justice of the U.S. Supreme Court and by the Director of the Administrative Office of the U.S. Courts. This board was created to address some of the unresolved problems facing the judicial system in the area of interpreter service. These include the certification of lesser-used languages such as Navajo and Haitian Creole, which are limited to specific geographic regions; fee schedules for freelance interpreters (certified and otherwise qualified court interpreters) who work in the federal courts; the training and orientation of interpreters; how to identify qualified interpreters for lesser-used languages; and the development of a Code of Professional Responsibility for interpreters who work in United States district courts (see Appendix 1).

Judicial Improvements and Access to Justice Act of 1988

The most significant amendments to Public Law 95-539 were enacted in 1988. The bill is bipartisan legislation that was introduced in the 100th Congress in 1987 by former presidential candidate Paul Simon, Senator Orrin Hatch of Utah, and others.

On 10 August 1988, the Committee on the Judiciary unanimously ordered the bill, S. 1867, favorably reported with an amendment in the nature of a substitute. The report submitted by Senator Joseph Biden, from the Committee on the Judiciary, states that this legislation is designed to enhance the effectiveness of the Court Interpreters Act of 1978, which established the right of non-English speaking and hearing impaired defendants and witnesses to competent interpretation services in the courts. The report states that in enhancing the 1978 Act, Congress recognized that "accurate interpretation is of paramount importance if the constitutional right of due process is to be meaningful for all people."[23] The committee which studied the bill considered that while the Court Interpreters Act of 1978 had "worked well in improving judicial interpretation services for Spanish speakers, the ten year history of the Act had yielded few visible improvements for other languages."[24]

Public Law 100-702, the Judicial Improvements and Access to Justice Act amended the Interpreters Act. The new act incorporates important provisions included in the failed 1985 bill, such as the requirement of guidelines for the selection of otherwise qualified interpreters. However, rather than listing the languages for which certification would be required, Public Law 100-702 states, in pertinent part:

> The Director may certify interpreters for any language if the Director determines that there is a need for certified interpreters in that language. Upon the request of the Judicial Conference of the United States for certified interpreters in a language, the Director shall certify interpreters in that language. Upon such a request from the judicial council of a circuit and the approval of the Judical Conference, the Director shall certify interpreters for that circuit in the language requested . . .[25]

Thus, on 19 November 1988, several amendments were enacted to the Court Interpreters Act of 1978 when the President signed Public Law No. 100-702, which went into effect immediately. This new law reiterates the mandate of 28 U.S.C. [United States Code] Section 1827 that the highest standards of accuracy be maintained in all judicial proceedings in which interpreters are utilized. The amendments include the following:

1. pretrial and grand jury proceedings are included within the definition of "judicial proceedings" to which the Interpreters Act applies. Thus, "presiding judicial officer" refers to any judge of a United States district court, a bankruptcy court, a United States magistrate, and the United States attorney for grand jury proceedings. This correction to extend the Court Interpreters Act to grand jury proceedings is indispensable if due process is to be maintained at all stages of the judicial process. The committee recognized that accurate interpretation is particularly significant at the grand jury level, for an error in the interpretation of the accused's testimony, or that of a witness, could result in wasted court time and money. More importantly, an interpretation error could result in the incarceration of otherwise innocent individuals;

2. both the district court and the U.S. attorney shall maintain a file of all persons who have been certified as interpreters by the Administrative Office of the U.S. Courts;

3. a process is established whereby the Judicial Council of an individual federal circuit can identify the needs of its linguistic population and request the certification of a given language or languages. The request would be forwarded to the Judicial Conference which in turn would request the certification of a language or languages, on either the national or regional level, to the Administrative Office of the U.S. Courts;

4. the Director shall certify interpreters based on the results of a criterion-referenced performance evaluation, an absolute measure of language and interpretive proficiency;

5. the Director shall provide clear guidelines to the courts on the selection of what is referred to as otherwise qualified interpreters, because court interpretation must have stringent quality control. As before, only in a case in which no certified interpreter is reasonably available may otherwise qualified interpreters be employed. Interim regulations issued by the Director to implement the 1988 amendments, define "otherwise qualified interpreters" and divide them into two categories: *professionally qualified interpreters* and *language skilled interpreters*. Interpreters of languages for which there is certification by the Administrative Office of the United States Courts cannot be considered as professionally qualified interpreters. To qualify as a professionally qualified interpreter, an interpreter must demonstrate either prior existing employment as a seminar or conference interpreter for the Office of Language Services of the Department of State, for the United Nations, or for related agencies for which examinations

are a condition of employment; or membership in good standing in a professional interpreters association which requires an application specifying a minimum of fifty hours of conference experience in the language(s) of expertise, and the sponsorship of three active members in good standing who have been members of said association for at least two years, and whose language(s) of expertise are the same as the applicant's, and who attest to having worked with the applicant as well as to the accuracy of the statements on the application. An interpreter who does not qualify as a professionally qualified interpreter, but who can demonstrate to the satisfaction of the court the ability to interpret court proceedings from English to a designated language and from that language to English will be classified as a language skilled interpreter.[26] While the fees for certified interpreters and professionally qualified interpreters are set at the same rate, fees for language skilled interpreters are set at a lesser rate (see Table 1.1);

6. the Director shall report periodically on the use and performance of interpreters (both certified and otherwise qualified);

7. the Director shall prescribe, subject to periodic review, a schedule of reasonable fees for services rendered by interpreters, certified or otherwise, and in so doing shall consider the prevailing rate of compensation for comparable service in other governmental entities;

8. upon the motion of a party, judicial proceedings in which an interpreter is used may be electronically sound-recorded. Section 705(e) lists some of the factors that the presiding judicial officer shall consider in making the determination about such a motion;

9. the preferred mode of interpretation is simultaneous rather than consecutive; and

10. the *summary mode,* the method of interpreting by which the interpreter summarizes and edits, is no longer authorized. The law, however, recognizes that flexibility should be given to the district court in deciding the particular mode to be used for the efficient administration of justice.

The provision of interpreters for the hearing impaired is likewise addressed in the 1988 legislation. In accordance with interim regulations, if sign language interpreting services are required, the presiding judicial officer shall seek the services of an individual who holds a Legal Specialist Certificate from the Registry of Interpreters for the Deaf, Inc. If no such certified person is reasonably available, the presiding judicial officer is responsible under the Act for ascertaining the competency of a proposed sign language interpreter, preferably an individual possessing a Comprehensive Skills Certificate from the Registry of Interpreters for the Deaf.[27]

In summary, as a consequence of these and other improvements, the federal courts will be better equipped to handle the linguistically diverse populations that find themselves before our judicial system.

Table 1.1
Fee Schedule for Court Interpreters in U.S. District Courts

Contractor Rates

Certified and Professionally Qualified

Full Day	$250.00
Half Day	$135.00

Non-Certified and Language-Skilled

Full Day	$120.00
Half Day	$ 65.00

Staff

Grade Level	Salary Range	Years of Experience as a Court Interpreter[a]
JSP-11	$31,116 - $40,449	1
JSP-12	$37,294 - $48,481	2
JSP-13	$44,348 - $57,650	3
JSP-14	$52,406 - $68,129	4

Source: Administrative Office of the United States Courts.
[a]Starting salary at the grade of 10 (0 years of specialized experience) is $28,322. At the grade 12 level and above, the years of specialized experience must have been at, or equivalent to, the next lower grade in the federal service.

Need for Interpreters

The number of cases requiring interpretation in the district courts has risen consistently since 1980. Statistics provided by the Administrative Office of the United States Courts document a dramatic increase in the use of foreign language interpreters in the federal courts from 1980 to 1990 (Table 1.2).

Table 1.2
Interpreter Use by Year,
Reported by U.S. District Courts, 1980-1990[a]

Year	Number of Times Used
1980	24,438
1981	30,998
1982	32,280
1983	39,905
1984	41,705
1985	46,511
1986	45,230
1987	40,389
1988	49,946
1989	56,415
1990	66,431

Source: Court Administrative Division, Administrative Office of the United States Courts.

[a]These figures are based on data on court interpreter use by language from 1980-1990. The figures refer to docketable events. If, for example, a case goes to trial and lasts one month, the record reflects only one docketable event, although interpreters may have been used over thirty times.

Information provided by the Administrative Office also indicates that some U.S. district courts, particularly in California and New York, have difficulty securing the services of freelance interpreters and filling vacant staff positions. Statistics gathered for 1988 demonstrate that the total number of proceedings in which interpreters were utilized by the federal courts continued to rise over prior years. That year, the courts reported that interpreters in seventy languages were needed in over 49,000 proceedings. (Table 1.3).

Certification was first developed for Spanish, the foreign language most frequently used in courts in the United States (Table 1.4). Approximately 95 percent of all federal proceedings requiring interpreters call for interpreters of Spanish. It is not surprising that Spanish is the language most in demand both in federal and state

Table 1.3
Interpreter Use by Language, Calendar Year 1988, Reported by U.S. District Courts

Languages	Number of Times Used	Languages	Number of Times Used
Spanish	46,064	Polish	8
Haitian Creole	538	Albanian	7
Cantonese	520	Cambodian	7
Arabic	307	Canjoval	7
Italian	244	Mein	7
Mandarin	180	Ga	6
Korean	170	Zuni	6
French	166	Bulgarian	5
Hebrew	161	French Creole	5
Greek	124	Hungarian	5
Vietnamese	123	Armenian	4
Urdu	113	Hausa	4
Navajo	111	Hintko	4
Tagalog	103	Norwegian	4
Portuguese	91	Czech	3
Farsi	89	Flemish	3
Thai	81	Ibo	3
Punjabi	68	Samoan	3
Russian	67	Sibuano	3
German	56	Yugoslavian	3
Serbo Croatian	51	Chamorro	2
Hmong	48	Fulane	2
Japanese	47	Icelandic	2
Hindi	44	Neapolitan	2
Gujarati	35	Swedish	2
Foochow	34	Yupik	2
Yoruba	24	Finnish	1
Bengali	23	Guinea	1
Laotian	23	Hakka	1
Apache	20	Indian	1
Dutch	20	Keres	1
Pushtu	14	Turkish	1
Sign	14		
Yiddish	11		
Nepalese	9	**Reported by Bankruptcy Courts**	
Wayuunaiki	9		
Indonesian	8	Spanish	9
Papago	8	Sign	4

Source: Administrative Office of the United States Courts.

courts since, according to the Cuban American Policy Center, in less than a decade the Hispanic percentage of the total U.S. population rose from 6.5 percent to 8.1 percent. Between 1980 and 1988 Hispanics experienced a 34 percent growth rate, compared to an 8 percent general-population growth rate. Their numbers increased from 14.5 million in 1980 to 19.4 million in 1988, and Hispanics became the nation's largest ethnic minority, surpassed only by African Americans. It is estimated that over the decade the number of Hispanic immigrants to the United States (documented and undocumented) averaged 250,000 annually.[28] According to the U.S. Census Bureau, immigration accounts for about fifty percent of the national increase in the last ten years. The Census Bureau also reports that the nation's Hispanic population is increasing at five times the rate of non-Hispanics.[29]

Table 1.4
Interpreter Use in U.S. District Courts, Calendar Years 1980-1990, Spanish

Year	Number of Times Used
1980	23,394
1981	29,754
1982	30,372
1983	38,224
1984	38,807
1985	43,109
1986	41,501
1987	39,874
1988	46,064
1989	53,300
1990	61,397

Source: Administrative Office of the United States Courts.

Federal certification for Haitian Creole and Navajo court interpreters is currently underway. In 1990, Haitian Creole and Navajo were among the ten most frequently interpreted languages in the federal courts (Table 1.5).

Table 1.5
Ten Most Frequently Interpreted Languages, Calendar Year 1990, As Reported by U.S. District Courts

Language	Number of Times Used
Spanish	61,397
Cantonese	709
Korean	447
Haitian Creole	417
Armenian	352
Arabic	224
Mandarin	204
Tagalog	196
Navajo	188
Turkish	176

Source: Administrative Office of the United States Courts.

Statistics reveal that the need for interpreters in the state court system far exceeds that of the federal district courts. For example, as reported in *Time* magazine in 1988, New York courts required the services of interpreters approximately 250 times a day.[30] In Dade County, in southern Florida, interpreters were utilized in 154,645 proceedings in 1988, and in 1989, interpreters made 155,395 appearances, translated 357 tapes, 135 documents and produced 5,552 pages of transcribed translations.[31] Compare these figures with the statistics for interpreter use in 1988 provided by the Supervisory Interpreter for the Federal District Court for the Southern District of Florida (Table 1.6).

Some states have enacted legislation providing for interpretation services in their courts. However, the legal basis for the right to a court interpreter is not treated uniformly by the states even though the need for interpreters in the state system is more acute than in the U.S. district courts. To date, none of the states have adopted the federal standards for interpreter certification. Those states which have statutes providing for the appointment of court interpreters have modeled them on Rule 28(b) of the Federal Rules of Criminal Procedure.[32] States that provide the statutory right to a court interpreter include Arizona, California, Colorado, Illinois, Massachusetts, Minnesota, New Mexico, New York, and Texas.[33]

Table 1.6
Total Docketable Events Requiring Interpreters in the U.S. District Court for the Southern District of Florida by Language, Calendar Year 1988

Language	Number of Times Used[a]
Spanish	4057
Creole	297
French	34
German	19
Portuguese	19
Arabic	10
Italian	7
Dutch	6
Hebrew	5
Hindi	5
Mandarin	4
Punjabi	3
Cantonese	2
Greek	2
Swedish	2
Finnish	1

Total: 4499 [Includes 26 cases requiring Spanish interpretation for Pre-Trial Services]

Source: Irene Tomassini, Supervisory Interpreter, U.S. District Court for the Southern District of Florida, January 1989.
[a] These figures reflect the number of criminal cases for which interpreters were provided by the Interpreters Office.

Although there are exceptions, most states do not require certification for court interpreters. A few states, among them California, New Jersey, New Mexico, and Washington, have initiated certification programs. Currently, several states are considering legislation designed to improve court interpreting services. At this writing, for instance, the legislature of the state of Florida is considering a bill designed to require a standard, uniform method to certify and otherwise determine the qualifications of the interpreters in Florida's courts.

New Mexico and California are the only states that have provisions for court interpreter services in their Constitutions. Article 2 § 14 of New Mexico's Constitution states that a defendant in a criminal case has the right "to have charge and testimony interpreted to him in a language he understands." Article 1 § 14 of the Constitution of California states that "a person unable to understand English who is charged with a crime has a right to an interpreter throughout the proceedings."

In conclusion, as a consequence of federal legislation and the high standards required for court interpreting by the federal government, states are now more aware of the impact of court interpreters in their judicial systems and of the disadvantage faced by persons with limited ability in English. Unfortunately, for those non-English-speakers who come into contact with the judicial system at the local and state level, the situation remains largely unchanged. Thus, much remains to be done before it is recognized nationwide that the professionalization of court interpreters, as well as the awareness of judges and other key court personnel regarding the role of the interpreter, are necessary for the smooth functioning of the legal system and for providing equal access to justice for all linguistic minorities.

Chapter 2

THE INTERPRETING PROCESS

Introduction

The need for systematic study of the interpreting process arises from the actual problems encountered during the production of interpretations. It is essential that the practical experiences of practitioners working in the field be integrated and placed in a theoretical context. It is equally important that the training of interpreters involve an appreciation for the theoretical basis of the process.[1] Theory and practice must not be dichotomous; scholars and practitioners should engage in a collaborative effort. In this chapter, I discuss some of the relevant information pertaining to language processing in interpretation, including simultaneous speaking and listening, and the importance of memory in interpretation.

The task of interpreting is extremely complex. Interpreters perform two functions simultaneously in the field of language and communication that otherwise are always carried out separately: 1) speech = the expression of our ideas, and 2) understanding, our comprehension of the ideas of the other speaker. Interpretation is a unique activity because these two processes are performed by the same person, often simultaneously, or nearly so. In place of the usual communication that occurs between speaker and listener—two individuals who reverse their respective roles in the course of communicating with one another—the communication takes place through an intermediary: the interpreter. Thus, an interpreter is at the same time both speaker and listener, although in reverse order: listening and then expressing the same verbal message, but doing so through a different linguistic system. The duplication of the processes involved in interpreting makes it easier to observe the interplay of linguistic systems and mental processes in humans.

The interpreting process reveals aspects of the relationship between thought and language that are not exposed in ordinary communication. As noted by Seleskovitch, interpretation theory studies the dual circuit which is, in duplicate, the same circuit that constitutes oral communication between two human beings. The presence of the interpreter inevitably alters the usual process of spoken communication between two individuals, as the outline below illustrates:

SPEAKER'S ACT OF SPEECH (Source Language, L_A) —>
INTERPRETER/LISTENER'S UNDERSTANDING (of speaker) —>
IDEAS OF THE INTERPRETER/SPEAKER (must be identical to those of the source language speaker) —>
INTERPRETER/SPEAKER'S ACT OF SPEECH (Target Language, L_B)[2]

Extralinguistic Knowledge and Understanding

The degree to which interpreters—as recipients of speech—understand the oral message depends on several factors: their knowledge of the original language; the relevant knowledge they possess of the subject under discussion; and awareness of what has already been said and what a given argument is endeavoring to demonstrate or to refute. This understanding of the situation will enhance an interpreter's capacity to comprehend the original message. What is characteristic of an interpreter is not so much his linguistic knowledge of two or more languages, but rather his capacity to decode a message in the source language (L_A) while simultaneously re-encoding it in the target language (L_B).

Extralinguistic knowledge plays a vital role beyond purely linguistic information because the interpreter's relevant knowledge of the subject under discussion enables him to recognize known factors and to construe the unknown. The crucial role that extralinguistic knowledge plays in understanding is best illustrated with Seleskovitch's example of the different reactions that two individuals may have to the same photographic slide of a safari vacation. The perception of the person who went on the safari and took the slide (the photographer) will contrast significantly with that of a friend who has no prior knowledge or experience with the object represented on the photographic slide he is shown (the viewer). For the photographer, an instantaneous view of the slide brings to mind an infinitely vaster experience than the visible symbols, because his recollections also include sensory and emotional experiences. To the viewer, however, the image evokes no more than previously experienced facts, totally inadequate to enable him to relive the actual experience of the photographer. Seleskovitch explains that "the difference in signification in the perception of the same slide by two persons having different experiences of the object represented is . . . explained by their difference in knowledge level. In the case of the photographer, the memories associated with the fraction of a second represented on the slide constitute the background knowledge used to interpret the image."[3] On the other hand, the viewer has limited background knowledge based on past experiences, if any, with safaris. An interpreter who lacks knowledge of the subject dealt with and developed in a speech or utterance is in the same position as a person who views an unknown photograph or slide. He would identify the language spoken and the words (in the same way as the viewer would recognize a category of living being or object on a photograph or slide), "but neither the ignorant interpreter nor the viewer would comprehend the meaning of the forms perceived."[4]

An example of the need for extralinguistic knowledge in interlingual communication may be found in the experience of foreign correspondents who must comprehend and report the messages of politicians in the United States. U.S. politicians are notorious for their frequent use of sports references in their speeches. President Bush, for example, stated in 1989 that his administration would "stay at the plate" until it ousted Panamanian dictator Manuel Noriega.[5] Upon hearing this, interpreters who are unfamiliar with baseball, but who have linguistic knowledge of the English language, will understand all the words. However, the true meaning of Bush's expression will be lost to them.

Words or phrases in isolation and entirely out of context cannot be linked to relevant knowledge and, consequently, are not amenable to interpretation. We are left with their lexical and grammatical meaning (identified by our knowledge of the language), but this merely enables us to recognize what is already known to us, it does not enable us to comprehend new information. Words thus constitute a potential communication; they only become "communication" when the speaker addresses them to a listener for a reason comprehensible to both parties.

What conclusions can be drawn about the relationship between extralinguistic knowledge and the formulation of the message? First, the formulation merely triggers the meaning. The meaning can only be construed in the listener's mind if he has some knowledge of the subject under discussion. This underscores the significance of relevant knowledge, because the kind of knowledge required for understanding is subordinate to the context. Second, the level of knowledge mastered by the interpreter who does not specialize in the subject matter under discussion can never equal that of the specialist whose knowledge is operational and enables a person to perform in a specific field of endeavor (e.g., a herpetologist) or assess the validity of the arguments put forward by the other speakers. An interpreter, however, must achieve a level of knowledge in a wide variety of fields, and that degree of knowledge must be adequate for understanding.

There are two cases in which a linguistic formulation may not arouse any meaningful knowledge and the interpreter/listener remains nearly as uninformed as before the words were spoken. This may occur when the words are out of context, as when someone asks for the translation of a specific word without giving any information about the substance of the message (e.g., "How do you say *date* in Spanish?"). Prior to answering such a question, interpreters must ask for the context or the way the source language word was used. Without the context, an interpreter would not know whether the word "date" was intended by the speaker to mean 'the day of the month' *(fecha);* 'an appointment or engagement for a set time' *(cita, compromiso);* 'the sweet, fleshy fruit of the date palm' *(dátil);* or any of the other meanings of that English word.

The second case may occur when interpreters are not given sufficient referential knowledge. In other words, if an interpreter is not given any information regarding the situation or the subject matter to be discussed, that interpreter may not possess the minimum level of knowledge that enables a person to interpret, that is, to understand. For example, in an extradition hearing involving the close associate of a former South American dictator, an interpreter who has not been informed of the identity of the person, or acquired any other information regarding the case could, upon hearing the prosecutor refer to the AAA, erroneously assume that the individual was referring to the American Automobile Association rather than to an organization known as the *Alianza Anticomunista Argentina* (Argentine Anticommunist Alliance), a reputed death-squad. A more humorous example is the misinterpretation of the word *Guatemalans* as *sandías* 'watermelons' in a court proceeding. This misunderstanding, brought about by the interpreter's lack of relevant knowledge regarding the case, was clarified when the defendant stated from the witness stand: *"Soy guatemalteco, no soy sandía"* ("I am Guatemalan, not a watermelon"). Moreover, it should be noted, the word *sandio(a)* signifies 'simpleton' or 'fool'.

Interpreters who receive insufficient referential knowledge must rely on linguistic meaning, and their translations will inevitably regress towards mere language-to-language code switching (literalness). In such cases, an interpreter will understand the words in their primary sense (the meaning they most frequently have for the interpreter or the meaning most recently associated with those words), not in their relevant sense. In these instances, any ambiguity in linguistic meaning will remain ambiguous for the interpreter. The interpreter who translates without understanding is not interpreting accurately, as in the example below:

> JUDGE: Do you waive further notice of this date?
> INTERPRETER: *¿Ud. despide que se le deje saber de otras informaciones en este caso?*
> (Do you wave [good-by] to receiving other information about this case?)

Interpretation focuses on the ideas expressed and aims at integral communication of meaning. Interpreters concentrate on finding the appropriate wording in L_B to convey a given wording in L_A, at a given moment and in a given context. Interpretation thus involves the identification of relevant concepts and their rewording in another language in such a way that source and target language utterances may correspond only in their temporary meaning in a given context. These rewordings do not necessarily constitute equivalent language units capable of reuse in different circumstances.

Due to a variety of reasons, the sound reaching the interpreter's ears is rarely of perfect fidelity. For instance, the speaker's pronunciation may be defective, the accoustics in the room may be poor, and the transmission of sound (whether direct or electronic) involves a loss factor and the sensory capabilities of different interpreters will vary. Therefore, perception of individual words always involves a certain amount of anticipation based on the interpreter's understanding of the meaning. The interpreter-listener differs from the ordinary listener in that the interpreter must concentrate much more intently on what is being said and follow the speaker's train of thought very closely. Interpreters can, on the basis of previous meanings, predict the probable forthcoming meaning. This predicting or anticipating process assists in hearing and understanding the acoustic forms of the words by comparing the relatively defective sounds reaching his ear with the anticipated meaning.

Relevant Meaning

It is important to note that dictionary equivalents are not experiential or phenomenological equivalents, and that language yields many meanings. Most words cover many facets of meaning, classified in an infinite number of ways according to the language under consideration. Consider the word *plant* (something that grows in the soil, or a factory, are two meanings that readily come to mind). The interpreter hearing the word "plant" is unlikely to think of a place where something is manufactured or built if the subject discussed is botany. Instead, the interpreter will automatically hear the relevant layer of meaning while the many other semantic layers stored with the same word remain dormant. The meaning of a sentence aimed at an audience is also more than the sum of relevant meanings carried by individual words, because the listener perceives the nonverbal part of the message at the same time as the words. That is why an interpreter does not process information in the same way as a Morse operator who transcribes a coded message into clear language.

In interpretation, there is no time to ponder a given word or sentence—the interpreter is forced to operate at the normal tempo of human speech. Average spontaneous speech in most languages is estimated to vary between 120 and 150 words per minute, but it may reach a much faster rate (220 words per minute).[6] The fact that few notes are taken in consecutive interpretation demonstrates the nonverbal nature of thought. For instance, students frequently make the mistake of rendering a consecutive interpretation of the original L_A speech—or part of it—in the source language:

QUESTION TO BE INTERPRETED: What is your occupation?
INTERPRETER: What is your job?

This indicates that the interpreter does not say one word in L_B for a word heard in L_A. The occasional rendering of a source language utterance in the source language, although using different terms, is an indication that the original message had assumed its nonverbal state in the interpreter's mind.

Memory

In interpretation, memory plays a very important role because interpreters are engaged in comprehending and recalling the context of what has been said. In consecutive interpretation, the interpreter must reproduce information at the end of a relatively long segment of speech (the length varies), and in simultaneous interpretation, the interpreter reproduces the message in L_B a few seconds behind the L_A speaker.

The memory of the simultaneous interpreter is concerned with several activities. In simultaneous interpretation, the interpreter must remember part of the earlier speech, render the target language version, and listen to and take in the rest of the speech that is being delivered while at the same time dealing with earlier segments. Figures and names pose the greatest retention problem and are among the mistakes made most frequently by simultaneous interpreters, who characteristically lag behind the speaker by two to three seconds.

Consecutive interpretation relies on memory processes for reconstructing a text. The interpreter is expected to reconstitute immediately a minimum of 120 words per minute in another language without omitting anything. Because the utterances by the original speaker may be rather lengthy, note-taking is an essential component of consecutive interpretation. Note-taking acts as a mnemonic device, an aid to trigger the memory of what the interpreter understood. Names and figures should be quickly jotted down because they are the most difficult to retain and recall. Owing to its importance in consecutive interpretation, note-taking is discussed more fully in chapter 3.

Contrary to common belief, it is not necessary for the interpreter to memorize long passages, or even to have the ability to do so. The interpreter's memory is involved in retaining the meaning which he extracts from the oral message. Thus, memory and understanding are inseparable in interpretation. Upon hearing the message to be interpreted, the interpreter rapidly analyzes it for complete understanding. The information which he assimilates is stored in the interpreter's short-term memory for immediate retrieval. This type of memorization is called *substantive* and may be distinguished from the type of memorization effort required when one must learn a passage, poem, speech, etc., by heart, that is, *verbatim*. When a person memorizes a text, it is the words (not the ideas those words carry) that he must commit to memory. This is not the type of memorization necessary in interpretation.[7]

The key factor in substantive memorization is comprehension, because a message which is not understood cannot be retained. Studies of memory retention indicate that the less meaningful the information, the more difficult it is to memorize and recall. Such studies have also demonstrated that memory is improved when one attaches meaning to utterances.[8] Compare, for instance, your capacity to recall the letters in examples 1 and 2. The twelve letters in each example are the same; they are, however, grouped in a slightly different way:

1. OKF BILB JY WCA
2. OK FBI LBJ YWCA

In the first example, the grouping of the twelve letters is devoid of any meaning. It is therefore unlikely that you will be able to remember many of them. But when the letters are organized into meaningful units, as in the second example, the ability to recall the twelve letters improves significantly. This difference in the capacity to remember information indicates that comprehension is essential and that items that make sense are easier to retrieve from the mental store.

Exercises for improving retention are extremely important, particularly for the performance of consecutive interpretation. For that reason, sample exercises are provided in Part II, together with suggestions for individual practice. The memory exercises stress concentration on the essential elements of the original speech or utterance, for one must analyze the message and retain the key elements. So-called natural texts, that is, those that reflect spontaneous speech, are ideally suited for this early stage of instruction. Formal written speeches, magazine and newspaper articles should generally be avoided.

Listening v. Hearing

Concentrated listening is necessary for comprehension and analysis. A distinction should be drawn between listening and hearing. Listening is a conscious, deliberate process. However, there are different ways in which individuals listen to a message, and this is determined by various factors, including the listener's interest in the subject. The term *selective listening* indicates that the message is not "taken in" in its entirety by the listener. Instead, one hears what one chooses to hear. By contrast, the term concentrated listening indictes that a mental effort is required of the listener. Because the objective of the interpreter is to follow the speaker's thought processes and understand the entire message, interpreters must engage in active concentrated listening. This mental effort is crucial because an interpreter "takes the place" of the speaker. Thus, without concentrated listening, understanding and accurate reformulation of the message would not be possible. In summary, interpreters must do the following:

CONCENTRATE when listening to the source language message;
COMPREHEND the meaning of the source language message in context by going beyond the literal meaning; and
FORMULATE AND EXPRESS the message accurately and completely in the target language.

Chapter 3

DEFINING THE TERMS

Translation v. Interpretation

Translation and interpretation are two tasks which require decoding of a message in one language and its encoding in a different language. *Translation* generally refers to the transfer of thoughts and ideas from one language (the source language) to another (the target language) by means of the written word. *Interpretation* refers to oral communication situations in which one person speaks in the source language, an interpreter processes this input and produces output in a second language, and another person (or persons) listen(s) to the interpreted target language version of the original speaker's message. The term "translation," therefore, refers to the processing of written language while "interpretation" refers to the processing of spoken language. Translation converts a written text into another written text, while interpretation converts an oral message into another oral message. *Sight translation* is a hybrid form by which interpreters give an oral rendition into the target language of a text written in a source language. Both translation and interpretation serve to eliminate barriers to communication across languages and cultures; translators and interpreters function as linguistic intermediaries or mediators.

Translation and interpretation call for language processing of a source language that has to be transformed into an output in a target language, while keeping the content of the message intact. Both tasks require complete fluency in the languages involved, share common characteristics, and have similar goals. However, the modes of processing are different in translation and in interpretation, and they represent two distinct professions. The basic differences in the use of the oral versus the written mode have several ramifications, as discussed below.

Translation and interpretation differ from each other in several ways. In translation, the source message which is written in (L_A) must be studied, analyzed and subsequently transformed into the target language (L_B) as a written text. Hence the translation is contained in a permanent setting. This text, regardless of its quality, "is static, immutable in its form and fixed in time. And the translation, equally circumscribed within a written text, is intended, as was the original, for a public the translator does not know."[1] Interpreting, however, represents an entirely different operation. In interpretation, a spoken message in a source language (L_A) must be immediately transformed and communicated orally in the target language (L_B). Thus, another basic difference in the use of the oral versus the written mode involves time constraints. Because interpreters must process and deliver their final product instantly, they perform at a speed which is considerably greater than that of translators. Language processing in interpretation is achieved through different techniques or modes. But regardless of the method used, the interpreter is present with both speaker and listener(s) and participates in a dialogue. The interpreter's words are aimed at a listener (or listeners) to whom he transmits the message directly.

Modes of Interpretation

Interpretation has been defined as an activity which allows two or more persons who do not speak the same language to communicate orally. This can be accomplished in several ways; thus, the different modes of interpreting are: simultaneous interpretation, consecutive interpretation, summary interpretation, and sight translation. In court interpreting all four may be used, although the summary mode is used rarely. Selection of a particular mode is generally contingent upon the situation and the availability of simultaneous interpretation equipment. Instruction in interpretation should adhere to the following sequence recommended by Weber: sight translation, consecutive interpretation, and simultaneous interpretation.[2] In this chapter each mode is introduced in that order, followed by remarks on summary interpretation. The materials included for interpretation practice in Part II of this book are arranged in the same sequence.

Sight Translation

Sight translation is the oral rendition into a target language of material written in the source language. According to Weber, it is "the process through which every translator must go before putting anything on paper. Moreover, it is really what translators do if they dictate their translations."[3] In court, sight translation is used when foreign language documents are introduced as evidence without an English-language translation. In such a situation, the interpreter is generally asked to read the source language text into the record in the target language. This mode is also used when non-English speaking defendants must "read" crucial documents pertaining to their case, prior to signing them or making other binding decisions. These include presentence investigations (PSI), indictments, and plea agreements. In these instances, the interpreter sight translates the written material off-the-record for the benefit of the defendant(s).

Court interpreters must be able to sight translate quickly, accurately, and be prepared to deal with unanticipated difficulties. Due to the wide variety of writing styles, which range from quasi-illiterate to very technical or formal, and the diversity of subject matter of the documents which interpreters may be called upon to sight translate, sight translation exercises should be performed regularly. Additionally, practice in sight translation helps develop: the appropriate conduct before an audience; public speaking quality, poise, voice, and presentation; the skills that are necessary for accurately transposing a message from a source to a target language at a high rate of speed; the swift eye-brain-voice coordination which is vital in the simultaneous interpretation of prepared written texts (such as the Court's instructions to the jury) that are often read at top speed by the judge; self-confidence in court interpretation, since a visual message is easier to interpret that an oral one; vocabulary; and familiarity with legal terminology and concepts.

Consecutive Mode

In the consecutive mode, the interpreter conveys a message in the target language in a sequential manner after the speaker. This mode requires that the source language speaker pause at intervals in order to allow the interpreted message to be relayed. In court, the consecutive mode is used principally in interview situations, at the witness stand in trials, and whenever a non-English-speaking defendant or witness speaks for the record during the pretrial process, in depositions, sentencings and other legal proceedings.

The consecutive mode is also preferred in many other types of interpreting situations, such as in diplomatic interpreting or high-level talks, welcoming addresses, speeches for banquets or similar occasions, press conferences, and two-language negotiations for industry or business. Interpreters may unexpectedly be called on to interpret in this mode if, for instance, simultaneous equipment is not available or if it fails.

In consecutive interpretation, the importance of the delivery of the message should not be overshadowed by the requirements of accuracy and completeness. Applications of *pragmatics* to research on court interpreting indicate that alterations made by the court interpreter count a great deal in shaping the impressions that mock jurors form, both of the testifying witness and of the examining attorney. Pragmatics may be loosely defined as the study of "the use of language to do things, focusing on what a person is doing with words in particular situations."[4] Berk-Seligson's studies show that the participation of an interpreter in the examination of a witness affects the impressions that mock jurors form of that witness. Her research indicates that the "perceptions of some of the witness's social/psychological attributes—namely, convincingness, truthfulness, intelligence, and competence—are affected by pragmatic alterations made by the interpreter."[5] Thus, consecutive interpreting involves public performance, and the quality of the delivery may alter the content of the message. In court, the jury does indeed judge; the quality of the interpretation may affect the jury's perception of witnesses or defendants.

Court interpreters often make a distinction between so-called long consecutive and short consecutive. The distinction between "long" and "short" consecutive derives from the length of the source language message retained by an interpreter before offering the target language interpretation. Unlike conference interpreting, the "short consecutive" method is the norm in the legal setting. This is due to the emphasis placed in the courtroom on a "verbatim" (as close to the original as possible) rendition of the primary speaker's message.

Public speaking skills are necessary in the execution of consecutive interpretation. For that reason, instruction in public speaking is often required of students enrolled in interpretation and translation training programs. These skills include those discussed in the session on sight translation as well as voice control and unobtrusive behavior. Eye contact and body language must be considered in performing this oral communication skill. Voice quality and patterns are extremely important to the consecutive interpreter. People with an abrasive voice or distracting mannerisms will have difficulty in their work, and systematic treatment of such problems within a course is one way of alerting the individual to possible trouble areas in this respect.[6]

When interpreting in the consecutive mode, court interpreters must be able to "go into" two languages. For instance, when a non-English-speaking witness testifies, the interpreter (who is situated next to him at the witness stand) interprets the attorney's questions from English into the witness's native language. As the witness answers, the interpreter listens and subsequently renders the English interpretation of the response for the benefit of all English-speaking individuals in the courtroom. It is critical to realize that *it is the interpreted version of the testimony and not the witnesses' original source language utterances which become part of the official court record.*

Interpreters must be faithful to the original message. If the primary speaker says, "I want to know if you were present on the day they arrived," the interpreter must not say: "He said he wants to know if you were present on the day they arrived," or "He wants to know if you were present on the day they arrived." Instead, the corresponding first person subject should be used (interpreters should aspire to live up to the label of a "faithful echo"). Thus, when interpreting in the consecutive mode, questions and answers should be interpreted into the target language exactly as they were posed in the source language.

1. ATTORNEY: When did you call Mary?
   INTERPRETER: *¿Cuándo llamó (Ud.) a Mary?*
2. WITNESS: *La llamé el día del juicio.*
   INTERPRETER: I called her the day of the trial.

However, in those (hopefully rare) instances when interpreters must speak "as the interpreter," this should be done in the third person:

> INTERPRETER: Your honor, the interpreter did not hear the question.

While interpreting, interpreters must **not** engage in personal conversation with any of the parties. The interpreter's function is to interpret *only* what has been said. Therefore, when a witness responds to a question by saying, "I don't understand," in the source language, the interpreter must say, "I don't understand," in the target language. Interpreters should not repeat the utterance for the witness or attempt to explain what was said.

Pauses by the primary speaker are necessary in order to allow interpretation of his remarks. Some speakers make natural pauses during their testimony, but most individuals who testify in court are not adept at working with interpreters, and this compounds the difficulty of the interpreter's task of retaining the complete message with all its nuances. It is therefore important for court interpreters to have some control over how much is said before beginning a consecutive interpretation. Sometimes, due to the lack of coherence of a witness, or the excessive length or complexity of an utterance (which may make it difficult for the interpreter to retain all that was said, including hesitations, repetitions, etc.), the interpreter may find it necessary to interrupt the speaker at an appropriate interval. However, interruptions must be kept to a minimum and accomplished through a discreet "pause" or "stop" signal to the speaker (a hand gesture, a nod of the head, or eye contact). In cases in which these signals do not suffice, it may be necessary to "interrupt" the speaker by beginning the interpretation before the witness has finished speaking. All aspiring interpreters, even those who intend to work as court interpreters exclusively, should be trained in both the long and short forms of consecutive interpretation, because such training will make it possible for them to retain greater segments or units of information, thereby reducing the number of instances in which they need to interrupt the speaker. In addition to the court-related material provided in Part II, a variety of prepared texts, such as the welcoming speeches provided by David and Margareta Bowen in *Steps to Consecutive Interpretation*, are extremely useful for this exercise.

There is no consensus among professional court interpreters regarding the reproduction or imitation of gestures and emotions. Some believe that interpreters should imitate the speaker's gestures and emotions while others regard the interpreter as a linguistic conduit and not an actor. At all times professional conduct and accuracy must prevail. Interpreters should strive to deflect attention from themselves and to be as inconspicuous as possible, and imitation of certain gestures should always be avoided. For example, if a witness indicates size (e.g., the length of a knife) with his hands, interpreters must refrain from attempting to duplicate such a gesture, since in such cases it is impossible to preserve accuracy. Likewise, sounds (e.g., a whistle) should not be reproduced; it is sufficient to state, "The witness has just whistled." Nonverbal communication is further discussed in chapter 4.

It cannot be over-emphasized that at all times the interpretation must faithfully reflect the speaker's message, style, tone, and register. The interpretation must always convey exactly what was said, taking "language level" into consideration; slang, obscenities, and formal language must also be expressed in the interpreted version. For example, if a witness testifying in Spanish states, *"Oye, dime por qué me trajeron pacá estos tipos,"* it would be incorrect for the interpreter to alter the message, as in the following rendition: "Your Honor, I would like to know why these gentlemen have brought me to court." In other words, the interpretation must be accurate and rendered in the appropriate speech style. Interpretations should not be literal, that is, word for word. Naturally, it would be incorrect to translate the statement, *"Me tomó el pelo,"* as, "He took my hair." Instead, the correct interpretation into English is, "He pulled my leg." It is the meaning which must be conveyed. If a mistake is made on the stand, the interpreter has a responsibility to make it noted for the record as soon as he becomes aware of it.

Interpreters engaged in consecutive interpretation must always carry a note pad and writing instrument. In positioning themselves in the courtroom, care should be taken to avoid obstructing the jury's view of the witness on the stand. Microphones should be used whenever possible. Interpreters should have a free hand for taking notes and a surface on which to place the note pad. It is also advisable to carry reference materials such as glossaries or a bilingual dictionary.

Videotaping several performances is instructive and extremely helpful to the novice interpreter. Videotapes offer the opportunity to self-critique as well as to monitor progress, and through their use, beginners are immediately confronted with their tendency to turn away from the microphone, to edit utterances, to omit or add testimony, and to mumble. Additionally, videotapes allow interpreters to see the consequences of their own body language and gestures which may interfere with accurate communication. A self-assessment form, such as the one included in section 2, Part II (Consecutive Interpretation Practice), has proven to be particularly helpful for beginners in the evaluation of their own sight translation and consecutive interpretation performances.

Note-taking in Consecutive Mode

Interpreters must always be prepared to take notes when interpreting in the consecutive mode. Clearly, note-taking is a useful tool for consecutive interpretation, because jotting down "key reminders" aids the memory. It is certainly possible to work for a short time without notes, relying on memory alone. However, a notation system will enormously improve the quality of the end product and it is essential for remarks running to more than a few sentences. If a text is brief and relatively simple, memory may be relied upon, as in the statement, "Mr. Brown, please state your name for the record." On the other hand, a more complex statement may require note-taking: "Mr. Brown, aside from the meeting you had with Fred Jones on the night of August 1st, had you met with him or with any of his associates at Ridewell Tire Company prior to the time he reached an agreement with the government on September 10?"

The notes, however, do not substitute for attention and the concentrated listening which are vital to interpreting. There is no need to write much, but many interpreters find it helpful to record dates, numbers, proper names, lists, and addresses. Note taking should be simple and individualized, and designed to assist the memory. As a rule, interpreters must not make mathematical conversions of measurements (e.g., meters into yards or feet, kilos into pounds, kilometers into miles), temperatures (e.g., centigrade into Fahrenheit), or foreign currency (e.g., *pesos* into dollars). Note, however, that the correct Spanish translation of the U.S. English "one billion" (1,000,000,000) is *mil millones* (one thousand million) rather than *un billón*.

There is no universal note-taking system nor are there rules about whether to take notes in the source or the target language. The process is highly individualized and no doubt there are as many different systems as there are interpreters. Practice in note-taking during consecutive interpretation will therefore help each individual develop his or her own note-taking system. There are, however, some general precepts and symbols that are best understood through examples,[7] and it may be helpful for students to see the instructor's own notes.

Notes are only symbols that contain a message; therefore, it does not matter in which language the notes are taken. Interpreters retain ideas and not the source language words. Words are only retained and jotted down if they are of extreme importance and if they carry a message of their own. Generally, this type of note-taking is based upon international cross-cultural symbols. Examples include the following: (♀) = woman; (♂) = man; (↑) = increase; (↓) = decrease; (>) = more; and (<) = less. In addition, it is useful to: pluralize by placing an (s) above the word^s or symbol^s; indicate negation by placing a slash (/) through the word; emphasize by underlining several times; use a wavy line (∼) to indicate "maybe"; draw a triangle

(△) to represent "defendant"; and abbreviate proper nouns (e.g., F^{co} = Francisco, M^{a} = María). Abbreviations should not be ambiguous and if an initial could cause confusion (e.g., "C" may refer to Cuba, Colombia, and Costa Rica, if all of those countries are being discussed), it will be necessary for the interpreter to note several letters of the word (e.g., Col = Colombia, CR = Costa Rica, and Cu = Cuba). Arrows are very versatile and may be used to indicate time frame (e.g., before and after), and verb tenses. The equal sign (=) may be used to show cause and effect. Link words are very important to comprehension. Short English words such as "but" and "so" are useful for conveying opposition and consequence. The symbols for therefore (∴) and because (∵) are also an important aid. Symbols should not be used if they do not carry meaning for the individual interpreter.

When taking notes, interpreters should afford themselves the luxury of space and use large blank sheets of paper, because it is more important to show relationships than to write down every single item.[8] Relationships can be shown through the use of indentation, lines, arrows, and the position of the items on the page. By writing notes vertically on the page, interpreters are able to convey a greater amount of information than if they write across the page. This is possible because a relative or subordinate relationship may be indicated by placing one note beneath another. Through this method, the page layout also contains information. For example, indentation should be used for noting enumerations or lists. This transfer of words to ideas to visual cues will help jar the memory during consecutive interpretation.

Memory-span experiments indicate that the capacity of the short-term memory is limited, and that information in short-term store is lost within approximately 15-20 seconds. Research also indicates that the capacity of short-term store is constant; it can store approximately seven "chunks" or "bits" of information. The long-term store is of virtually unlimited capacity. Information which we have more or less available to us, such as our ability to speak a language, the names of the days of the week, etc., is stored in the long-term memory. A *chunk* of information may be defined as "anything that has some unitary representation in the long-term store."[9] For instance, a digit (e.g., the number 2), a letter, such as *H*, or a word, such as *court*, are all chunks. A proverb such as "The early bird catches the worm," may also be considered as a chunk because such a phrase has a unitary representation in the long-term memory. This has important implications for consecutive interpretation, because if a person has the ability to remember approximately seven items—regardless of how information is contained in each item—it is possible to retain a considerable amount of information in the short-term store.

How can interpreters increase their short-term memory store capacity? Since only seven letters or numbers can be held in the short-term store when they are unrelated to one another, interpreters can judiciously recode many low-information chunks into fewer high-information chunks. In chapter 2 we discussed that memory is improved when one attaches meaning to utterances, and that by organizing twelve apparently unrelated letters (OKFBILBJYWCA) into meaningful units (OK FBI LBJ YWCA), the ability to recall the twelve letters improved dramatically. Note that the first grouping is composed of twelve unrelated letters (chunks), which is beyond the short-term store capacity. In the second grouping, however, there are only four chunks, because each group of letters (e.g., YWCA) has a unitary representation in the long-term store and is thus encoded as a single chunk. This means that by organizing the information into meaningful chunks and by taking notes, capacity in the short-term store is immediately increased. For example, in the phrase, "The undercover agent told me to use the payphone to call him at 576-8219," if the interpreter does not write down the telephone number, his short-term store will be "occupied" by those seven digits, thus reducing his capacity to recall the rest of the message.

Shorthand should be avoided in consecutive interpretation, because shorthand notes are automatically taken in the source language and must be deciphered at the moment of interpretation, thereby slowing down the process. It must be emphasized that words as such are unimportant for interpreters, since in order to retain all the information contained in the original utterances, interpreters must concentrate on meaning alone. Additionally, learning new symbols (shorthand) would further strain the interpreter's memory. Thus, shorthand notes would constitute an unnecessary burden on interpreters and rather than facilitating their work, would further complicate the task of consecutive interpretation. Notes are of no value and may instead become a hindrance to the interpreter if he has to decipher them.

In order to place note-taking within the context of the interpreting process, let us summarize the sequence of processes which any foreign language interpreter must go through before rendering an interpretation. The process involves: hearing, comprehension, and analysis of the source language message. While the message is analyzed, the interpreter retains the essential ideas which he quickly grasps and jots down. To get to the substantive message, it is helpful to establish a relationship between the parts of the message. In organizing the content of the source language message, it is also important to have a mental picture of the message and visualize what is being said. Finally, the interpreter reconstitutes and conveys the message in the target language.

In conclusion, the activities of analysis and note-taking are intimately linked: notes are used to convey ideas, not specific words. In general, only words that are of extreme importance, as well as numbers, figures, names, addresses, telephone numbers, license plate numbers, etc. should always be taken down. As summarized by John A. Henderson, "notes should be few and concise and go to the heart of the matter."[10] This process requires the identification of key ideas. Note-taking is a direct consequence of the rapid analysis that has taken place and the mental image of the essential elements of the message, because utterances must be quickly analyzed by the interpreter prior to determining which words or symbols to write down.

Simultaneous Mode

This mode has been described as one of the most demanding human information processing tasks. Simultaneous interpretation demands that the interpreter speak almost contemporaneously with the primary speaker whose words are being interpreted. The interpreter is simultaneously playing two roles in the field of language communication that otherwise are always practiced separately: speech and comprehension. In performing a simultaneous interpretation, as Lambert has observed, the interpreter has to "juggle" several activities: 1) the interpreter receives part of a sentence in L_A ("chunk" 1); 2) the interpreter begins translating and conveying chunk 1 in L_B; 3) at the same time as the interpreter is vocalizing chunk 1, chunk 2 is being processed auditorily and stored until chunk 1 has been interpreted. "Furthermore," notes Lambert, "while emitting the translation of chunk 1, the interpreter is continuously monitoring his/her output to ensure its correctness."[11]

In court, much of the interpreter's work is done in the simultaneous mode. This mode is used when rendering an off-the-record rendition of all that is said in the courtroom for the benefit of the non-English speaking defendant(s). Other interpreters use this mode, for example: when interpreting during certain discussions or negotiations; for international conferences; for formal speeches, mostly of a general or political nature; for technical and scientific papers, which are almost always read; and for lectures, which are normally prepared in writing.

The following description of simultaneous interpreting represents an interpreter's own view of this activity:

> . . . The speaker speaks, and you are speaking too. If memory plays little part, neither does the personal element in the reconstruction of speech. Your sentence must, of necessity, follow the pattern of those which the speaker has pronounced. Circumlocutions are impossible. You cannot hear ahead. Your rendering will naturally tend to be verbatim, but, of course, what you say must make sense, and word for word translation may not. As you are following the speaker you start a sentence. But as you start a sentence you are taking a leap in the dark, you are mortgaging your grammatical future; the original sentence may suddenly be turned in such a way that your translation of its end cannot easily be reconciled with your translation of its start. Great nimbleness is called for to guide the mind through this syntactical maze, whilst at the same time it is engaged upon the work of word-translation. Listening intently, translating half unconsciously, consciously intervening to redress the forms and balances of syntax, touching up, putting in fillers—these are some of the demands of simultaneous interpretation.[12]

It may appear to those unfamiliar with the process, that simultaneous interpreters listen and speak at the same time. However, because the interpreter does not perform a word-for-word translation but is rather transferring the thoughts and ideas of the primary speaker into the target language, there is a time lag that may vary from a split second to a few seconds.

To understand more fully what is involved in simultaneous interpretation in the courtroom, let us examine what occurs when, for example, we speak contemporaneously. When we speak spontaneously, our words do not come out in spurts. That is, we do not first think out what we are going to say and then stop thinking while we speak. Likewise, we do not stop speaking in order to mentally compare what we are going to say next. On the contrary, our speech is continuous, it involves two superimposed processes in a cause and effect relationship: mental impulses and their oral expression. It appears, however, that the words are uttered at the exact moment the following thought is conceived. On the contrary, "at the precise moment the product of the conceptualizing process is uttered, the mind is already focused on further development of the thought which is to be expressed in the following statement."[13]

Interpreters do essentially the same thing when they are interpreting in the simultaneous mode as when they are speaking. Interpreters hear the next source language unit or segment of speech while uttering the preceding one in the target language. They hear their own message while at the same time listening to the meaning of the words being spoken by the source language speaker, and they retain this meaning in order to deliver it immediately after completing the previous utterances in the target language. The interpreter's memory stores the meaning of the speaker's words and not the words themselves.

Segmentation or "chunking" of the L_A in units-to-be-encoded in the L_B is characteristic behavior of interpreters. Goldman-Eisler (1972) suggested that simultaneous interpreters have their own ways of segmenting the input and that there are three ways in which the source language message may be segmented: 1) encoding the chunks of speech between pauses as they occur in the source language (*identity*); 2) starting to encode before the source language chunk has ended (*fission*); and 3) stringing two or more input chunks and then encoding (*fusion*). Of a large number of of responses from six professional interpreters working from and to English, French and German, Goldman-Eisler found 11% identity, 48% fission, and 41% fusion responses. Goldman-Eisler concluded that whether simultaneous interpreters used input chunks or imposed their own, segmentation appeared to be a function of the language being translated, and that larger chunks were stored after interpreting German than English or French.[14]

Another important feature of simultaneous interpretation is the ear-voice span (EVS). This is the time between the moment a message unit reaches the ear and the moment it is reproduced in the target language. The interpreter must group a certain amount of material before beginning to interpret, the amount varying with the position in the sentence of certain key words such as the verb. However, because of limitations in short-term memory capacity, an interpreter cannot afford to lag too far behind the source-language speaker. Goldman-Eisler analyzed the linguistic structure of the words comprising interpreters' EVS when simultaneously interpreting from and to English and French and from

German to English. The majority of EVS were found to consist of at least a complete predicate expression; the average EVS appeared to be between four and five words. Studies by Barik indicate that the interpreter characteristically lags behind the speaker by two or three seconds.[15] Goldman-Eisler concluded that an interpreter makes use of his own chunking as well as the segmentation produced by the speaker. Segmentation, therefore, is an active processing which is a function of both of the languages involved in the interpretation.

A speaker's words or message cannot be predicted. This is a factor that makes interpreting a stressful profession. Moreover, simultaneous interpreters cannot wait for the speaker to develop his entire idea before the implications of each chunk of speech can be understood fully. Consequently, in order to accurately comprehend the meaning of the speaker's statements, interpreters must compensate for the quick speed at which the process of analysis-expression is to be carried out. A thorough knowledge of the subject matter (preparation) and as much relevant information about different aspects of the legal proceeding as possible (information), are essential in this regard.

Shadowing

Prior to attempting to interpret in the simultaneous mode, it is useful to practice *shadowing* exercises, so as to become familiar with the techniques of listening and speaking simultaneously. Shadowing is the technique of listening to a source language message and at the same time repeating (in the same language) what one hears. This transfer of input from the auditory to the vocal mode is a comparatively simple type of processing. Shadowing does not require the complex analysis and transformation of input necessary in simultaneous interpretation, which requires analysis of both input and output at a number of levels. In shadowing, speakers simultaneously repeat what they hear, but in the same language. Short speeches on a variety of subjects in the two working languages constitute a good introduction to this technique.

Once shadowing can be handled without difficulty, the additional step of switching from one linguistic code to another is introduced. Such advanced exercises should include authentic materials presented in ascending degree of difficulty, including opening and closing arguments, direct and cross-examination of a witness, direct examination of an expert witness, and a judge's charges or instructions to the jury (see section 4, Part II).

Summary Mode

In the summary mode the interpreter condenses and summarizes. This method is seldom used in court interpreting because it lacks the accuracy and completeness which are absolutely necessary in the legal setting. use of the summary mode was authorized by the Court Interpreters Act of 1978, which included a provision that read, in pertinent part:

> The interpretation provided by certified interpreters pursuant to this section shall be in the consecutive mode except that the presiding judicial officer, with the approval of all interested parties, may authorize a simultaneous or summary interpretation when such officer determines that such interpretation will aid in the efficient administration of justice . . .'

That provision was changed in 1988. Subsection (k) of Public Law 100-702, § 709, states that the interpretation provided by certified or otherwise qualified interpreters "shall be in the simultaneous mode for any party to a judicial proceeding instituted by the United States and in the consecutive mode for witnesses. . . ."[16] Thus, court interpreters must generally avoid the use of this mode unless there is a prior stipulation by all parties involved as to its use.

Effects of Listening Conditions

Skills involving the sharing of attention and the processing of information are particularly susceptible to the detrimental effects of environmental noise. It is not surprising, therefore, that simultaneous interpreters are particularly sensitive to the listening conditions. Gerver has documented the effects of noise on the performance of simultaneous interpreters.[17] Twelve professional conference interpreters interpreted into English six prerecorded excerpts from articles in the French edition of the UNESCO Courier. The passages were heard without noise, with a moderately noisy background, and against a very noisy background. The results indicated that as noise increased, more was omitted and more errors were made in interpreting; in spite of the increase in errors, the ratio of simultaneous interpreters' corrections to errors (of commission) remained almost the same in all three listening conditions; the ear-voice spans remained fairly constant in good and bad listening conditions. These results suggest that to maintain a constant ear-voice span in difficult listening conditions, the simultaneous interpreters in this study were prepared to sacrifice accuracy by lowering their response criteria, that is, by accepting more errors without attempting to correct them.

Good listening conditions, then, are an essential element for a good performance, for one cannot interpret what one cannot hear. Good acoustics, adequate physical location of the interpreter in the courtroom, appropriate equipment, and the use of microphones by all the source language speakers, contribute to this end.

Equipment

The only equipment necessary in sight translation or consecutive interpretation is a note pad and writing instrument. However, special equipment is necessary in order to effectively carry out simultaneous interpretation. Although it is possible to interpret simultaneously in court without the use of such equipment (the interpreter is situated in close proximity to the non-English speaker(s) and whispers the interpretation) this method does not work effectively for more than one or two persons. This "whisper" method is frequently utilized in proceedings involving only one defendant, such as sentencings, initial appearances, bond hearings, arraignments, pretrial detention hearings, and indictments.

The basic equipment needed for simultaneous interpretation includes transmitters and headsets (wireless or not). Interpreters speak into the transmitter and defendants hear the interpretation through the headsets. The use of such equipment makes it possible for interpreters to whisper into the transmitter. Consequently, the interpreter's voice does not "compete with" or drown out what is being said by the source language speaker. Unfortunately, many courtrooms are not equipped with simultaneous interpretation equipment, even though use of a transmitter and headsets improves audibility, increases physical comfort, reduces strain on the voice, allows greater concentration for the interpreter, and makes physical distance between interpreters and defendants possible.

Wireless equipment allows for maximum mobility. If acoustics are poor or if the primary speaker does not speak into the microphone, the interpreter should be able to move to a position in the courtroom which is most advantageous for listening. Occasionally, videotapes, graphs, maps, and other visual materials are displayed to the court and the jury and are often outside the interpreter's field of vision. If the interpreter is unable to see these visuals, it is advisable for him to move to a better position, without unduly disrupting the proceedings.

Unlike conference interpreters, court interpreters are not isolated in booths or consoles. However, physical distance between the interpreter and the defendant, whenever possible, is desirable. Unnecessary communication on the part of the defendant with the interpreter is thereby discouraged, thus underscoring the interpreter's neutral role in the legal process.

Interpreters should follow several basic rules when handling simultaneous interpretation equipment. For instance, interpreters should: always test the equipment prior to its use; make certain that the microphone is turned on while interpreting, and off at all other times; have back up equipment immediately available, should any component fail; control the volume on the receiver to ensure that the interpreter's voice is heard clearly by the listener(s) and is comfortable for the interpreter; keep a proper distance from the microphone and maintain this distance; and use the cough or interrupt buttons whenever necessary.

It is important to become familiar with the equipment and feel comfortable with it prior to a first attempt at simultaneous interpretation. As a first exercise, beginners should listen to a good simultaneous interpretation in order to learn what the interpreted discourse should be. The elements of a good simultaneous interpretation include the following: the target language rendition sounds effortless; the interpreter's voice sounds pleasant and inspires confidence; the interpretation does not sound like a "word-for-word" translation; and the interpretation is complete. The innuendos, inflections, nuances, as well as the style and register of the original speaker must be maintained.

Number of Interpreters to Cover a Trial

The concentration and effort required to carry out the task of interpreting is extreme, and interpreters should not work alone, all day, on one case. The *Court Administration Bulletin*, a monthly journal of the Court Administration Division of the Administrative Office of the United States Courts, reports that the *Interim Court Interpreter Regulations* issued in 1989 allow the presiding judicial officer to "use the services of multiple interpreters where necessary to aid interpretation of court proceedings." This is done "to assure that the quality of interpretation does not decrease due to interpreter fatigue."[18] During a trial, someone is always speaking, and it is seldom the same person. The interpreter, however, must process the words of everyone in the courtroom. For that reason, he is the only person in the courtroom who is constantly listening, interpreting and speaking. Consequently, interpreters should work in teams of two (occasionally more interpreters may be assigned to lengthy, multi-defendant trials).

The U.S. district court regulations call for the use of interpreters in tandem, a standard that originates from the profession of conference interpreting. These standards have been established by organizations and agencies such as the United Nations and the State Department, which have used conference interpreters for many years. The United Nations policy is to switch or rotate interpreters every twenty minutes. Two interpreters work together (in the simultaneous or consecutive mode, as required by circumstances and the nature of the proceedings) and they alternate rendering the interpretation. The non-speaking interpreter remains present to listen, follow the testimony, assist as necessary by taking notes and looking up difficult terms, or "take over" for the other interpreter should he need an unscheduled break.

Because the consideration of findings and testimony from experts indicate that an interpreter should not work alone in court proceedings, and that thirty minutes is about the limit of efficiency for interpretation, this is the standard that should be followed in court.[19] However, in many courtrooms interpreters are called upon to interpret alone, without relief, in complex trials for much longer periods of time. Under such circumstances, the quality of the interpretation will inevitably suffer.

Chapter 4

LANGUAGE AND CULTURE

Un idioma es una tradición, un modo de sentir la realidad, no un arbitrario repertorio de símbolos.
—Jorge Luis Borges, prologue to *El ojo de los tigres*

Cross-Cultural Awareness

Communication between peoples of various cultural backgrounds and languages has increased in modern times due to rapid changes in technology, as well as expanded trade, travel, and migration. Because differences in cultures can cause misunderstandings, society needs professionals in the field of intercultural communication who are able to cross linguistic and cultural barriers. Interpreters and translators play a significant role in intercultural communication, and as the frequency of contact between peoples of various cultural backgrounds and languages increases, so to will the need for translators and interpreters. Although language is the prime factor in linguistic interchange across cultures, accurate communication is based on other important components as well. Some of these components are discussed in this chapter.[1]

The objective of the court interpreter is to convey precisely, accurately, and completely in the target language the information contained in the source language. Consequently, factors such as dialect, educational level, register, specialized terms, style, and nonverbal cues will influence the interpreter's choice of expression.

Translation and interpretation are complex activities that require substantially more than the simple substitution of words and phrases in one language for equivalents in another. Because languages are dynamic and ever-changing, interpreters and translators must keep abreast of changes in their working languages and in the cultures in which those languages are spoken.

An examination of the interpreting process reveals that although there is a central core of linguistic activity, interpretation also involves extralinguistic factors. This process includes, of course, the nuances of culture. In my view, *semiotics*, the study of sign systems or structures, can contribute much toward understanding the interpreting process, because semiotics studies the art of communication. It emphasizes *how* things mean as well as *what* they mean. Communication involves non-linguistic codes (e.g., gestures) and paralinguistic codes (e.g., intonation). Clearly, the process of interpretation, in addition to the transfer of meaning contained in one set of language signs into another set of language signs through linguistic knowledge, also involves extra-linguistic criteria: language and culture are inseparable.

To understand how translators and interpreters handle factors that transcend purely linguistic phenomena, consider Eugene Nida's model of the translating process (Figure 1).

Nida explains that rather than going directly from one set of surface structures to another, a competent translator first analyzes the source language message into "its simplest and structurally clearest

Figure 1

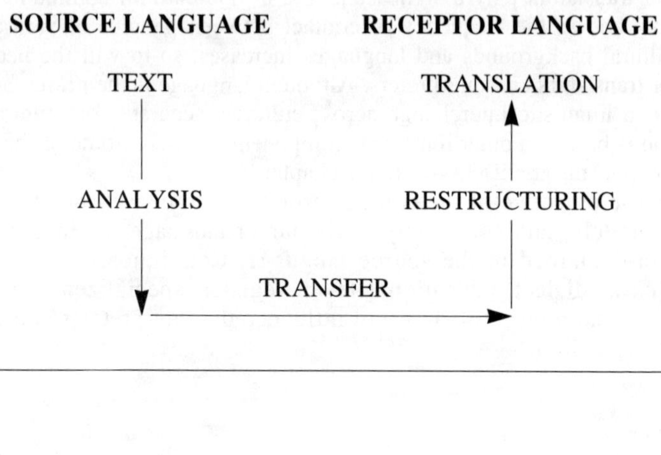

forms, transfers it at this level, and then restructures it to the level in the receptor language which is most appropriate for the audience which he intends to reach."[2] Nida designates the language into which one translates as receptor language rather than target language. He uses the term 'receptor' to emphasize that the translated message must be decoded by those who "receive" it.

Using Nida's diagram, Bassnett-McGuire demonstrates the complexity involved in transferring meaning from one linguistic code to another. Her discussion of the translation into French, German, and Italian of the seemingly simple lexical unit "hello", is also helpful in understanding interpretation. For example, dictionaries give *ça va?*, *hallo*, and *âllo*! for French; *wie geht's?* and *hallo* for German; and *ola*; *pronto?* and *ciao* for Italian equivalents of this standard English form of greeting. English does not distinguish between the word used when greeting someone face to face and that used when answering the telephone, while French, German and Italian do make that distinction. *Pronto* can only be used as a telephonic greeting. The German *hallo* can be used as a telephonic greeting and can also be yelled *Hey!* to attract someone's attention on the street. *Ciao*, used on arrival and departure, is a word of greeting linked to a moment of contact between individuals either coming or going and not to the specific context of arrival or initial encounter. Bassnett-McGuire illustrates the stages involved in translating "hello" into French (Figure 2).

Figure 2

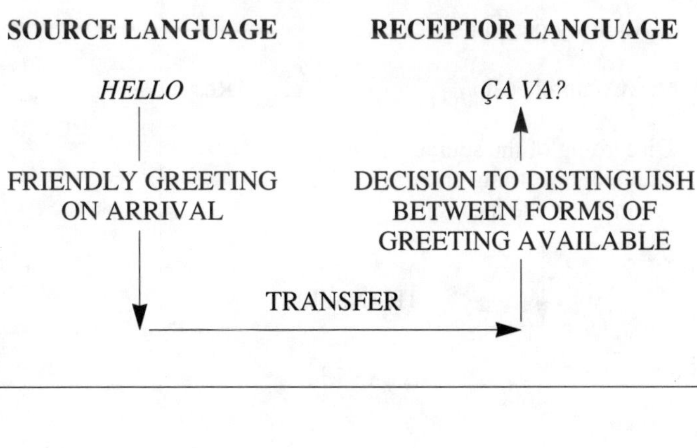

In translating "hello" one must first extract from the term a "core of meaning." During the translation process, "the notion of greeting has been isolated and the word *hello* has been replaced by a phrase carrying the same notion."[3] Interpretation encompasses the same analysis, transfer, and restructuring involved in translation. However, the rate at which interpreters work (120-220 words per minute are processed in simultaneous interpretation) is one of the several significant differences between the two processes.

When I add Spanish to this example, the interpreter or translator has many options from which to choose, including: *hola*, *¿qué hay?*, *¿qué hubo?*, and *¿qué tal?*. *Diga*, *oigo*, *mande*, and *¿bueno?* are likewise possible as telephone greetings. Selection of one among these and other possibilities entails knowledge of the various dialects of Spanish spoken in the United States and of the numerous varieties of Spanish in Spain and Latin America.

In Figure 3, I have followed Nida's model of the translating process and incorporated the stages involved in interpretation, namely: 1) auditory perception of a linguistic utterance in the source language; 2) comprehension of the message through a process of analysis and *exegesis*. Exegesis may be defined as "the process of

Figure 3

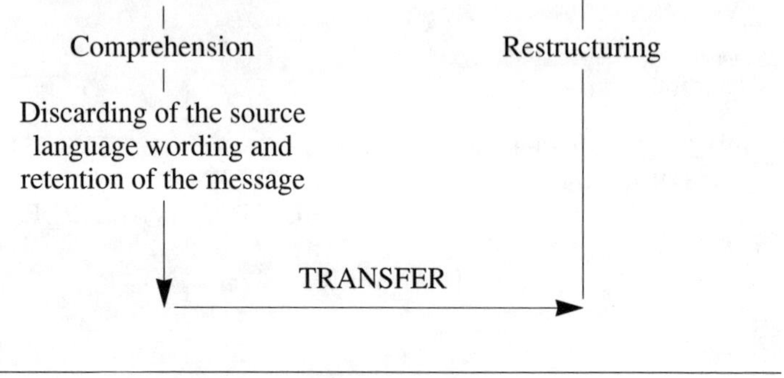

reconstructing the communication event by determining its meaning (or meanings) for the participants in the communication;"[4] 3) immediate and deliberate discarding of the source language wording; 4) retention of the mental representation of the message (concepts, ideas, etc.); and 5) production of a new utterance in the receptor or target language which expresses the original source language meaning in its entirety and with all its nuances.[5]

In Figure 4, I substitute the word "hello" used in Bassnett-McGuire's illustration (Figure 2) with a phrase taken from an actual courtroom proceeding— "The jury will be charged this afternoon" —to summarize the process involved in the interpretation of this sentence into Spanish.

Figure 4

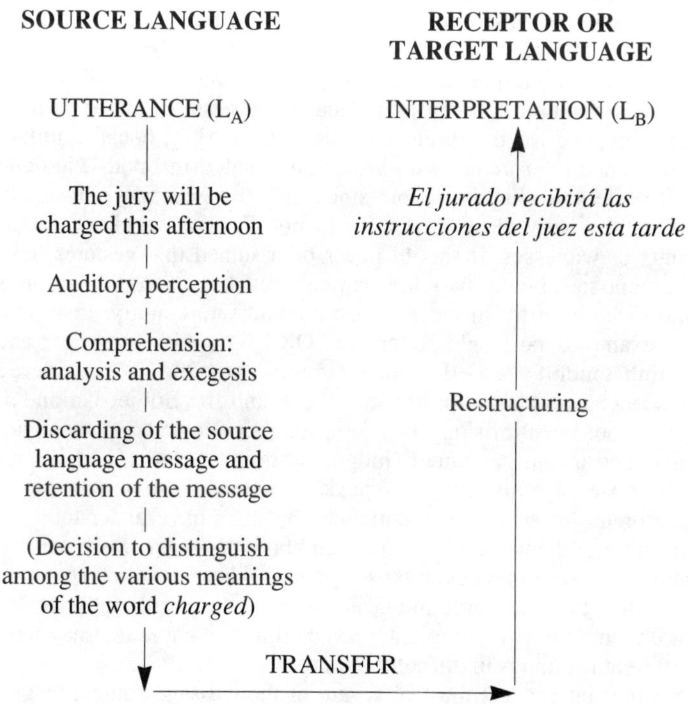

During the comprehension process the verb *charged* is analyzed. A person familiar with courtroom procedure and legal language is able to distinguish between the various meanings of this verb (e.g., to give an electric charge to; to accuse or blame; to attack; to fix or ask as fee for payment; to restore the active materials in [a storage battery]; to impose a task or responsibility on; to command, instruct, or exhort a right or authority) and choose the target language wording which conveys the original source language message correctly.

Nonverbal communication

Communication can involve feelings and emotions as well as actual message content, or factual information. To convey fully the total message from one person to another, court interpreters must be sensitive to the nuances of all aspects of a communication situation. Thus, attention must be paid not only to the words, but also to tone, changes of intonation, facial cues, and gestures, because the full context of an interpreted statement involves verbal as well as nonverbal communication. Body language and gestures are of particular relevance for interpreters in the legal setting, because unlike conference interpreters who are often isolated in booths, judicial interpreters are highly visible since they are generally physically situated in very close proximity to non-English-speaking defendants or witnesses. It should never be assumed that gestures have the same meaning in two different cultures. In fact, certain gestures significantly differ in meaning from country to country. In Brazil, for example, the Anglo-American "OK" sign, with forefinger and thumb touching and the other fingers extended, is considered obscene; it is also impolite in Greece and the Soviet Union.[6] It would not be surprising, therefore, for monolingual and monocultural courtroom personnel (judges, attorneys, clerks, and jurors) who observe a non-English-speaking witness testify through an interpreter, to erroneously conclude that they have understood the meaning of the witness's gestures and body language. Such persons may be unaware that even those gestures whose meaning seems so clear that they can serve in place of words (i.e., the thumbs-up sign or drawing the index finger across the throat like a knife, may have different meanings in different cultures.

Court interpreters must be aware of the message content of gestures, even those gestures the meanings of which seem unambiguous;

even those signs which often replace words, have different meanings in different cultures. For example, twirling the index finger around the ear, a gesture used in the United States by Anglophone Americans to mean "crazy", is used in the Netherlands to indicate someone is wanted on the phone.[7]

Biculturalism in Court Interpreting

According to Edward Sapir, language is a "guide to social reality" and no two languages are ever sufficiently similar to be considered as representing the same social reality.[8] Thus, the worlds in which different societies live are distinct worlds, not merely the same world with different labels attached. Sapir's theory, endorsed by Whorf that language determines perception and that users of different languages perceive the world differently,[9] has been disputed by more recent research; it is, however, agreed that language expresses perception and the categorization of experience.[10]

The transfer involved in the process of interpreting from a source to a target language is not automatic because language is a metaphor for cultural and personal experience. Each language is composed of a different set of metaphors, based on cultural and personal assumptions and experiences that can be very similar, or remarkably different, at the cultural or personal level. All languages belong in a cultural framework and exist within that framework. Language has therefore been called the "heart within the body of culture."[11] The word *culture* is used here to mean "the way of life of a people or society, including its rules of behavior; its economic, social, and political systems; its language; its religious beliefs; its laws; and so on. Culture is acquired, socially transmitted, and communicated in part by language."[12]

Biculturalism entails the ability to interpret experiences in the manner appropriate to both cultures involved. Monoculturalism implies ethnocentric interpretation, regardless of the language or the context of the experiences.[13] The distinction is one of degree and bilinguals, as researchers have pointed out, are not *de facto* bicultural.[14] Interpretation requires a deep familiarity with the languages involved (bilingualism) and their respective cultures (biculturalism). In court interpreting, biculturalism plays a significant role in preserving the rights of non-English speakers who come into contact with our judicial system, because to interpret speech is to transpose it with its entire semantic, emotional and aesthetic baggage into a language using different modes of expression. To interpret, one must initially comprehend the message perfectly. Such comprehension enables the interpreter to detach the message from its verbal support and subsequently reconstitute it with all its nuances in another language. Interpretation, then, is "a constant exchange and interchange of mentalities, of one cultural universe with another."[15]

Language has been defined as a set of conventional symbols that allow, or provide the means for self-expression, for sharing ideas, thoughts, or information. What is meant by conventional symbols? Words are abstract symbols that represent something or mean something because we have implicitly agreed to associate the word with the "thing." Words are not the object or the feeling, just a convention that represents it. For example, *table* merely represents the object; the word "table" is a symbol. We could use any other symbol to represent the same object. In the same way a word like *fear* merely represents the emotion.

Can we say without qualification that *pájaro* and *bird* mean the same thing? It depends on how one defines *pájaro* and *bird*. It also depends on whether native Spanish speakers conceptualize the same thing when they hear the word *pájaro* as native English speakers do when they hear the word *bird*. This is in turn complicated by country, region of origin, and even by personal experience. Thus, the word *pájaro* may convey a very different image or mental representation to a person from a rural area than to someone from an urban area in the same region of the country, not to mention the different image that the word may convey to individuals from different geographic locations.

It has been stated that because Eskimos, for example, need to distinguish minute differences in atmospheric conditions in order to survive in their harsh northern environment, they have developed the vocabulary to express those varying conditions. According to some sources, their language has over one hundred different ways of designating what we call *white* in English.[16] There are more than thirty different words for *snow* in the Eastern Arctic dialect of Inuktitut, at least fifteen for *wind*, and countless others to describe every facet of winter weather. Thus, the word *apimajuq* means *snow-covered*, *apisimajuq* refers to *snow-covered but not snowed-in*, *qaliriiktaq* is *a snow layer of poor quality for an igloo*, and *qiasuqqaq* is *thawed snow that refroze with an icy surface*.[17] Other cultures do not need such fine distinctions. Equivalence is not word for word, but rather message equivalence: "Words in one language do not carry the same connotations as do similar words in another language. Past history and experience as well as current cultural contexts are all embodied in the language itself."[18]

Because words are conventional symbols, they have to be considered in the context of the system or society in which they serve as conventions. There are cultural, social, legal, religious, economic, historical, and educational differences among countries, and all of these aspects of the cultures of different countries are inextricably bound up in their languages. Does this mean, then, that most words have no exact translation in other languages? Any language can, of course, express whatever it has to, but until the necessity arises, a specific language may not have a mechanism that enables it to convey this concept. Perkins points out, for example, that when Chinese speakers came into contact with our culture and the necessity to express contrary-to-fact statements—those situations that in English and Spanish are expressed with the subjunctive—they had to devise a way in their language to convey the notion.[19]

Words mean very little unless we place them in a context. Context involves placing a word among other words, and it is also concerned with the situation in which the words are uttered. The place of origin and the intended meaning of the speaker, among other factors, must be taken into account by the court interpreter. The Japanese word *hai* serves well to illustrate linguistic ambiguity and what is meant by "the intended meaning of the speaker" because *hai* is a versatile and frequently used word. Every language has its ambiguities, but the problem is amplified in Japanese by a cultural abhorrence of dissensions. *Hai* means *yes* but it can also mean *no*. Fujiko Hara explains: "This seeming contradiction and lack of logic is offensive and a mark of insincerity to a Western mind. Understand the 'yes' portion of the sentence as a demonstration of good will and the negative part as the substance of the message."[20] These observations suggest that Japanese/English interpreters must be trained to comprehend the unspoken thought; fluency in a foreign language does not compensate for ignorance, inexperience in handling Japanese language matters, or cultural idiosyncrasies.

Thus, meaning is found in the context of words. Words are symbols; what must be interpreted is the meaning represented by the words, not the words themselves. This may best be illustrated with the ritual of offering a toast when drinking (e.g., "Here's mud in your eye"), and by idiomatic expressions and proverbs.

Idiomatic Expressions

What is an *idiom*? The original meaning of this word in Latin refers to "the word signified" or language itself. In English, it has come to mean an expression whose meaning (as a whole) cannot be inferred from the meanings of its elements (or parts).

The interpretation of idioms takes us a step further in considering the issue of meaning and interpretation. The Spanish idiom, *Juan no tiene pelos en la lengua*, demonstrates the kind of shift that occurs in the process of interpreting. A literal translation would yield the following: *Juan does not have hair on his tongue*. Naturally, the meaning of the original phrase has been lost; instead, an accurate interpretation would provide the phrase: *Juan is outspoken*, or *Juan speaks his mind.*

What is the Spanish equivalent of the following English idiomatic expression: *Every cloud has a silver lining?* A literal translation into Spanish would make no sense at all to a native speaker of that language. Interpreters and translators must be sufficiently familiar with both the target and source language cultures to be able to understand idioms and provide equivalent idiomatic expressions, where required. The Spanish phrase, *No hay mal que por bien no venga*, for instance, would convey the meaning of that popular English expression.

Cultural Miscommunication

In the legal setting, interpreters must be alert to possible cultural miscommunications resulting from differences that may arise because the person involved in a legal proceeding is from a civil-law country where there is no presumption of innocence until proven guilty,[21] or that person may not understand the process itself because the word for *trial* in their native legal system connotes a proceeding where there is virtually no possibility that there will be a finding of not guilty. Moreover, there are cultural differences in degree of formality and forms of address (some languages use a polite or formal form and an informal form of "you" while English uses only one form) which could interfere with communication. Miscommunication may also arise when the person's body language and gestures are different from those of the majority culture of the United States. For example, many Haitians and Hispanics who look at the floor when asked a question, may be doing so as a result of a culturally learned respect for the judge as an authority figure and not because of guilt.[22]

The following exchange, which took place during a deposition serves as an example of culturally learned responses. The plaintiff (in a civil suit) is a male Hispanic. When questioned by a female attorney, through a female interpreter, he emphatically and proudly denies having physical impairments although he is suing for damages as a result of an accident:

> ATTORNEY: Mr. X, is there anything you cannot do now that you were able to do prior to the accident?
> INTERPRETER: *Sr. X, ¿hay algo que usted podía hacer antes del accidente que ahora no puede hacer?*
> PLAINTIFF: *Yo lo puedo todo.* (I can do it all; I can do everything).

Language is an expression of culture. The different legal, cultural, and social background of individuals is reflected in their speech. Cultural fluency, which is necessary in accurate interpretation, includes knowledge of varieties of language and forms of personal address, as well as an awareness of the different meanings of gestures and nonverbal communication.

The Interpreter as Bilingual

> *Becoming bilingual is a way of life. Your whole person is affected as you struggle to reach beyond the confines of your first language and into a new language, a new culture, a new way of thinking, feeling, and acting. Total commitment, total involvement, a total physical, intellectual, and emotional response is necessary to successfully send and receive messages in a second language.*
>
> —H. Douglas Brown,
> *Principles of Language Learning and Teaching*

The concept of bilingualism presents many theoretical and methodological difficulties. It is a complex issue that raises questions which cannot be answered in the present state of knowledge in the study of languages in contact. In this section, bilingualism will be addressed only as it applies to an activity which, by its very nature, demands bilingual competence. It must be underscored, however, that interpretation cannot necessarily be performed by any bilingual person. It is an activity of bilingual processing that can only be performed by bilinguals "who process the two languages in such a way that the message remains intact while the code is changed."[23]

Bilingualism is a phenomenon that has existed since the beginning of language in human history. It is improbable that any language group has ever existed in total isolation from other language groups, and the history of languages is replete with examples of language contact which have led to some form of bilingualism. Today, it is practically impossible to identify a genuinely monolingual country, that is, one that does not contain one or several linguistic minorities whose members use, to some extent, both the majority and minority languages. Japan perhaps most closely approximates a monolingual country, with a small Korean community (0.7%).

Definitions of bilingualism range from a nativelike competence in two languages to a minimal proficiency in a second language. Most definitions refer to linguistic skill and neglect nonlinguistic factors. Thus, the word *bilingual* may refer to all degrees of linguistic accomplishment, and a person's bilingualism is a matter of degree. For instance, Grosjean defines bilingualism as "the regular use of two languages." He notes that most bilinguals "use their languages for different purposes and in different situations, and hence 'balanced' bilinguals, those who are equally fluent in both languages, are probably the exception and not the norm."[24]

Ideally, an interpreter should fit Thiery's description of the so-called true bilingual, that is, someone who is "taken to be one of themselves by the members of two different linguistic communities, at roughly the same social and cultural level."[25] However, although most professional interpreters are highly proficient in two or more languages, those who are perfectly balanced, that is, who have reached an equivalent competence in those languages and can pass as monolinguals in each language, are rare.

A bilingual's dominant language is the one which is preferred or easier to use. In many cases this is the first language learned, but the second or third learned language could become the bilingual's dominant language. Anderson points out that linguistic dominance may have two consequences for interpreters. First, because it is generally easier to understand a language than to speak it with facility, bilinguals who interpret into their dominant language will be expected to meet with more success than when interpreting from it. Second, the greater the linguistic dominance the more likely an interpreter will identify with the speakers of the dominant language, rather than with clients speaking the "other" language.[26] However, at all times interpreters must act as a "faithful echo" of the remarks of **all** parties, therefore casting themselves in the role of the nonpartisan, a sometimes difficult, but necessary task. Personal detachment is essential for accurate interpreting. In court, personal detachment results in maximal attention to faithful interpretation, even to reproduction of intonation and gestural signs. Communicative content must not be manipulated (i.e., angered words blunted, profanity "cleaned up" or omitted).

Grosjean believes that much of what we know about bilingualism today is tainted, in part at least, by a monolingual, fractional, view of bilingualism. He advances the view that bilinguals are not two monolinguals in one person, but different, perfectly competent speaker-hearers in their own right. This "wholistic" view proposes that the bilingual is an integrated whole which cannot easily be decomposed into two separate parts. The bilingual is not the sum of two complete or incomplete monolinguals. Rather, a bilingual has a unique and specific linguistic configuration because the "coexistence and constant interaction of the two languages in the bilingual has produced a different but complete language system."[27] Likewise, the bicultural person is not two monoculturals; instead, the bilingual combines and blends aspects of the two cultures to produce a unique cultural configuration. According to this wholistic view of bilingualism, the bilingual has developed competencies to the extent required by his needs and those of the environment. The bilingual uses the two languages separately or together, for different purposes, in different domains of life, with different people.

It is beyond the scope of this book to review the extensive literature dealing with bilingualism.[28] I do wish to emphasize, however, that the occupational demands of the interpreting profession make it imperative for interpreters to engage in a continuing learning experience and to strive to improve their competencies in all their working languages.

How can interpreters develop linguistic and cultural competence in each language? Certain types of educational experiences can increase the level of desirable skills found in good interpreters. Reading on a wide variety of subjects is necessary to expand knowledge and vocabulary. Travel abroad, in my view, is essential. Overseas study or travel encourages flexibility and leads to a wide background of knowledge—both of which are necessary for interpreters. A number of researchers have found that people who live outside their home country for long periods of time learn a great deal about themselves because they are inevitably challenged in the other culture. Behaviors that fit well into their "home" culture do not work as well in the other culture, forcing the person to reexamine the basis of the behavior and how it fits different situations. Thus the person learns that certain behaviors are suited to certain situations only, and thus encouraging greater mental flexibility in problem solving. A person having experienced such *intercultural experiences* will be more flexible, more aware of subtle communication variables, and will have more knowledge on which to draw in the role of interpreter.

This chapter has emphasized that culture is an orderly way of coping with the infinite complexities of reality and that language symbolically represents the culture that uses it. Language therefore conveys a great deal of information about how a culture views the world. Cultural fluency in court interpreting implies not only knowledge of regional or dialectal meanings of words and expressions, but also of the meanings of gestures and unspoken reactions. It also implies cognizance of cultural justifications for reactions, of degree of formality of address, and an awareness that a non-English-speaking person may come from a different legal and cultural background. Cultural competence, therefore, is a crucial factor in court interpreting.

In conclusion, fluency in two languages and knowledge of their corresponding cultures are necessary starting points for competent interpretation. Equivalence in interpreting results from the relation between signs themselves, the relationship between signs and what they stand for, and those who use them. Thus, the final product, the interpreter's mediating act of speech, is a complex system of decoding and reencoding on the semantic, syntactic, and pragmatic levels. An interpreter is a unique bilingual in that he is able to use his fluency in two languages in complex information-processing activities.

Chapter 5

INTERPRETING NONSTANDARD LANGUAGE

The previous chapter dealt with the relationship between language and culture and with the importance of linguistic and cultural fluency in court interpreting. In this chapter, other issues affecting court interpretation in bicultural and bilingual communities are considered. This discussion focuses on linguistic phenomena resulting from the constant interaction of English and Spanish: code-switching, language borrowing, and the use of deceptive cognates. The challenge of interpreting drug-related language and regional varieties of Spanish is also addressed.[1] Although the focus is on the Spanish spoken in the United States, the principles under discussion are applicable to other bilingual communities.

Language Variety

A *dialect* may be defined as a speech variety within a language. When a language is spoken by a large number of people who live in an extensive area, where groups have often been isolated from one another, as in the case of Spanish and English, there will be dialectal diversity due to the geographical spread of the language. Although linguists may differ on whether the differences between two speech communities reflect two dialects rather than two languages, the term "dialects" is used here to mean "mutually intelligible versions of the same basic grammar, with systematic differences between them."[2]

The dominant or prestige dialect is often called the *standard* dialect. Language "purists" generally consider the dialect used by the upper socioeconomic classes, the dialect used for official printed documents and in literature, and the dialect taught in the schools, as the correct form of the language. This notion of the standard dialect as the only correct form of a language is promoted in some countries by official academies of scholars who decide what usages constitute "proper" language. For instance, Spain has the *Real Academia de la Lengua*, which periodically updates its dictionary of accepted Spanish words. The French Academy has vigorously opposed the use of "Franglais," that is, words of English origin which have been borrowed and adapted by speakers of French (e.g., *le drugstore, le weekend, le camping*).

One dialect is not "superior" to another. In addition to regional dialects, social dialects and changes brought about by contact with another language, there are other differences in speech related to education, age, occupation, personality, emotional state, and in the case of bilinguals, degree of bilingualism. Thus, each individual has a unique way of speaking. The term *idiolect* refers to the "unique characteristics of the language of an individual speaker."[3]

Obviously, competence in the standard form of the source and target languages is essential in the preparation of interpreters. However, court interpreter training should also stress proficiency in the use of nonstandard speech.[4] The diversity of speech encountered by court interpreters includes the formal legal language spoken by judges and attorneys, the technical jargon of expert witnesses such as forensic chemists, and the nonstandard speech and slang of drug dealers, addicts, and persons of variable educational and cultural backgrounds. Thus, the practice materials in Part II contain samples of standard and nonstandard usages of language.

Nonstandard Spanish

This section focuses on the nonstandard speech which is characteristic of the language spoken in bilingual and bicultural communities throughout the United States. In Spanish-speaking communities, this means that interpreters must be equipped to deal with language-switching[5] or *code-switching* (the alternate use of two languages in the same utterance or conversation) and with what is commonly called *Spanglish*. "Spanglish" may be defined as "a speech variety which is rich in the use of loan words and shows a certain degree of grammatical interference from English."[6] It is characterized by the borrowing of words and phrases from one language (English) and incorporating them morphologically, phonologically and syntactically into another language (Spanish). Court interpreters must be aware of these varieties of language, since they are likely to interpret for individuals who code-switch and use "Spanglish."

Many of the examples used throughout this chapter are drawn from actual cases in the courts of the Southern District of Florida, the busiest trial court in the federal judiciary. The linguistic changes experienced as a consequence of the demographic transformation of southern Florida are representative of developments taking place in many other communities throughout the country (Table 5.1). Dade County, also known as Miami or, more accurately, Greater Miami, is not unlike other ports of entry into the United States. It is similar in demographics to other major metropolitan areas such as New York, San Francisco, Los Angeles, Chicago, and San Diego. Greater Miami includes a collection of twenty-seven municipalities and unincorporated areas, the largest being the cities of Miami, Hialeah, and Miami Beach. In this area, which is larger than Rhode Island or Delaware, there was an increase of 64.4 percent in the Hispanic population from 1980 to 1990.[7] Although Cubans make up the largest group of Spanish speakers in southern Florida (over 600,000 live in Dade County alone), in recent years a constant flow of immigrants from other Latin American countries has changed the makeup of the area's Hispanic population. Thus, Greater Miami's Hispanic community is a heterogeneous mix of individuals from the different Spanish-speaking countries in the world, including some 105,000 Nicaraguans, over 75,000 Colombians, 36,000 Salvadorans, 48,000 Puerto Ricans, 21,000 Dominicans, 19,000 Hondurans, 16,000 Mexicans, and smaller groups of Hispanics from most of Latin America and Spain.[8] The result is a complex sociolinguistic situation which is reflected in the Spanish spoken in the courts, a dynamic linguistic "mirror" or microcosm of society.

According to the U.S. Census Bureau, the ethnic and racial makeup of the population of the United States changed more dramatically in the past decade than at any time in the twentieth century, with nearly one in every four Americans having African, Asian, Hispanic or American Indian ancestry. Census data indicate that the nation's Hispanic population has grown by approximately 53 percent since 1980, rising to over 22 million people.[9] The number of Hispanics is rising at five times the rate of non-Hispanics, and immigration accounts for about 50 percent of the national increase in Hispanic population. California, Texas, New York, and Florida have the highest Hispanic populations. Illinois, New Jersey, Arizona, New Mexico, and Colorado also have significant Hispanic populations.[10]

Table 5.1
Percentage Change in Hispanic Population in the United States Since 1980

State	% +/-	State	% +/-
Alabama	-26	Montana	22
Alaska	87	Nebraska	32
Arizona	56	Nevada	131
Arkansas	11	New Hampshire	103
California	69	New Jersey	50
Colorado	25	New Mexico	21
Connecticut	71	New York	45
District of Columbia	85	North Carolina	33
Delaware	64	North Dakota	20
Florida	83	Ohio	17
Georgia	78	Oklahoma	50
Hawaii	14	Oregon	71
Idaho	45	Pennsylvania	51
Illinois	42	Rhode Island	132
Indiana	14	South Carolina	-9
Iowa	28	South Dakota	31
Kansas	48	Tennessee	-4
Kentucky	-20	Texas	33
Louisiana	-6	Utah	40
Maine	36	Vermont	11
Maryland	93	Virginia	101
Massachusetts	104	Washington	79
Michigan	24	West Virginia	-33
Minnesota	68	Wisconsin	48
Mississippi	-36	Wyoming	5
Missouri	20		

Source: U.S. Census data adapted from "U.S. Population Trends," *Miami Herald* (11 March 1991): 10A.

Language Contact and "Spanglish"

Languages constantly evolve. Extant words assume new meanings, others fall into disuse, words from one system may be incorporated into another. Finally, technological developments demand formations of new words to express novel ideas, processes and concepts. Language contact occurs when one language comes into pervasive contact with another, usually as a consequence of human migration. The evolution of language is accelerated in such areas of contact, especially when bilinguals mix languages by borrowing words and phrases from another language and incorporating them phonologically, morphologically and sytactically into the base language.

"Spanglish" is a language variety of Spanish created in many Spanish-speaking communities in the United States by socio-historical circumstances. It is also referred to as *Tex-Mex*, *español revuelto*, and *español mixtureado*.[11] Sometimes, words in language A (Spanish) will take on new meaning simply because they sound like words in language B (English) (e.g., *groceri* or *grocería*, which signifies a rude remark or gesture in standard Spanish, is often used in bilingual Spanish/English communities to refer to a grocery store). Loan words are common in this speech variety and although there is some grammatical interference from English, the differences with standard Spanish are mostly lexical.

As Lucía Elías-Olivares has observed regarding the "Español Mixtureado" spoken in a Chicano community, words and phrases "which have undergone the process called relexification, and calques have become a part of the Spanish repertoire of speakers, most of whom do not recognize their English source."[12] A *calque*, or *loan-translation*, may be defined as the borrowing of a word or phrase from one language in a manner that transfers the usage of the lending language (e.g., English), but the form of the element belongs to the borrowing language (e.g., Spanish). For example, in the phrase, *Creo que ella va a correr para alcalde* (I think she is going to run for mayor), the meaning of the English phrase "to run [for office]" has been adopted by Spanish. Elías-Olivares explains that

> when a speaker says *la mira* (the meter) or *la jira* (the heater) or *Ella me ticha español* (She teaches me Spanish) and has no notion of the origin of the word we no longer have interference but integration. When a speaker says *Lo puso patrás* (He put it back) instead of *Lo regresó a su lugar* or *Lo volvió a poner en su lugar* we are not in the presence of a bilingual who is experiencing interference from

English when speaking Spanish but in the presence of a variety which is the habitual system of communication of a number of speakers who sometimes do not speak English.[13]

Consider the following example recorded for a newspaper article on the Nicaraguan community in southern Florida:

1. *Los nicaraguenses son **bizneros**.*
   Nicaraguans are business-minded.

Note that the word *biznero* as used by the Nicaraguan quoted above, is the phonological and morphological adaptation of "business person or business-minded person." However, that same word may have a different connotation for others. For example, Cubans who immigrated to the United States during or after the Mariel boatlift of 1980, may understand that word to refer to illicit activity, because in Cuba *biznero* generally referred to someone involved in the black market.[14] The same process of adapting an English word phonologically and morphologically into Spanish is involved in the following example:

2. *¿Quiere que se lo **rapee**?* ('to wrap,' *envolver* in standard Spanish)
   Would you like me to wrap it for you?

The following speech samples, drawn from legal proceedings, are illustrative of the phenomenon of language integration, the result of which is "Spanglish." In each case the presence of English is mainly of a lexical nature rather than morphological or syntactical:

1. Q: What were your duties on the job site?
   (Interpretation of the question)
   A: *Yo era el **bajolista**. Yo era el que manejaba el **bajó**.*
   (Bajó = a back hoe; ***retroexcavadora*** in standard Spanish)
2. *Las conocí a ellas ahí en el **bildin**.* (Building)
3. *Necesita **pushin.*** (Pushing)
4. *Estoy en **estanbai**.* (Stand-by)
5. *El estaba ahí de **guachimán**.* (Watchman)
6. ***Bitiar** un caso.* (To beat a case) [*Salir absuelto de un caso*]
7. *Sra, ¿quiere que le **apunten** un abogado*? (appoint)
8. *Mi respuesta fue que no tenía otro **chois** porque ya lo estaban haciendo.* (Choice)
9. *El avión está **lisiado**.* (Leased)

10. *Ahí hay alguien que se lo estaba* ***likin*** *a ellos.* (Leaking)
11. *Yo* ***failiaba*** *los papeles.* (To file)
12. ***Loncheamos*** *juntos.* (To have lunch)
13. *Me dijo que estaban* ***redi.*** (Ready)
14. *...había dejado pasar ese* ***dil.*** (Deal)
15. *Bueno, dentro del* ***fail*** *venían las órdenes de que yo tenía que cobrar.* (File)
16. *Yo tenía un* ***tiquete*** (Ticket)
17. *Había un* ***bonche.*** (Bunch)
18. *El* ***principal*** *de la escuela.* (the principal = *el director* in standard Spanish.
19. *Me enseñó un* ***sampo.*** (A sample)
20. *Cambiar* ***de mente*** (To change your mind = *Cambiar de opinión*)
21. ***Estaba supuesta a...*** (I was supposed to = *Se suponía que yo...*)
22. *Lo pagó* ***cash.*** (Cash = *en efectivo*)
23. *Tomar un* ***chance*** (To take a chance = *Correr un riesgo*)
24. *Yo lo llamé por teléfono y él me dijo que no lo* ***badeara.*** (bother)

The following exchange, which occurred during the cross-examination of a Hispanic witness in a trial, serves as an example of the pervasiveness of nonstandard forms of the Spanish spoken in bilingual communities in the United States:

ATTORNEY: Did you have a choice, sir, to sign the paper?
INTERPRETER: *¿Pudo usted elegir si firmar o no ese documento, señor?*
WITNESS: *Por supuesto que no tuve* ***chois.***
INTERPRETER: Of course I had no choice.

Code-switching

Another nonstandard mode of communication resulting from language contact involves the use of a variety of Spanish together with English, what is known in linguistics as code-switching. In code-switching there is a constant alternation of the two languages in the middle of sentences or between sentences.

Code-switching among Spanish-English bilinguals living in the United States is one of the most salient characteristics of this speech population and has been the subject of comment and research by educators, psychologists, linguists, anthropologists, and literary investigators. Code-switching can involve a word, a phrase, a sentence or several sentences. This alternate use of two or more languages in the same utterance or conversation is an extremely common characteristic of bilingual speech, and it has only recently received the unbiased attention of researchers.[15]

Switching is different from borrowing a word from the other language and integrating it phonologically and morphologically into the base language. In code-switching, the switched element is not integrated. Instead, there is a total shift to the other language:

1. *Las computadoras están* **down**.
2. *Los niños están en el* **day care**.
3. She was, like, ***muy antipática***.

It is a complete shift (including pronunciation) to the other language for a word, a phrase, or one or more sentences. These examples, however, could be considered 'borrowing' depending on the pronunciation of the English words.

Code-switching appears in the literature of many Hispanics in the United States, as exemplified by the following excerpts from a bilingual Chicano poem by Sylvia Alicia Gonzales. Her poem titled "El Poeta" provides an outstanding example of bilingual sentences:

El poeta es la voz de una gente
Pouring forth their sufferings and struggles
Como las aguas de una fuente
El poeta es el palpitar de un pueblo
Beating regularly their frustrations and pain
Así pues, tras el grito viene el eco.

Poeta, tú eres el orgullo de mi raza
Describe to everyone my town and cities
De muchos colores son las flores de la plaza
Negra la noche cuando con desprecio la aplastan
Tell them about a culture and a language
Que hace muchos años fue raptada
Tell them of the squallor and neglect
Una cultura rica sobreviviendo de la pobreza.

Cuéntales poeta...
Cuando mi raza llora

Lloro con ellos.
When my people are angry
Ya verás como peleo
Seeking justice for my people
Hasta el día que muera.

Como la voz, el corazón y el orgullo de la raza nueva
Con mis dos idiomas te dedico estas letras...[16]

Court interpreters encounter code-switching in a variety of settings, in formal court proceedings as well as in more informal settings, such as in the offices of attorneys where depositions are generally taken. This linguistic phenomenon is perhaps most often encountered by interpreters who transcribe and translate audio or video tapes of defendants and witnesses who are unaware that they are being monitored. The following excerpts belong in that category. They are taken from a conversation between two Cuban males, recorded by undercover federal agents:

Voice 2: "*El piloto*, I don't know if you got any guy *que es, pues gran piloto. Tú sabes, que...* who would *hacer la cosa así, con un piloto. Pero la cosa es lo siguiente: El vuelo sale desde el punto que uno quiere que salga.* It comes in *con un* flight plan, *entra —pam, pam. Aterriza en [location], pasa* Customs, *y de ahí sale pa' donde uno (unintelligible). Vaya,* **a** typical flight."

* * * * *

Voice 2: "*... porque el radar te* picked up..."

* * * * *

Voice 1: *... Porque hay... hay radares que te cogen.* Right on the water, even the boats. They get the boats *también* like that."

* * * * *

Voice 2: "*... Eso es seguro, yo le tengo que decir a él, 'Oye, mira, yo te entro el vuelo de tal punto a tal punto. Cuando yo lo tenga, yo te lo traigo'* and that's it, I mean, there's nobody else to talk to. Except me, *yo y* [name], there's nobody else in the middle. *Tú no tienes que conocer a más nadie, yo no tengo que conocer a más nadie. Tú no tienes que cobrárselo, yo lo tengo que cobrar...*"

* * * * *

Voice 2: *¿Tú sabes? Pero este tipo te dice, 'Oye, mañana a tal hora.* I'm there *de tal hora a tal hora.' Y el tipo es Jefe de Customs, ¿me entiendes? Que ahí, por ese lado, no hay tormento. Y el tipo es familia mía. Vamos,* we've used him before, *tú conoces gente que...*

Voice 2: *Este tipo*, I used to pay him thirty percent. *De lo que, de lo que se cobraba. Hiciste* nine hundred thousand, *el tipo cobraba trescientos mil pesos. Cuando tú llegabas ahí y aterrizabas, como Pedro por tu casa. Llegabas, bam, bam, chequeabas, y* that was in front of [name] International Airport.

* * * * *

Voice 1: ...You know, what I'm saying is, *yo te puedo vender el avión, financiárselo a quien sea ¿tú me entiendes? Buscarle* financing *a la persona que legítimamente lo pueda* afford, *¿no? Y* — and you do it, and you go for it *y tú sabes que conmigo, yo soy una tumba, yo soy incapaz de hablar nada de nada — nunca.*

* * * * *

Voice 2: *Ahí no hay ese tormento*, you don't... you don't have to, *tú sabes*, be jumpy about it. *La cosa es que tiene que poder llegar aquí...*

* * * * *

Voice 1: Let me figure something out, *porque yo... puedo hacer un inventico, que...* and you're gonna think this is nuts, but it's not nuts because I have seen it; and I sold one of these airplanes, but somebody else did this. *Era un* Beechcraft, Twin-Air, Excalibur *que... valdrá ciento cincuenta mil dólares. El avión con veinte [unintelligible] no más se consiguen las alas de un* King-Air, *que es* prop-jet *y se le ponen las alas esas...*

* * * * *

Voice 2: *El es piloto.* You might have seen him in [location]. *El tipo, es un tipo que anda en un* [make of car]...

* * * * *

Voice 2: ... *yo tengo un tipo que... vamos, que es primo mío. El tipo*'s worked for Customs for years...

* * * * *

Voice 2: *¿Tú no conoces ningún tipo que tenga un avión* that would do something like that?

* * * * *

Voice 2: *Pero*, you know how Customs works out in [location]? *Tu sabes, que tú entras pa' dentro y el avión te lo chequean estos tipos de* Customs, *¿tú sabes?* And you got certain times to come in. You can't come in *a cualquier hora, ahí por [location].*[17]

Code-switching generally takes place unconsciously and speakers are often unaware that they are switching from one language to another. The main concern of such bilingual speakers is with communicating a message or intent, and they know that the other bilingual person will understand them whether they use one or two languages.

The mixing of languages presents a problem for all concerned in the legal process, particularly for the court reporter and the interpreter. Most persons requiring the services of an interpreter in court are Spanish monolinguals who speak little or no English. Yet their speech (even that of recent immigrants) incorporates English words. When interpreting for someone who uses both languages, interpreters should be guided by common sense and the goal of accurate and complete interpretation. It is not necessary, for example, for the interpreter to repeat (in English) a phrase uttered in English by the person whose speech is being interpreted. In most instances, the presiding judicial officer will immediately instruct the witness to speak only in Spanish so as to avoid confusion.

Deceptive Cognates

"False" or deceptive cognates are frequently used in bilingual enviroments and are among the most common pitfalls for court interpreters, who must be aware of the possible usage of these *faux amis* (false friends) so as to avoid error. False cognates are words which have the same root in both languages and consequently "look alike" but which often have different meanings. In some usages, the meanings of some of these words may coincide; thus, they must be embedded in a context.

The following examples represent some of these *palabras engañosas* or deceptive cognates which are often encountered by court interpreters:

1.	SPANISH	ENGLISH
	actualmente	actually
	(at the present time)	(*en realidad*)

From an exchange on the witness stand:

WITNESS: Actualmente estoy trabajando en el club. (At the present time I'm working at the club.)
INTERPRETER: Actually, I'm working at the club.

2.	SPANISH	ENGLISH
	discutir	discuss
	(to argue)	(*hablar, comentar*)

From a cross-examination of a witness during a trial:

ATTORNEY: Did you have a discussion with your uncle about the package [which contained the cocaine]?
INTERPRETER: *¿Tuvo Ud. una discusión con su tío acerca del paquete*?
WITNESS: *¿Discusión? No, nosotros no discutimos.* (Argue? No, we didn't argue)
INTERPRETER: Discussion? No, we didn't discuss it.

Consider the possible consequences of the misinterpretation of another deceptive cognate, the Spanish verb *ignorar*:

3.	SPANISH	ENGLISH
	ignorar	to ignore
	(to be unaware)	(to disregard)

ATTORNEY: Why didn't you [obey the law]?
INTERPRETER: *¿Por qué no cumplió con la ley?*
DEFENDANT: *Porque la ignoraba.* (Because I was unaware of it)
INTERPRETER: Because I ignored it.[18]

Other deceptive cognates commonly used in Spanish/English bilingual communities include the following: *una aplicación* instead of *una solicitud* for 'application form' (*aplicación* may refer to 'diligence,' or 'the application of a remedy'); *molestar* 'to bother' instead of *abusar sexualmente* for 'to molest'; *soportar* 'to stand,' 'to bear' instead of *apoyar*; *mantener* for 'to support'; *casualidades* instead of *víctimas* for 'casualties' (*casualidad* = 'coincidence'); and *crimen* instead of *delito* for 'crime' (*crimen* refers only to violent felonies).[19]

Court interpreters encounter deceptive cognates regularly. However, because some Spanish speakers may use the words with their English meaning, interpreters must be aware of this possibility. When in doubt about the speaker's intended meaning, interpreters should first ask the judge for permission to request a clarification.

Drug-Related Language

The availability and abuse of illicit drugs, and the criminal activity associated with their production and distribution are among the most serious problems faced by our society. It is therefore not surprising that most of the criminal cases filed are drug related. For example, 95 to 98 percent of the criminal cases filed in the U.S. District Court for the Southern District of Florida in 1988 involved illegal drugs.[20] The Drug Enforcement Administration reports that more than three times as much cocaine is seized in Miami than anywhere else in the United States (Table 5.2). Nonetheless, drugs are a multibillion-dollar underground industry in many communities throughout the United States, and cocaine, for instance, finds its way into the country through different ports of entry.

Table 5.2
Cocaine Seized in the U.S. from October 1987 to September 1988

Total Nationwide	122,973 pounds
Miami	54,569 pounds
New York	18,007 pounds
Fort Lauderdale	15,201 pounds

Sources: John Fernandez, Drug Enforcement Administration; *Miami Herald* files.

Cocaine is smuggled in, among other things, blue jeans, flowers, freezers, frozen yucca, pulleys, fruit juice, and refried beans. Often it is stashed in freighters and concealed on passenger planes. According to DEA sources, an estimated 80 percent of the cocaine confiscated in southern Florida in 1988 was controlled by Colombia's Medellin cartel.

Examples of drug-related language illustrate the importance of understanding words in their relevant meaning as opposed to understanding them in their primary sense, that is, the meaning they most often have for the listener. Court interpreters are witnessing firsthand the genesis and proliferation of a nonstandard

Spanish lexicon, largely due to the constant interaction of Spanish and English, the presence of regionalisms, and the slang associated with the enormous volume of drug trafficking in the community. This situation in not unique to southern Florida. Other multilingual communities throughout the United States are experiencing similar situations. Thus, the Miami experience applies to much of the United States.

In chapter 2 it was emphasized that interpreters must go beyond the literal meaning of words and retain the message which the words convey in context, because while certain language units such as figures and names can be considered permanent matches with language units in another language (e.g., one = *uno*; Germany = *Alemania*), speech equivalents are a different matter. Speech equivalents are contextual; they always stem from meaning.

In dealing with "actual speech instead of with *langue*, one is obliged to recognize the existence of a plurality of codes or code varieties in the same linguistic community."[21] In the context of drug-related cases, Spanish speakers, regardless of country of origin, often use standard words to indicate something other than their primary meaning or principal denotation (the meaning they most often associate with a specific word). For example, the relevant meaning (or intended meaning) of *una bolita*, a standard Spanish word whose primary meaning is 'a small ball,' when used in the context of the illegal importation of drugs, may be 'a pellet,' a small rubber-enclosed packet of cocaine smuggled into the United States in the digestive system of so-called swallowers or *tragones*.

In court, *aparato* may signify 'apparatus' or a 'key,' that is, a kilogram of an illegal substance, and *perico* may allude to 'parakeet' or 'cocaine.' *Un marimbero* also could mean 'a marimba player' or 'a marijuana dealer.' *Coso* is a common word used to refer to cocaine, and *un coso* may refer to a kilogram of cocaine, although it may also allude to another object, article, or 'thing'. Many words are designated to mean cocaine since drug dealers rarely use the actual word 'cocaine' to refer to that illegal substance. Often words such as *material*, *documentos*, even *juguetes* 'toys' are used.

Not long ago, the word 'crack' was virtually unknown to street drug abusers. Today it is probably heard on a daily basis by mainstream society, and new drugs such as 'crank' threaten to become another epidemic throughout the United States.

Geographic Variation

Language provides a variety of different labels to refer to an object or an action. Moreover, the social meaning of a term shifts with the situation. Regional dialects may differ in the words people use for the same object, as well as in pronunciation. As Giglioli has pointed out, selection among referentially equivalent linguistic forms –be they two languages, two varieties within a language, or lexical choices within a variety– carries primarily social information. Sociolinguistic choices may inform the hearer about the speaker's social and regional origin.[22] These observations have important consequences for court interpreters.

A consequence of the diverse Spanish dialects spoken in the United States today is the need for interpreters to be cognizant of the geographical varieties of the language. Obviously, certain lexical items may be used in one region or country where Spanish is spoken, while a different vocabulary is used in another region or country to mean the same thing. Conversely, the same vocabulary item may carry a totally different meaning within the same language, from one region or country to another. *Bodega*, *chapa*, *almacén*, and *kilo*, are frequently encountered examples of this phenomenon. These words tend to have different meanings for Cubans and Colombians: to a Colombian *bodega* generally means 'warehouse' whereas to a Cuban it refers to a "mom and pop" type of grocery store, what is known as a *colmado* in Mexico; *chapa* can indicate 'door lock' (Col.) or 'license plate' (Cub); and for a Cuban *almacén* may refer to 'warehouse,' but for Colombians and Panamanians it generally refers to 'a store.' Finally, when *kilo* is used as the abbreviated form of kilogram it is usually a reference to illegal drugs; however, Cubans use the same word to refer to 'cents' or 'pennies.' Depending on the context, the country of origin, and the intended meaning of the speaker, then, "*No tengo ni un kilo*" could signify "I don't even have a kilo [of an illegal substance]" or "I don't even have a penny (I'm broke)."

It is important for interpreters to be provided with information that will enable them to make wise sociolinguistic choices regarding the speaker for whom they are interpreting. Such knowledge will reduce the potential for misunderstandings—often embarrassing. Throughout much of the Spanish-speaking world, the verb *coger* means 'to get,' 'pick up,' 'grasp,' 'catch,' 'gather,' whereas in Argentina and Uruguay, for instance, it is used as a profanity. Consequently, use of the verb *coger* should be avoided when interpreting for persons from these countries when the intended meaning of that word is 'to get,' 'to take,' etc. Because it is not always possible to know the country of origin of the person for whom one is interpreting, interpreters must make every attempt to use words which will be as widely understood as possible. For example, *depósito* would satisfactorily carry the plurality of meanings of the problematic 'warehouse.' Knowledge of language varieties can be acquired through direct contact with speakers from other countries, or through indirect contact (e.g., movies, radio or television broadcasts, print media, and literature).

When interpreting for speakers of a local area (especially for uneducated individuals) the particular form used in the area may facilitate communication. The word *duffel bag*, where drugs are often carried in the course of illegal importation into the United States, is more clearly understood by a Colombian as *tula*, while a Cuban is likely to refer to the same item as *gusano*. The latter is also the label given by the Cuban government to those individuals who left the island after Castro's revolution, many of whom carried their belongings in elongated duffel bags.[23] A Peruvian is not likely to use the word *aguacate* but will refer to 'avocado' as *palta*; 'beans' are *porotos* to someone from Chile or Argentina, *frijoles* to Mexicans and Cubans, *habichuelas* to Puerto Ricans, and *judías* to Spaniards. Likewise, a Chilean mother will comfort her crying *guagua* 'baby', while a Cuban and a Canary Islander may take a *guagua* 'bus' to work. Most English speakers who reside in the United States are probably familiar with the word *taco*, a staple of Mexican food; however, in Chile that same word refers to 'a short stocky person' or 'an obstruction' or 'impediment,' and in Spain, the word may refer to an 'expletive' or profanity.

In the United States there exists a language repertoire composed of varieties of Spanish which do not conform to the rules of the standard variety of the language. These varieties –which reflect the fluid state of language evolution– serve to fulfill the communicative needs of the speakers. Consequently, extraordinary demands are placed on court interpreters, who must have knowledge of the different varieties of the language.

Linguistic flexibility and cultural fluency are developed through study, reading, travel, as well as personal contact with persons from the various countries where the interpreter's working languages are spoken. Wise sociolinguistic choices will likely be made by interpreters who have benefited from contact with a wide range of native speakers from a variety of countries and backgrounds. Experience (personal or academic) with the standard and nonstandard forms of the working languages is very important for court interpreting.

In conclusion, familiarity with regionalisms, code-switching, "Spanglish", deceptive cognates, and drug-related language is of prime importance in developing the communicative competence which is so vital in the legal setting. Thus, successful court interpreting in a bilingual setting requires knowledge of at least two sets of sociolinguistic rules (the standard and nonstandard forms of two languages), together with an ability to use varieties meaningfully.

BRIEF GLOSSARY OF NONSTANDARD SPANISH

Nonstandard Spanish	English	Standard Spanish
army	army	ejército
baquear	to back	apoyar
bil	bill	cuenta (en restaurante, etc.)
bonche	a bunch	un montón, puñado
breiks	brakes	los frenos
carpeta	carpet	alfombra, tapete, tapiz
cashier	cashier	cajera(o)
cofi	coffee	café
dropear	to drop	dejar caer; darse de baja
espreswey	expressway	autopista, supercarretera
flonquear	to flunk	fracasar, fallar (un examen o curso)
frisar	to freeze	congelar, helar
ganga	gang	pandilla, banda (de malhechores)
guachimán	watchman	vigilante, sereno, velador
introducir	introduce	presentar (una persona a otra)
liqueo	a leak	gotera (en el techo); salida, escape (de gas, aire, etc.)
lonchar	to have lunch	almorzar
magasín	magazine	revista (publicación periódica)
marqueta	market	mercado
mayor	mayor	alcalde
populación	population	población
pushar	to push	empujar, impulsar
un shopin	shopping center	centro comercial
taipear	to type	escribir a mquina, mecanografiar
trostear	to trust	confiar en, fiarse de

BRIEF GLOSSARYOF DRUG-RELATED LANGUAGE[a]

Spanish	English
aparato	key or kilo of an illegal substance; apparatus
basuco	cocaine sulfate, base or paste (a preliminary coca product prior to conversion to cocaine HCL)
bipear	to beep
biper	beeper
blanquear dinero (Spain)	to launder money
bombardear	to air drop (contraband from a plane)
caballo	stud, dude, guy; heroin
caleta (Col.)	stash
cargamento	shipment, load
casa de encaletamiento	stash house
celada	trap, trick, sting (operation)
clavo (Cub.)	a secret compartment (place where money or drugs are stashed)
clorhidrato de cocaína	cocaine hydrochloride
coca	coke, cocaine
consignas	deposits (money)
contra-celada	reverse sting (undercover operation)
cortar	to cut (mix drugs with another substance in order to increase the amount of the drug and make it less potent)
cualude	qualude
chiva, chivato (Cub.)	snitch, informer
decomisar	to seize, confiscate
diluyente	a cutting (diluting) substance
drogadicto	drug addict
embalao; embalado	high on drugs
[agente] encubierto	undercover agent
espidbol	speedball (mixture of cocaine and heroin)
estar en la marimba	to be dealing drugs
estar tirando material	to be dealing drugs
estupefaciente	stufefacient, narcotic
gusano (Cub.)	duffel bag
hacer vueltas (Col.)	to run errands
hacerle la cama a alguien (Cub.)	to set somebody up

hierba	grass
informante	informer
kilo	kilo, kilogram
lavandero	money launderer
marimba	dope, marihuana
marimbero	drug dealer (esp. marijuana dealer)
material	material (any type of drug)
mayimbe (Cub.)	big chief, big shot, honcho
mercancía	merchandise
narcotrafico	drug traffic
ocupar	to seize, confiscate, to take possession
parada (Cub.)	a deal
parqueadero (Col.)	parking lot
parqueo (Cub.)	parking lot
pase	line (doses of cocaine)
pase	pass, permit; license (Col.)
patana	barge
pateador	kicker (person who kicks drugs out of planes during air drops)
pepas	cocaine pellets
perico	cocaine
pitillo	joint; cigarette (Spain)
placa	badge; license plate
porro (Spain)	joint
producto	product (any type of drug)
rendir	to cut drugs
samplita	a small sample
sampo	a sample
sicario	hit man, hired assassin
soltar prenda (Cub.)	to give something away, especially information
traficante	dealer, trafficker
tragón	swallower
traqueteo	negotiation, business
tula (Col.)	duffel bag
tumbar	to rip off
tumbe	rip-off
varillo	joint
volado(a)	high
yerba (var. of hierba)	grass

[a]This glossary represents the consensus of several federally

certified court interpreters and is based on many hundreds of proceedings in federal courts. A version of this glossary appeared in the *Jerome Quarterly* (Nov.-Dec. 1989): 6-7.

NOTE: The brief glossaries included in this section contain examples of nonstandard and drug-related words and phrases encountered by interpreters in legal settings. Keep in mind that words may have multiple meanings and that their use is determined by context. Because languages are instruments of communication, constantly adapting themselves to the needs of the different groups who use them, interpreters need to continually acquire new vocabulary. Thus, the compilation of wordlists or glossaries is an integral part of an interpreter's preparation. Students should add words or phrases to these lists to reflect the particular linguistic characteristics of the geographic area where they reside.

Chapter 6

INTERPRETING IN COURT

Introduction

Mastery of the techniques of interpretation and linguistic and cultural fluency in the source and target languages are obviously not the only requirement for competent court interpretation. It is also necessary to have an understanding of court proceedings and of the language of the court. In this chapter the reader is introduced, in necessary brief and generalized fashion, to the various stages that confront participants in a full-length legal proceeding. The interpreter's function and the modes of interpretation he must employ are discussed. The role and function of interpreters in various types of immigration hearings are also considered, and a glossary of immigration-related terms is included in this chapter. A bilingual glossary of legal terms is provided elsewhere in this book.[1] This is not intended to be an exhaustive description of the law, of rules of procedure, or of legal terminology. Rather, the purpose of this section is to introduce aspiring court interpreters to court proceedings in which they are likely to be utilized.

It is important to keep in mind that the legal system in the United States differs from that of most other countries. In contrast with the law of Spain, Italy, and most of Latin America, which is based essentially upon the Roman law and is called civil law, the law of the United States, and that of most English-speaking states is called *common law*.[2] Common law refers to early English laws, developed by judges, which incorporated Anglo-Saxon tribal custom, feudal rules and practices, and the everyday rules of behavior of local villages. Common law became the standardized law of the land in England and eventually formed the basis of the legal system of the

United States. It is judge-made law rather than a fixed body of definite rules. A cornerstone of Anglo-Saxon justice is that the accused is presumed innocent until proven guilty beyond a reasonable doubt in a court of law.

An important distinction which must be drawn to avoid confusion is that the term *civil law,* as that term is used here, is not synonymous with Roman law. As explained in chapter 1, a case at civil law is usually one between private persons and private organizations, but the government may also bring civil (and criminal) action(s) against an alleged offender. A case at criminal law is always brought by and in the name of the government (whether local, state, or federal). Criminal and civil proceedings are discussed in the sections that follow.

Prior to interpreting in formal court proceedings, interpreters may be administered an oath such as the one below. This practice and the oath itself vary widely from court to court.

INTERPRETER'S OATH

> You do solemnly swear that you will faithfully and accurately interpret from English into [Spanish] and from [Spanish] into English such testimony of the witnesses, and such other matters as may be required of you by the Court, according to the best of your ability, so help you God?

Criminal Cases: From Offense to Sentencing

In chapter 1, it was established that a criminal action is the procedure by which a person accused of a crime is brought to trial and either found not guilty or found guilty and sentenced. Criminal proceedings are brought against individuals or groups who are accused of committing one or more 'antisocial acts' that society, through its governmental process, defines as a 'crime' in public law.[3]

The various stages involved in a criminal case are complex. In the interest of clarity and conciseness they are summarized in the sections that follow. I wish to underscore, however, that the description offered here is, by necessity, an outline of the essential framework of the legal proceedings under consideration. It is not within the scope of this book to take into account the manifold practices, procedures, and safeguards that surround this aspect of the judicial process of the United States.

Apprehension

Apprehension refers to the arrest of a person on a criminal charge. Unless a prospective defendant voluntarily surrenders to the authorities, the arrest may take place while he is committing a crime, while fleeing, or as a result of an arrest warrant. Although there are exceptions, an interpreter will generally not be present at the time of arrest. The interpreter's role usually begins when the accused is brought to court. Occasionally interpreters will be called to assist the officer who 'books' or processes the accused in the 'lock-up,' a detention area often located inside the courthouse or adjacent to it.

Charging Documents

Complaint

An accusation of crime may be set forth in a document known as a *complaint.* In a criminal case it is a sworn allegation made in writing to a court or judge that an individual is guilty of some designated offense. This is often the first legal document filed regarding a criminal offense. The complaint can be filed by the victim, the police officer, the district attorney, or other interested parties. If it appears that there is *probable cause* to believe that the defendant has committed a crime, a warrant for arrest will be issued. Probable cause is determined at the preliminary hearing, which, unlike grand jury proceedings, is public and attended by the accused and the defense attorney. In most states an information may be used in place of a grand jury indictment to bring a person to trial. The magistrate judge may also, at the request of the prosecutor, issue a *summons* ordering the defendant to appear before the magistrate at a stated time and place, rather than having the defendant arrested and brought to court.

Information

An *information* is a written accusation, a formal charging document, made by a prosecutor on his oath of office without the intervention of a grand jury. It accuses a person of committing some criminal offense. However, the Fifth Amendment to the Constitution of the United States requires the federal government to prosecute 'infamous' crimes only upon presentment of an indictment by a grand jury.

Indictment

An *indictment* is a written accusation returned by a *grand jury* charging one or more individuals with a specified crime or crimes after determination of probable cause. The grand jury is usually comprised of twenty-three registered voters chosen at random (sixteen constitute a quorum for the transaction of business). Members of the grand jury hear the evidence adduced by the prosecution and issue formal criminal accusations if they are satisfied that a trial should be held. Thus, the grand jury serves an investigatory function; it does not decide a defendant's guilt or innocence.

The prosecutor, who represents the government and presents evidence to the grand jury that a crime has been committed, does not have to prove the case beyond a reasonable doubt (as in a trial). He does, however, have to present sufficient evidence to show that it is more likely than not that the crime was committed and that the persons under investigation probably committed it. If the prosecutor presents enough evidence to establish probable cause, the grand jury returns what is known as a *true bill*, and an *indictment* will result. If the prosecutor is not successful in establishing a *prima facie* (on the face of it) case, the grand jury returns what is known as *no bill*.

The federal grand jury is concerned only with federal crimes. There are also grand juries impaneled in many of the states and those grand juries investigate only state crimes; they derive their authority from the constitutions, laws, and rules of court of the states where they are impaneled. Some states only use grand juries to investigate crime and corruption among public officials in a limited number of cases. Other states have replaced it with the information.[4] State and federal grand juries are similar and their work is essentially the same, but some rules do vary (e.g., the number of grand jurors).

There is considerable disagreement about the origin of the grand jury. By most accounts the institution of the grand jury antedates the Magna Carta, the first English constitutional document, granted in 1215 by King John, at the demand of his barons.[5] The first English grand jury consisted of twelve men who were summoned to inquire into crimes alleged to have been committed in their community. They functioned as accusers or witnesses, rather than as judges. With time, as the modern grand jury developed in England, proceedings became secret and the grand jury became independent of the Crown. Consequently, a grand jury may indict or refuse to vote an indictment, regardless of the recommendations of judge, prosecutor, or any other individual. When the English colonists came to America, they brought with them many of the institutions of the English legal system, among them the grand jury, which was to be included in the Bill of Rights.[6] The Fifth Amendment to the Constitution of the United States provides in part that:

> [no] person shall be held to answer for a capital, or otherwise infamous crime, unless on a presentment or indictment of a Grand Jury...

In contrast to the *trial jury* (also called the *petit jury*) which listens to the evidence offered by the prosecution and the defense (if the defense chooses to present evidence) during a criminal trial, the grand jury hears only the evidence tending to show the commission of an alleged crime. It determines—without hearing evidence for the defense—whether a person should be tried. A grand jury is not completely free to compel a trial of anyone it chooses. The prosecutor must sign the indictment before an individual may be prosecuted. Thus, the government and the grand jury act as checks upon each other.

Grand jury proceedings are strictly confidential. This secrecy extends to interpreters, who take an oath that they will not divulge the nature or content of the grand jury investigation unless ordered to do so by the appropriate judicial authority. The foreperson administers the oath sworn to by the interpreter at the beginning of each proceeding. In the Southern District of Florida, interpreters are required to undergo a background check and obtain security clearance before they may interpret at grand jury hearings. This practice, however, is rather recent and does not extend uniformly to other parts of the country. Because of the need for secrecy, only authorized persons may be present in the grand jury room while evidence is presented, i.e., the jurors, the prosecutor, the witness under examination, the court reporter, and the court interpreter (when needed). Prosecutors must not be present, however, while the grand jury deliberates or votes on an indictment.

Witnesses are called to testify individually. Each witness, as he appears to give testimony, is sworn by the grand jury foreperson (or, in his absence, by the deputy foreperson). The prosecutor advises witnesses of their rights, explains the reason they have been called to testify, and conducts the questioning. Members of the grand jury have the right to ask questions of the witnesses. Witnesses must appear unaccompanied by their attorneys, although they may step outside the room to consult with them before answering any questions. Defendants under subpoena to appear before the grand jury may answer questions or decline to do so under the Fifth Amendment.

The entire interview process is conducted in the consecutive mode. The interpreter's English rendition of the witness's words (and not the original foreign language testimony) is taken down by the court reporter.

In summary, the grand jury has the responsibility of determining whether the evidence presented indicates that a crime was probably committed. Thus, before a person can be subjected to a trial, the grand jury must be satisfied that there is probable cause to believe that a crime has been committed and that the accused has probably committed it.

Initial Appearance

The *initial appearance* is the first appearance of the arrested suspect before a magistrate or judge for consideration of bail. The suspect must be given an initial appearance within a "reasonable time" after arrest. In some cases, the accused "may only be advised of his rights and assigned counsel."[7] For petty offenses, this step often serves as the final criminal proceeding, either by adjudication by a judge or guilty plea. Although initial appearances are conducted somewhat differently in different courts, they may proceed as described below.

The defendant's name and case number are called. The accused steps forward to face the judge. When an interpreter is needed, he steps forward to stand next to the defendant, facing the judge. The judge asks the defendant to state his name and age. Any dialogue with the defendant is interpreted in the consecutive mode in a clear, audible voice. Everything else that is said in the courtroom is whispered in the simultaneous mode to the defendant. In some courtrooms, simultaneous interpretation equipment is used for these proceedings. Where that practice is followed, the interpreter does not need to stand next to the defendants because they are able to hear the simultaneous interpretation through headsets.

The judge informs defendants of their rights, what is commonly known as the Miranda warning. *Miranda* is the result of two U.S. Supreme Court decisions (Escobedo v. Illinois, 378 U.S. 478, and Miranda v. Arizona, 384 U.S. 436) which require that a police officer, or other law enforcement agent, inform individuals under arrest of certain constitutional rights, such as the right to remain silent and the right to have an attorney present (see Part II). Although aimed at protecting an individual during in-custody interrogation, the warning must also be given when the investigation shifts from the investigatory to the accusatory state, that is, when suspicion begins to focus on an individual.[8]

The judge asks the defendant if he has an attorney. If the defendant is not represented by counsel and claims to be indigent, the judge will place the defendant under oath to answer questions about his financial ability to hire an attorney. Once it is determined that the defendant qualifies for court-appointed counsel, the judge will appoint an attorney, usually a public defender.

Preliminary Hearing

Pursuant to the Federal Rules of Criminal Procedure, a defendant has a right to a probable cause hearing within ten days of the date of his initial appearance, if incarcerated, or twenty days if released on bond. Should an indictment have been returned against him, that serves as a showing of probable cause. However, if no indictment has been returned, the government is required to present sufficient evidence before a magistrate judge to constitute probable cause. That proceeding is a preliminary hearing. Where an indictment has been returned, an arraignment takes its place.

A *preliminary hearing* is held before a magistrate judge to determine whether the arrested person should be released or held for trial. The person charged with a crime has the right to be represented by an attorney. During a preliminary hearing the state is required to produce enough evidence to establish that there is probable cause to believe that a crime was committed and that the defendant committed it. If the evidence does not indicate that there is probable cause to believe that the accused has committed the crime, he is discharged and the case dismissed. If, however, there appears to be probable cause, the accused will either be held in custody or released on bail to await the decision of the prosecutor or the grand jury on whether an *information* or an *indictment* will be filed against him.[9]

Thus, a preliminary hearing is the first screening of a criminal charge in federal court and in many state courts, and its function is to determine whether there is sufficient evidence to continue with the case and to require the defendant to post bail or be held for trial. It is also called a *preliminary examination*, *probable cause hearing*, and *bind over hearing*.[10]

Arraignment

The *arraignment* is an initial step in the criminal process wherein the accused is formally charged with an offense (i.e., read the charges against him in a charging document or accusatory instrument and asked how he pleads to those charges). Possible pleas are "guilty" or "not guilty" or, where permitted, "nolo contendere." In the federal system, however, the court must enter a plea of not guilty to the indictment at the arraignment stage, even if the defendant wants to plead guilty.[11] In addition, the accused are advised of their rights.

Many defendants in the criminal justice system have their first contact with the courtroom when they are arraigned on an indictment by a grand jury. The indictment states the facts constituting the crime and cites the particular law which the defendant is alleged to have violated. Often, the defendant has already retained an attorney.

At the arraignment, when the judge calls the defendant's name, the attorney announces his presence and the fact of representation. Attorneys generally waive the reading of the indictment in open court, enter a plea of not guilty, request a trial by jury and a standing discovery order. *Discovery*, another commonly used term, refers to the physical evidence, including law enforcement agency's reports, papers, documents, tape recordings, and other materials that comprise the government's case. Judges generally respond that the not guilty plea has been entered, that a standing discovery order has been signed, and then instruct the defense attorney to check the trial date with the judge who will preside over the trial.

During this proceeding, any dialogue with the defendant is interpreted in the consecutive mode. The simultaneous mode is used to interpret everything else that is said in the courtroom. As always, the interpreter's function is to communicate exact meaning. It should be underscored that the attorney-client privilege applies to the interpreter as well. Additionally, interpreters must not express their opinion about the case nor engage in private dialogue with defendants.

Pre-Trial Motions

A *motion* is an oral or written request asking the court to make a specified finding, decision, or order. In this section several of the most common motions that attorneys may file prior to trial are mentioned: a *motion to dismiss*, a *motion to suppress*, a *motion to sever*, and a *motion for a change of venue*. Interpreters are frequently needed during these proceedings.

A *motion to dismiss* is a request by the defendant asking the court to dismiss the charges against him because the indictment was not validly brought, the court has no jurisdiction over the offense with which the defendant is charged, or any other fact which would cause the court to dismiss the charges against the defendant.

At a *motion to suppress*, a defendant requests the court not to allow certain evidence to be admitted at the trial because it was obtained illegally, that is, in violation of the defendant's constitutional rights (e.g., a search of the defendant's home was carried out without a valid search warrant). Defendants may also file motions to suppress statements made to law enforcement officers at the time of arrest. Defendants may argue, for example, that the statements were coerced, or that the law enforcement officials failed to properly advise them of their Miranda rights.

A *motion to sever*. In a criminal case involving two or more defendants, one (or more) of them may feel that they will not get a fair trial if tried with the other(s). Defendant(s) will thus request a separate trial.

A *motion for a change of venue*. If the defendant feels that the conditions in the judicial district where the trial will be held are such that a fair trial is not possible, he may request that the trial be transferred to another jurisdiction.

During all pre-trial hearings, the interpreter must simultaneously interpret all that is said in the courtroom. If a non-English-speaking witness testifies, then the interpreter will use the consecutive mode.

Guilty Plea

A *plea* is an answer to formal charges by an accused. Defendants may choose to plead guilty to all the crimes with which they are charged rather than going to trial. In order to enter a plea to less than all of the charges, however, a *plea bargain* must be agreed to by the prosecutor. Plea bargaining refers to the discussions between the defense counsel and the prosecution by which the accused agrees to plead guilty for certain considerations. Most guilty pleas are entered as a result of such a plea bargain in which both parties—defense and prosecution—generally yield something. For instance, the prosecution may agree to drop a count of the indictment and the defendant agrees to give up the right to a jury trial. The advantage to the prosecution is that a conviction is obtained without the time and expense of lengthy trial proceedings. Judges are entitled to reject the plea. The judge must be convinced that the defendant is indeed guilty of the alleged charges before accepting the guilty plea. The terms of the plea are usually written down. This document, commonly called a *plea agreement*, must be signed by all the parties involved (see Section 1, Part II).

The proceeding known as a *change of plea* takes place in the courtroom. The judge is on the bench, the prosecutor at counsel table, and the defendant generally stands at a podium facing the judge. The defense attorney and the interpreter are situated next to the defendant. The consecutive mode is employed when interpreting the dialogue between the defendant and the prosecutor or the defendant and the judge. Everything that is said in the courtroom about the defendant and the case must be interpreted for the defendant in the simultaneous mode.

At this proceeding defendants are told that by pleading guilty they are giving up certain constitutional rights. The judge explains these rights, which include: the right to a trial by jury; the right to cross-examine any witnesses brought by the prosecution to testify against the defendant; the right to present evidence and to bring witnesses to testify on his behalf; and the right not to testify in the trial, if so desired.

Judges must be satisfied that a plea is made knowingly and voluntarily, that no one has coerced or forced the defendant or made promises (other than those contained in the plea agreement) in order to get the defendant to enter a guilty plea. The judge will go over the terms of the plea agreement with the defendant. Defendants are also asked if they are under the influence of medication, alcoholic beverages, or other chemical substances that could impair their understanding of the proceedings. The judge may also ask defense attorneys if they have any doubt as to the defendant's competence to enter a guilty plea.

The prosecution is asked by the judge to give a factual foundation for the plea. The prosecutor gives an oral summary (profer) of the case the government would have presented had the case been tried by a jury. The defendant is then asked if the prosecution's version of the case is accurate. It the defense does not have any objections to the profer, the judge then asks the defendant how he pleads to the charges. After the judge accepts the guilty plea, a sentencing date is set.

Prior to sentencing a *presentence investigation report* (PSI) must be completed by a probation officer. These reports contain information about the defendant's background, education, previous employment, family, the defendant's own statements concerning the offense, prior criminal record, interviews with friends or acquaintances, and other relevant information which will help the judge in determining the appropriate sentence. The report is required in felony cases in federal court and in many states. It is optional with the judge in some states, and in others it is mandatory before convicted offenders can be placed on probation. The PSI may also include information about a defendant's mental and physical condition. The report is also referred to as the social history report in the case of juvenile offenders.[12]

While there may be variations in this proceeding, it is generally carried out as just described. The many questions asked are designed to ensure that the plea conforms to all constitutional requirements. At all times the interpreter must be thorough and accurate.

Special terms are used in pre-trial proceedings. Knowledge of legal terms and their target language equivalents is essential prior to interpreting in court. Interpreters should request a copy of the indictment whenever possible and review it as well as other documents that they may be asked to sight translate in court (see Section 1, Part II).

Criminal Jury Trial

In a jury trial guilt is determined by the decision of a group of individuals who represent the community as a whole. This section focuses on various steps of the trial process in which interpreters are utilized: jury selection, opening statements, presentation of evidence, closing arguments, charges to the jury, and verdict.[13]

Jury Selection

The judge directs the marshal's or sheriff's officers to bring a panel of jurors to the courtroom where the case is to be tried. Generally the judge, the attorneys, defendants, interpreters, the court reporter and the clerk are in place and ready to begin before the prospective jurors enter the courtroom. When using special equipment for simultaneous interpretation, it should be set up and tested prior to the time the jury is brought into the courtroom.

Jury selections are interpreted in the simultaneous mode. Defendants must be able to "hear" everything as if they were native speakers of English. A defendant must be able to aid the defense attorney in the selection of the jurors who are going to try his case.

The officers will bring a large group of people (the number will vary) who will be asked to take seats in the courtroom. Attorneys receive printed lists of prospective jurors by name and number. It is a good idea for interpreters to obtain a list of the names of the prospective jurors because there is a potential for confusion if names are mispronounced. One of the officers or the judge's clerk will begin to draw names and will ask jurors to take the designated seat in the jury box when their name and number are called. Although criminal trials are decided by twelve persons, fourteen names will usually be drawn, so as to guarantee alternates in case a juror becomes sick or is otherwise incapacitated.

The judge introduces himself, the lawyers and the defendant(s). The judge briefly tells the jurors what the case is about, and explains that they will be required to answer a series of questions. This is the process known as *voir dire* (French for see and speak).

The questions asked by the judge and the attorneys concern prior jury experience, knowledge of the case and of the parties involved in the trial, or anything else that might prevent the jurors from being fair and impartial in trying the case. Jurors may give their answer at sidebar (at the judge's bench), if so desired. Any jurors who demonstrate bias by their answers may be excused. If any of the impaneled jurors is challenged or excused, other potential jurors are chosen to replace them. The questioning continues until fourteen persons are selected by the lawyers.

Jurors may be dismissed because they are biased, have prior knowledge of the case, or demonstrate that they are unable to render a fair and impartial judgment in the case. This is known as *challenge for cause*. A *peremptory challenge*, on the other hand, is the dismissal of a potential juror by either the prosecution or the defense for unexplained discretionary reasons. Both sides are granted a number of peremptory challenges, with which they can dismiss without cause, one at a time, prospective jurors from the jury pool. When all of the lawyers announce that the jury is satisfactory, the jury selection process is complete and the jury is sworn. An oath is administered—generally by the clerk—in which jurors are asked whether they will well and truly try the case and return a true verdict according to the evidence.

OATH TO TRY THE CASE

> You and each of you do solemnly swear that you will well and truly try the issues herein between the U.S. and [name(s) of defendant(s)], and a true verdict render according to the evidence and the charge of the Court, so help you God. Do each of you take this solemn oath?

After the jurors are all seated, the judge makes some preliminary remarks about the need for impartiality, their role in the case, and explains to the jury that they are to select a foreperson from among themselves.

Opening Statements

During a trial, all remarks made by the judge, attorneys, and anyone else present in the courtroom are interpreted in the simultaneous mode for the defendant(s). After preliminary statements by the judge to the jurors, the government prosecutor addresses them. The prosecutor delivers an *opening statement* which outlines what the government intends to prove, how it intends to prove it, and what it believes the evidence will show (see section 4, Part II). The prosecutor is followed by the defense attorney(s), who may or may not offer an opening statement at this time. When opening statements are concluded, the judge tells the prosecutor to call his first witness. The prosecution always presents its case first.

Presentation of Evidence

The presentation of evidence may take the form of *witnesses* or *exhibits* such as drugs, photographs, or maps. In other words, evidence is either testimonial or physical. When physical evidence is introduced, a witness is generally necessary to identify and explain its relevance to the case. During the trial everything is interpreted in the simultaneous mode unless one of the witnesses who is to testify is non-English speaking and requires the services of an interpreter. As in other proceedings, the consecutive mode is used from the witness stand.

When a witness is called to the stand he is asked to raise his right hand and take the familiar oath: "Do you solemnly swear to tell the truth, the whole truth, and nothing but the truth, so help you God?" After the witness responds, he is asked to state his name and spell the last name for the record. Once this has been done, the questioning begins.

The sequence of questioning is as follows: *direct*, *cross-examination*, *redirect*, and *recross*. The party calling the witness asks what are known as direct questions. The attorney attempts to get that person to tell his story. Cross-examination is designed to emphasize inconsistencies and may get quite heated (see Section 4, Part II). Theoretically, cross-examination is restricted to topics covered in direct examination. Redirect examination is designed for clarification purposes; the direct examiner can take the opportunity to correct misapprehensions caused by the cross-examination. If there is any recross-examination, it is supposed to be limited to the clarification of redirect examination.

Objections may be expressed by either of the parties. Witnesses are instructed not to answer until the judge has ruled on the objection and the witness's response should not be interpreted until the judge has ruled on the objection. Objections may be *overruled*, in which case the witness will answer, or *sustained*, in which case the witness must not answer. In the interest of fairness, arguments regarding objections should be interpreted in the simultaneous mode for both the non-English-speaking witness as well as for the non-English-speaking defendant(s). After all, English-speaking witnesses are able to hear these statements. Sidebar discussions, on the other hand, are made at the bench and are generally not intended to be heard by anyone other than the judge, court reporter, and the attorneys. Objections may also be raised regarding physical evidence that one of the parties wants to introduce.

When attorneys want to introduce an object as evidence, they mark it for identification. Exhibits are usually marked consecutively; often they are marked in advance in order to save time during the trial. When attorneys ask that exhibits be admitted they generally use the phrase: "Your Honor, I would like to move exhibit [X] into evidence." If there are no objections by the opposing party, the exhibit is usually admitted. If there are objections, the judge rules after a legal argument.

After all the prosecution's evidence has been presented, the prosecutor will "rest." At this stage in the trial, the judge dismisses the jury temporarily because important legal issues must be resolved outside the jury's presence. For instance, defense counsel may claim that the government did not prove the elements of the offenses and that the defense is entitled to a judgment of acquittal. The judge will rule on this and on any other matters that the attorneys raise.

At the conclusion of these issues, the defense case, if there is to be one, begins. This is conducted much the same way as the prosecution's case. However, the defense may choose not to put on a case at all. After both parties rest, they have a right to rebuttal testimony. Once all the evidence and rebuttal witnesses, if any, have been presented, the testimonial portion of the trial is over and the jury is then prepared to hear the attorneys' closing arguments.

Closing Arguments

Closing arguments resemble opening statements, except that during these summations the attorneys argue what they did prove and what the other party failed to prove. This is the time when each party argues its side and attempts to persuade the jury.

Jury Instructions

The instructions on the law that the judge gives to a jury after closing arguments and prior to deliberations are known as the *charges to the jury* or jury instructions. Interpreters should request a copy of the jury instructions. Knowledge of terms such as "knowingly and willfully," "burden of proof," "presumption of innocence," and "beyond a reasonable doubt" is essential. (see Section 4, Part II). Interpreters should also be familiar with the charges set forth in the indictment (e.g., conspiracy and possession with the intent to distribute a controlled substance).

Prior to reading the jury instructions, the judge and the attorneys may hold a "charge conference" during which time the attorneys may object to a particular portion of the charge or request a supplemental charge or instruction. Should a non-English-speaking defendant be present at this conference, everything that is discussed must be interpreted in the simultaneous mode for him.

Once the jury has been instructed, the judge thanks the alternate jurors for their participation in the case and excuses them from the courtroom. Now the case "goes to the jury," that is, the jury may begin deliberating the facts of the case.

Verdict

When the announcement is made that a unanimous verdict has been reached (this can take from thirty minutes to several days), all the participants in the case are called to their places in the courtroom. Everyone stands as the jury files into the jury box. The foreperson hands the verdict form to the clerk who then reads it. Everything is simultaneously interpreted for the defendant(s). (see the verdict form provided in Section 1, Part II).

After the verdict has been read the jury is polled, that is, each juror is asked to state that he agrees with the verdict as recited. Each juror is expected to answer affirmatively. If a juror expresses disagreement with the verdict, a mistrial will be declared. Should everything go smoothly, however, the jury's role is over. The judge thanks the members of the jury and discharges them.

Defendants who are acquitted are free to go. If, however, the defendant was convicted, a sentencing date will be set. Matters of bond are also discussed at this time. The trial is officially over.

Sentencing

All defendants who are guilty—whether by plea or by conviction—must be sentenced. The sentencing procedure begins with a presentence report prepared by the probation department. Presentence investigations are conducted after the end of the trial or pleading, and prior to the sentencing. As previously discussed, the ensuing report of an investigation carried out by the probation department is used by the judge in determining an appropriate sentence. Both parties may comment on the PSI report and may request changes, additions, deletions, or other modifications.

The judge asks if the defendant wishes to address the court, if so, this must be interpreted in the consecutive mode. Other witnesses may be brought to speak on the defendant's behalf and to plead for leniency. Often, they are family members or close friends and associates, and at times, sentencings can be highly emotional events. Naturally, interpreters must maintain their objectivity and impartiality throughout this and all proceedings.

Sight translation may be required at the time of sentencing. Letters and other documents may be presented by the defense at this time. After both sides have spoken, the judge sentences the defendant, who is then generally remanded to the custody of law enforcement officials.

Civil Cases

A civil case proceeds along the same lines as a criminal case, although they differ in many respects and different terms may be used. A civil action is a lawsuit that is brought to enforce a right or gain payment for a wrong, rather than a court action involving the government trying to punish a crime. Important differences of opinion, disputes, or controversy may be settled in the court through the judicial system. The dispute brought before the court is called the case, suit, or action. The party who complains or sues—the injured party—is the *plaintiff*. The party whom the plaintiff accuses of wrongdoing is the defendant.

The suit begins when the plaintiff files a *complaint*, which is the formal written statement in which the plaintiff presents the facts as he believes them to be, and demands the relief to which he believes to be entitled. To *file* a document is to submit it to the court by placing it in the official custody of the clerk. This is generally done by an attorney hired by the plaintiff, who draws up the complaint and files it in the clerk's office. A defendant is then required to file an *answer* to the complaint, consisting of his version of what happened. Plaintiffs and defendants are the parties to the suit. They are also called *litigants*, and the court proceedings, the *litigation*.

The procedure by which individuals are notified that they are being sued and that an answer must be filed within a given time is called a *summons*. This is a *writ*, a formal command from the court which is served (delivered) by a law enforcement officer. The complaint and the answer make up the *pleadings*, the formal allegations of the parties of their respective claims and defenses for the judgment of the court. Once the answer is filed, the issue has been *joined*, meaning that the parties have agreed to the basic issues constituting the dispute.

Pre-trial

Both parties need to have as much information as possible in order to prepare a case before it comes to trial. *Discovery* is the procedure for obtaining information from the opposing party. This is done through interrogatories, depositions, or motions to compel production of documents.

Interrogatories are written questions served on an opponent, who is required to serve written answers under oath. A *deposition* is an oral statement made under oath before an officer of the court and taken down in writing, generally by a court reporter. Interpretation, when necessary at these proceedings, is in the consecutive mode.

A motion, as discussed previously, is an application made to the court for an order or ruling. Both sides have the opportunity to argue before the judge in open court in a proceeding called a *hearing*. The judge will either grant or deny the motion. Motions may include a motion to compel production of documents, to amend the complaint, to dismiss the case altogether, to ask for a change of venue, to extend time, and to request judgment on the pleadings without the necessity of trial or additional showing to the court. During this time the judge may call a pre-trial conference, a meeting between the attorneys for the two parties. At this meeting, the attorneys may be encouraged to consider whether it would be wise to settle the case.

Trial

The parties are entitled to a trial by jury, but if a jury has not been demanded, or if the case is not triable by jury, it is tried by a judge without a jury. The size of the civil jury is determined by the local rules of the district. Often, six or more persons will be selected to try the case. Trials proceed in much the same way as criminal trials.

After the jury returns its verdict, if either party feels that the verdict is wrong, a *motion for judgment N.O.V.* (notwithstanding the verdict) may be made. Such a motion asking the court to render a judgment different from the jury's verdict can be granted only if the evidence introduced at the trial fails to support the verdict of the jury. Generally, however, at the end of the trial the judgment is entered.[14]

Interpreting in Immigration Proceedings

The dramatic increase in recent years in the need for interpretation services in immigration proceedings, has necessitated the hiring of full-time interpreters by the U.S. Department of Justice for current and future vacancies for many field offices around the country. This trend is expected to continue.[15]

This section is intended to serve as an introduction to the role of the foreign language interpreter in immigration proceedings. Its purpose is to provide basic information about the Executive Office for Immigration Review (EOIR), the different types of immigration proceedings, the role of the interpreter in these proceedings, and the special terms and phrases utilized in immigration hearings).[16]

Functions of the EOIR Interpreter

The most significant functions of the EOIR interpreter occur during proceedings in which interpretation is provided for the non-English speaking respondent, applicant, or witness, for the attorneys, and for the judge. EOIR interpreters are expected to perform clerical functions such as updating information concerning individual cases while they interpret. At this writing, immigration interpreters are not required to pass a nationwide certification examination such as the one developed for federal court interpreters.

The oath of office developed for EOIR interpreters according to the *Interpreter's Handbook* made available by the Office of the Chief Immigration Judge is as follows:

> OATH OF OFFICE
>
> I (name) do solemnly swear (or affirm) that I will support and defend the Constitution of the United States against all enemies, foreign and domestic; that I will bear true faith and allegiance to the same; that I take this obligation freely, without any mental reservation or purpose of evasion; and that I will well and faithfully discharge the duties of the office on which I am about to enter. So help me God.

Office of the Chief Immigration Judge

The Office of the Chief Immigration Judge (OCIJ) supervises and directs the activities of the Offices of the Immigration Judges (OIJ) which conduct more than 100,000 immigration hearings annually, and are located in twenty-one cities. Under the guidance of the Director, the Chief Immigration Judge and four

Assistant Chief Immigration Judges, develop operation policies for the OIJs, oversee policy implementation, and evaluate the performance of the OIJs.

Each Office of the Immigration Judge (OIJ) is staffed with Immigration Judges who conduct the various hearings. The OIJ Management Officer, under the supervision of an Assistant Chief Immigration Judge, manages and supervises the everyday activities of the field office. This includes supervision of support staff such as language clerks and language specialists. The Management Officer is also the liaison with the local INS (Immigration and Naturalization Service) and other agencies or organizations which are involved in immigration matters. Not all hearings are held in the twenty-one field offices. Hearings may also be held at other locations, such as at INS detention centers, as well as state and federal detention centers or penal institutions.

At present, the mode of interpretation used most often by EOIR interpreters is the consecutive mode. The EOIR *Interpreter's Handbook* states that the summary mode must not be utilized due to the inherent danger of omitting necessary information or incorrectly summarizing what was said. The simultaneous mode is utilized by EOIR only in exceptional circumstances.[16]

Types of Immigration Hearings

The four principle types of immigration proceedings conducted by the OIJs are: 1) *deportation*; 2) *exclusion*; 3) *rescission*; and 4) *bond redetermination*. All of these proceedings involve a person whom the Immigration and Naturalization Service (INS) has charged with violating the immigration laws of the United States. That person, who is referred to as an *alien*, is called a *respondent* in a deportation case, and an *applicant* in an exclusion case. Each type of hearing is briefly described below.

Deportation Hearing - Deportation cases generally occur when INS alleges one of the following violations of the immigration laws of the United States: 1) that a respondent entered the country illegally, that is, without being inspected by an immigration officer; and 2) that a person entered the country legally with a visa, but later violates a condition of the visa. For instance, if the visa is for a specified time period and the person stays beyond the visa expiration date, that person is subject to *deportation proceedings*.

The charging document issued by the INS when they believe a respondent is deportable is called an *Order to Show Cause (OSC)*. Deportation proceedings begin when the OSC is filed with an

Office of the Immigration Judge. At the deportation hearing the government (INS) must prove that a respondent is deportable for the reasons stated in the Order to Show Cause.

Bond Redetermination Hearing - When INS detains a respondent who is under deportation proceedings and conditions that person's release from custody by requiring posting of a bond that will guarantee the respondent's appearance at the hearing, the respondent has the right to ask an Immigration Judge to redetermine the bond. A *bond redetermination hearing* is separate from the deportation hearing and has no bearing on subsequent deportation proceedings. In a bond redetermination hearing, the judge can change any of the conditions of the bond over which Immigration Judges have authority. Thus, the bond can be raised, lowered, the amount of the bond can be maintained or it may be eliminated altogether.

Exclusion Hearing - An *exclusion hearing* involves a person who tries to enter the United States but is stopped at the point of entry because INS finds the person to be inadmissible (e.g., the INS officer believes that the applicant's entry papers are fraudulent). In order to charge an applicant in exclusion proceedings, INS issues a document called an "I-122" and files it with an OIJ. In these cases, INS has sole jurisdiction over the custody status of an applicant. In an exclusion proceeding an applicant technically has not entered the country and the burden of proof is on the alien who must prove admissibility to the United States. Such hearings are not open to the public unless the applicant requests otherwise.

Rescission Hearing - If INS discovers, within five years of granting adjustment of status, that a respondent/applicant was not entitled to lawful permanent residence status (LPR), INS issues a Notice of Intent to Rescind. If the respondent/applicant requests a hearing before an Immigration Judge, INS will file Notice with the OIJ and the proceeding to rescind (*rescission hearing*) the individual's lawful permanent residence status begins. In these proceedings, as with deportation cases, the government has the burden of proof to show that rescission is warranted. An individual who loses LPR status may then be subject to deportation proceedings.

Uniform Docketing System and the Master Calendar

When the OIJ receives a charging document, support staff enter the case information into the EOIR computer data base called

ANSIR (Automated Nationwide System for Immigration Review), and also create a file called the Record of Proceeding (ROP). The support staff assigned to assist the judge during the *master calendar hearing*—usually the interpreters—generally schedule twenty-five cases for each half day master calendar session.

At the master calendar, the judge explains all respondents/applicants who do not have an attorney of their rights and provides them an opportunity to seek counsel at their own expense. For those individuals who are represented by an attorney, the judge established representation for the record by ensuring that the attorney has filed the appropriate notice of appearance form with the OIJ, and also assures that the respondent/applicant has been fully advised by counsel of his rights. At the master calendar hearing, the judge is usually able to complete simple issue cases, but for more complex cases, the judge uses the session to establish whether deportability or admissibility of the respondent/applicant is a contested issue. The judge may also discuss the types of discretionary relief from deportation. All utterances are interpreted in the consecutive mode from the target language (English) into the source language and vice versa.

Potential Relief From Deportation

The variety of forms of potential relief from deportation range from simple grants of voluntary departure to complex waivers of deportation. All these forms are granted or denied by the immigration judge assigned to the case. They include: *voluntary departure*, *request for asylum*, *suspension of deportation*, and *adjustment of status*. A brief description of each one of these forms of relief is offered below.

Voluntary departure enables respondents to leave the country at their own expense within a time limit specified by the judge. This type of relief makes it possible for respondents to reenter the United States after leaving provided that they obtain the proper visa for reentry. By contrast, an order of deportation removing an alien from the country at the government's expense bars that person from legally reentering for five years from the date of deportation (even with an otherwise valid visa), unless granted a waiver by the government of the United States.

In order for individuals to be granted a request for asylum, they must prove that they have a well grounded fear of persecution because of race, religion, nationality, political beliefs, or membership in a social club if they are returned to their country of origin.

A suspension of deportation may be requested by a respondent who has been living illegally in the United States for at least seven years. For this relief to be granted, the respondent must prove good moral character, extreme hardship if returned to the country of origin, as well as seven years of continuous physical presence in the United States.

Adjustment of status is a type of relief available for a respondent who is deportable but is eligible for lawful permanent resident status due to a number of factors, such as marriage to a citizen of the United States.

After a judge determines what type of relief a respondent/applicant seeks, a date is set for the respondent/applicant to file the appropriate application for relief. The judge then schedules the case on the individual calendar for a hearing on the merits of the application.

Individual Calendar

At the individual calendar hearing, the judge hears testimony from the respondent/applicant and witnesses for either party. An EOIR interpreter is provided for non-English speakers. The judge will generally render an oral decision in the case after hearing testimony. The decision includes a finding of facts, the establishment of deportability or excludability, a statement of the relief sought, the application of existing case law, and the judge's conclusion about the case. After announcing the decision, the judge gives each party an opportunity to waive or reserve appeal. The judge's decision becomes final if both parties waive appeal, but regardless of whether the appeal is reserved or waived, a form order referred to as a *minute order* is given to the parties before they leave the court. This form summarizes the judge's decision.

GLOSSARY OF IMMIGRATION-RELATED TERMS (Spanish/English)

This glossary includes basic terms used in a variety of proceedings by EOIR interpreters. It should be remembered, however, that individual words and phrases may have different meanings in different contexts. Although many of the terms that appear in the legal glossary provided elsewhere in this book are often used in immigration hearings (e.g., prosecutor), they have been excluded from this list in order to avoid repetition.

ENGLISH	SPANISH
adjustment of status	ajuste de estado (legal)
advice (n.)	consejo
advise (v.)	informar, poner en conocimiento
alien	extranjero(a)
alien registration number	número del expediente; número de registro
alien registration card	número de registro de extranjero; tarjeta verde mica
alien smuggler	contrabandista de extranjeros; coyote; pollero
amnesty	amnistía
applicant	solicitante; demandante; aspirante
application	solicitud
to make an application	formular una solicitud
appeal for reconsideration	recurso de suplicación; apelar para reconsideración; súplica de reconsideración
appear	comparecer
arrest record	antecedente penales; prontuario policial
asylum hearing	audiencia sobre asilo
attorney general	procurador
attorney of record	abogado del caso
bag-and-baggage letter	carta de 30 días para salir del país
baptismal certificate	certificado de bautismo; fe de bautismo
bar association	colegio de abogados
Board of Immigration Appeals	Tribunal de Apelaciones de Immigración
bond reduction	reducción de fianza
bond reduction hearing	vista para pedir rebaja de fianza
border	frontera

border crossing point	lugar de cruce de la frontera
border crossing station	garita de la frontera; garita fronteriza
border patrol	patrulla fronteriza
breach of bond	incumplimiento de las condiciones de la fianza
capital offense	delito que conlleva la pena de muerte
charging document	documento de acusación; instrumento de acusación
City Hall	Ayuntamiento
claimant	reclamante
conscientious objector	objetor de conciencia
conscription (draft)	conscripción (fem.)
cross the border	cruzar la frontera; (col) saltar la línea
customs	aduana
customs officer	inspector de aduana
death certificate	acta de defunción; certificado de defunción
death flights	vuelos de muerte
death squads	escuadrones de la muerte
deceased	fallecido; difunto
deportability	deportabilidad; validez de los cargos de deportación
deportation hearing	vista de deportación
determination	decisión; fallo
economic hardship	dificultades económicas
employer sanctions	sanciones contra patronos
employment authorization	permiso de trabajo; autorización para trabajar
expunge	borrar; cancelar
extended voluntary departure	prolongamiento de salida voluntaria; aplazamiento de la salida voluntaria
fingerprints	huellas digitales; impresiones dactilares
forfeit bail (v.)	perder la fianza
furnish bail	depositar la fianza
good moral character	solvencia moral o buena conducta moral
habitual criminal	delincuente consuetudinario
harbor	amparar; abrigar
hardship	dificultades; sufrimiento
extreme hardship	dificultades extremas
undue hardship	sufrimiento innecesario
hereinafter	en adelante
heretofore	hasta ahora
identification card	cédula de identificación
immediate relative	pariente cercano

immigrant	inmigrante
immigration hold	orden de entrega al departamento de Inmigración; detención para Inmigración
Immigration Judge	Juez de Inmigración
Immigration and Nationality Act	Ley de Inmigración y Nacionalidad
Inmigration and Naturalization Service (INS)	Servicio de Inmigración y Naturalización
immigration officer	agente de inmigración; (col) la migra
impeach	impugnar; desacreditar
indigent	indigente; sin recursos económicos
individual calendar	lista de casos individuales
ineligible	no eligible
informer	informante; soplón; chivato (Cub); orejas (Central America)
issue (n.)	el punto controvertible; asunto; cuestión
issue (v.)	emitir; expedir
issued in	expedido(a) en
kin	familia; parientes
knowingly	a sabiendas
lawful permanent resident	residente permanente legal
law officer	agente; representante de la autoridad
lenient	indulgente; clemente
maiden name	apellido de soltera
marital status	estado civil
marriage fraud	matrimonio fraudulento
master calendar	lista de audiencia preliminar
mortgage (n.)	hipoteca
mortgage (v.)	hipotecar
murder (n.)	asesinato
murder (v.)	asesinar
native	oriundo; nativo
non-immigrant	no inmigrante; con visa temporal
oath	juramento
O.R. (own recognizance)	libertad bajo palabra
overturn	reevocar
pardon	absolución; indulto; perdón
pending court action	acción judicial pendiente
political asylum	asilo político
port of entry	puerto de entrada
preference alien	extranjero con preferencia para inmigrar
preference classification	clasificación de preferencia para inmigrar
private (mil)	soldado raso
raid	redada; incursión

recidivist	reincidente
refugee	refugiado(a)
relief from deportation	recurso contra la deportación
resident alien	extranjero residente de los EE.UU.
respondent	compareciente; demandado
responsible relative	pariente responsable
siblings	hermanos y hermanas
spouse	cónyuge; esposo(a)
status	estado; condición; posición
stay of deportation	prórroga de la deportación; aplazamiento de la orden de deportación
summary deportation	deportación por el oficial de inmigración sin intervención judicial; deportación sumaria
summons	auto de comparecencia; citación
supporting documents	documentos comprobatorios
suspension of deportation	suspensión de deportación
taxes	impuestos (m)
temporary restraining order (TRO)	orden inhibitoria temporal
temporary stay	aplazamiento temporal
transcripts	transcripciones (fem)
trial attorney	abogado del juicio
unarmed	desarmado
unconstitutional	anticonstitucional
undocumented	indocumentado
union	sindicato; unión (P. Rico)
unlawful	ilegal
violation of human rights	violación de los derechos humanos
voluntary departure	salida voluntaria
waiting period	período de espera
waiver of rights	renuncia de derechos
warrant of arrest	auto de detención; orden de arresto
well-founded fear of persecution	temor a la persecución con bases bien fundadas
whereabouts	paradero
withholding of deportation	detención temporal de deportación
work permit	permiso de trabajo

Chapter 7

COURT INTERPRETING AS A PROFESSION

Introduction

This final chapter focuses on general concepts regarding court interpreting as an emerging profession. The principal issues addressed in this section concern the criteria for accurate interpretation, the challenge of interpreting so-called legalese, general rules of conduct for interpreters, training, federal certification, and the future of court interpreting in the United States.

In his classic 1953 study, "Toward a Science of Translating," I.A. Richards called translation "probably the most complex type of event yet produced in the evolution of the cosmos."[1] I concur with Richard Brislin's statement that "while it is easy to overemphasize the significance of one's own specialty, the proficiency and range of skills demanded of a good translator and the magnitude of the task of translating from one language to another make the quote by Richards defensible."[2] Although these quotations refer to the work of translation, interpretation merits similar characterization.

Accurate Interpretation

It is generally agreed that in the United States court interpreting is intended to protect the rights of non-English speakers, that is, to put them on equal footing with speakers of English. However, proper court interpreting also serves to protect society-at-large from individuals who are guilty of crimes.

Clearly, interpretation is an essential component in the case of a non-English-speaking person who comes before our legal system. In reaching a decision about that person's guilt or innocence, the services of a court interpreter or legal translator are relied upon at various stages of the legal process. When the interpretation or translation carried out in that person's case is flawed, can we say that justice has been served? It stands to reason, then, that if innocent individuals could be unjustly punished as a result of inaccurate translations or interpretations, guilty persons could go unpunished. Thus, accurate interpretations are fundamental in avoiding miscarriages of justice.

To achieve that end, the interpretation must adhere to certain criteria. The elements necessary for a true and exact interpretation may be summarized in two general categories: **1) Accuracy**. There must be no errors, omissions, modifications or embellishments in conveying the speaker's message. The speaker's style and register must be maintained, otherwise the impact of the interpreter's words on jurors will be altered. If, for example, an interpreter "cleans up" the testimony of a witness by eliminating obscenities, the jury hearing only the English interpretation will receive an inaccurate impression of the witness. Likewise, if an articulate, highly educated person's testimony is interpreted with slang terms, grammatical errors and improper syntax, this interpretation may not be considered correct; **2) Objectivity**. The interpreter must have no personal interest in the outcome of the case nor be biased in any way. Prejudices, opinions, or personal feelings must not interfere in any way with the interpreter's formulation of the target language message.

The requirement of accuracy must be underscored because court interpreters play a vital role in the administration of justice. It is a unique kind of interpreting: unlike conference interpreting in which interpreters often work into one language, the court interpreter constantly switches back and forth between two languages. Additionally, in court one interprets for people from all walks of life. Nancy Festinger points out some of the demands connected with court interpreting:

> . . . we perform mental gymnastics, jumping from an attorney's constitutional argument in a motion to suppress, to a drug addict's slurred explanation, to a witness's deliberately elusive answer, to the socio-psychological jargon of a probation report, to the small print of a statute, to a judge's syntactically convoluted charge to the jury—often, all in the space of a few hours. We repeat patent

nonsense, veiled (or not-so-veiled) bullying, impassioned pleas, righteous indignation, stern admonishments, nit-picking questions, ironic remarks, barbed answers, tearful confessions, and through it all we must pay unflagging attention, betray no sign of annoyance or incredulity, all the while maintaining composure, impartiality and linguistic fidelity.[3]

Legal Language

In the previous chapter, we discussed that interpreters need to be cognizant of the legal process and the special terms used in court proceedings. In this section, I wish to underscore that in addition to familiarity with legal terms and phrases and their foreign language equivalents, court interpreters must be aware of the characteristics and unique style of legal language, what is commonly called "legalese."

Researchers as well as laypersons know that legal language differs from ordinary English. A number of studies of language and the law have sought to examine the characteristics of legal language in the United States.

Some of the characteristics of "legalese" include: an esoteric vocabulary; grammatical constructions that differ from ordinary usage; archaisms (e.g, "hear ye, hear ye"); terms of art, that is, technical words and phrases whose meanings are seldom disputed in the law (e.g., injunction); certain syntactic constructions that either had disappeared from ordinary English many years ago, or are used infrequently in normal discourse; redundancy; passive constructions; and numerous foreign language terms (e.g., voir dire, prima facie). It is, in fact, considered that the language of the law qualifies as a jargon.[4] In their examination of the comprehensibility of jury instructions, Veda and Robert Charrow write that what evolved from their study was "a concept of legal language as a distinct subset" (register) of English.[5]

Roseanne D. Gonzalez has observed that the social roles and attitudes within the trial situation are formally defined and frozen, and that the language used in court "reflects this formality in matters of procedural announcements and in matters of concretized phraseology."[6] She asserts that "procedural techniques within courtrooms are also ossified in action and language. For instance, the bailiff uses the language of eighteenth century England to 'empanel a jury,' to swear in witnesses, to adjourn for recess, and to inform a jury 'to retire'."[7]

It must be noted that most of the research on legal language has focused on written legal language and that the word "legalese" generally refers to the written rather than the spoken language. As a consequence, relatively little is known about the nature of spoken legal language. O'Barr and his colleagues, however, have studied language varieties used in an American courtroom. To avoid confusion regarding use of the word *legalese*, O'Barr uses the terms *written legal language* and *spoken legal language*.[8]

O'Barr has discerned four varieties of spoken legal language: 1) formal legal language (the variety that most closely parallels written legal language); 2) standard English (the variety typically used in the courtroom by lawyers, it closely parallels that which is taught as the standard in U.S. classrooms); 3) colloquial English (a variety which is less formal than standard English); and 4) subcultural varieties (a variety spoken by segments of the society who differ in speech style and mannerisms from the larger community). O'Barr explains that these varieties constitute all registers of court-talk observed and that most speakers "shift within their own repertoire in response to situational changes" and that "divisions among the varieties are not clear-cut, and the varieties for any individual may form a continuum or may be mixed in actual usage."[9] For example, the same attorney who uses formal legal language in a "charge conference" to discuss the judge's instructions to the jury, may use colloquial English during his closing argument in an effort to seek solidarity with jurors.

Foreign language court interpreters deal with all varieties of spoken and written legal language. Moreover, because they work with two language systems, the varieties of spoken English legal language defined by O'Barr are encountered in the foreign language as well. For instance, a foreign language court interpreter may be required to sight translate foreign language legal documents introduced as evidence in a trial. If one of the non-English speaking witnesses is an attorney, he is likely to use the variety of spoken legal language defined as "formal." Standard, colloquial, and subcultural varieties of the foreign language are regularly used, as we discussed in chapter 5.

Interpreters also need to be aware of the special meanings assigned to "everyday words" in the legal setting. For example, the word *bench* which in everyday language generally refers to a long seat for two or more persons, in the legal sense may refer to the office or dignity of a judge. Moreover, court interpreters must be aware that at times the ambiguity of legal language is intentional in order to allow for double meanings.

The lack of standardization of equivalent foreign language terms for the English terminology used in court proceedings in the United States constitutes a special challenge for interpreters. Although a few bilingual wordlists, glossaries and guides for court interpreters have been in existence for several years (see Appendix 5), little effort has been made to standardize the usage of foreign language equivalents for the legal terms used in court. As a consequence, legal terms are routinely interpreted differently by different interpreters. For example, a frequently used term such as 'arraignment,' is interpreted into Spanish as *instrucción de cargos*, *accusación formal*, *lectura de acusación*, *procesamiento*, or *presentación formal de cargos*, among other possibilities. The implications for non-English-speaking defendants and witnesses and for the entire legal process, are self-evident. A recently published dictionary of Spanish/English criminal justice terms has yielded the term *vista incoatoria* as the Spanish equivalent of arraignment.[10] That undertaking, by Benmaman, Connolly, and Loos, is the final product of a federally funded project to codify and standardize the Spanish translations of criminal justice terms. Their work represents a much-needed response to the "absence of a standardized vocabulary in Spanish which accurately reflects the concepts of Common Law" and to the need to promote "consistency and uniformity of usage by all persons needing to express the terminology of common-law procedures in Spanish."[11]

We have discussed the importance of knowing the differences in the cultures and the legal systems of the countries where the court interpreter's working languages are spoken. A conspicuous example in Spanish/English is the difference in the role, qualifications and functions of a notary public in the United States and the *notario público* in Spanish-speaking nations. Although the terms sound and look very much alike, the differences are striking and the consequences of those dissimilarities, far-reaching. In Spain and Latin America, the notario is an attorney who meets rigorous qualifications and whose authority approximates that of a judge, whereas in the United States a notary public need not have any knowledge of the law at all. Notaries in the United States generally carry out routine matters such as the authentication of signatures. Reports indicate that the confusion created by the apparent similarity between the Spanish and English terms is a nationwide problem.[12] Some notaries who are not lawyers and call themselves notarios públicos prey upon Spanish-speaking immigrants, charging them high prices for illicit legal advice. They are able to get away with it because "in many parts of Latin America a notario is a lawyer —often a lawyer with superior credentials."[13] California, Texas, and Illinois have taken measures to thwart this unethical practice. In Florida, a law which takes effect on 1 January 1992, bans the literal translation of the phrase "notary public" into a language other than English in advertisements for notary services. In addition, all notary advertisements must now carry the following disclaimer: "I am not an attorney licensed to practice law in the state of Florida, and I may not give legal advice or accept fees for legal advice."[14]

How can students prepare for interpreting legal language? The answer is found in three words: study, training, and preparation. A supervised internship in a court where students observe legal proceedings and the work of experienced, competent interpreters is, in my view, indispensable.[15]

An Emerging Profession

Good interpreters are language experts. However, the regular utilization of untrained bilinguals to interpret in many courts in the United States indicates a widespread lack of awareness about interpreting. The quality of a profession goes hand in hand with its rewards and the status society bestows upon its practitioners. So while court interpreters should be expected to train and strive to meet minimum standards such as those established by the federal government, society must recognize and reward their worth.

We have seen that court interpreting is a relatively young profession in the United States, having been recognized as such only since the passage of the Court Interpreters Act of 1978. Prior to that year, there was no uniform method in the United States of determining the qualifications and objectivity of the person called on to interpret. Sometimes even relatives of the non-English speaker or court personnel such as bailiffs were utilized. Many instances have been documented in which defendants were either denied the assistance of an interpreter altogether or were provided with an interpreter on an *ad hoc* basis. Schweda-Nicholson's study revealed that these "untrained (often unpaid) 'interpreters' may not have even spoken the required languages well enough; however, peoples' lives have hung in the balance while unqualified 'interpreters' have, for example, misinterpreted critical testimony."[16]

The *Ballad of Gregorio Cortés* depicts on film the tragic, true account of a Mexican-American's encounter with the law, his unjust incarceration as well as that of members of his family, and the fatal shooting of his brother—all due to the misinterpretation of a single word. The word *yegua* was erroneously interpreted as "horse" rather than "mare," thus setting off the largest manhunt in the history of Texas.[17]

Recognition of the specialized nature of court interpreting exists primarily in the federal court system. Most states have yet to take the necessary measures to ensure that court interpreting is performed only by trained and skilled individuals whose competence has been demonstrated through a standardized screening or certification process. This situation exists, in part, because many people still believe that any person who can speak two languages is able to interpret or translate accurately. As pointed out by Jack Leeth, who was involved with federal certification from its inception, "Most people believe that if you are bilingual, you can interpret. That is about as true as saying that if you have two hands, you can automatically be a concert pianist."[18] Nonetheless, the Court Interpreters Act of 1978 and subsequent amendments have underscored the importance of using qualified interpreters to ensure a true and accurate interpretation. Such measures have made educators aware of the level of expertise required for court interpreting and have contributed a great deal toward professionalizing this activity. However, because the requirements for court interpreting are not treated uniformly throughout the United States, one may legitimately ask if court interpreting is a profession.

Black's Law Dictionary defines a profession as a "vocation or occupation requiring special, usually advanced, education, knowledge, and skill; e.g. law or medical professions. [The term] also refers to whole body of such profession. The labor and skill involved in a profession is predominantly mental or intellectual, rather than physical or manual. . . .[19] By this definition, court interpreting is clearly a profession.

In addressing the issue of whether we are justified in calling court interpreting a profession, Benmaman examined the standard sociological definitions applied to the category of professional occupations and analyzed the field of court interpreting in relation to these various components. Her study indicates that court interpreting has many points of congruence with the professional occupations. For instance, the essential criterion of a "cognitive base of empirical, scientific and theoretical knowledge" has been met, since there is a substantial body of scholarship dealing with the theoretical analysis of the translation and interpretation process.[20]

Another basic element, that of prestige, respect, and authority, arises from the recognition by laypersons that the professional possesses extensive education in the theoretical knowledge of his discipline. A degree from an institution of higher education has therefore become the basic credential for a professional. Benmaman concludes that a degree or certificate in interpretation (preferably on a post-graduate level) from an established university program would accord respect, status, and marketability to its bearer. Unfortunately, the criterion of formalized education, essential in the professionalization of this occupation, has yet to be fully realized. Likewise, the ultimate autonomy and control of the profession by its own members, manifest by accreditation associations, and licensing regulations, is still beyond the grasp of the field.[21]

Another element associated with professional occupations, that of a professional culture, has begun to emerge in the field of court interpreting. A professional culture refers to the composite values, behavioral norms and shared symbols of a group, which permeate the workplace and extend well beyond. "It is an attitude towards work which views it as an end in itself, performed with affinity primarily for personal satisfaction and not monetary gains, and requiring total personal involvement."[22] In summary, what remains ahead for court interpreting is for the field "to rise within the professional hierarchy. It can do so by strengthening those attributes which have already emerged in a number of dimensions."[23]

General Rules of Conduct

A code of ethics is indispensable. The Administrative Office of the United States Courts has drafted a code of ethics, as have other professional organizations (see Appendixes 1 and 2). Similar proposed code of professional responsibility for court interpreters and legal translators have been formulated by state systems (e.g., New Jersey). To date, however, there is no national professional organization with the power to impose sanctions and with the autonomy to proceed with disciplinary procedures.

An examination of the rules of conduct and guidelines for court interpreters reveals that they generally take the following factors into consideration:

1. **Impartiality**. Interpreters must set aside any personal biases or opinions about the case in which they are interpreting and render a true and accurate interpretation. The interpreter's conduct, both

inside and outside the courtroom, must not give occasion for distrust of his impartiality and professionalism (e.g., interpreters must not discuss a case pending before the court or display personal feelings regardless of the nature and circumstances of the case). No one should be able to tell what the interpreter's reactions are to what he is interpreting;

2. **Confidentiality**. Court interpreters must not disclose confidential information acquired or available to them in the course of their official duties. Interpreters must not disclose privileged communications between attorney and client;

3. **Conflict of Interest**. Interpreters must inform the court it they are acquainted with one or more of the parties to an action or with any witnesses. Interpreters must not have any interest (direct or indirect) in the outcome of a case;

4. **Favors or Gratuities**. Interpreters must not accept money or other consideration or favors which might reasonably be interpreted as an attempt to influence the performance of their duties;

5. **Preparation**. Interpreters should obtain as much information as possible about all assignments and prepare or review any glossaries or other references which might be necessary; and

6. **Professionalism**. Interpreters must maintain a professional relationship at all times with everyone involved in the case and avoid the informal form of address (e.g., Spanish *tú*) when speaking to parties during court proceedings. Furthermore, interpreters must never give legal advice.

Training

Federal laws have not provided for interpreter training, although it is clear that a key factor in providing quality interpretation services in the judicial system is improved and expanded training of interpreters in all languages. It is only through "professional training and adequate compensation" that the judicial system of the United States will be able to develop "a competent corps of court interpreters."[24] Thus, state and private institutions must play a larger role in court interpreter training programs.

In the United States, programs which focus on conference interpretation have existed at institutions institutions of higher learning for several decades. Prominent examples are the ones at Georgetown University (established in 1949) and at the Monterey Institute of International Studies (established in 1965). Both programs continue to emphasize conference interpreting. Courses and programs of instruction in legal interpretation have been initiated at institutions of higher learning relatively recently. The program at Florida International University, for example, which consists of a year-round series of sequential courses (33 hours of academic credit) leading to a Professional Certificate in Legal Translation and Court Interpreting, was initiated in 1979.

An American Translators Association survey conducted in 1981 revealed that some seventy-seven institutions of higher learning reported offerings in translation and/or interpretation. With few exceptions, these offerings included summer institutes, workshops, continuing education courses, and undergraduate courses in translation, and did not reflect organized, structured programs such as those offered in centers for professional training in European universities. Nonetheless, these offerings in U.S. colleges and universities demonstrate an increasing interest in interpretation and translation as a primary occupation.[25]

Federal Certification

A few states (e.g., California, New Mexico, Washington, and Massachusetts) require interpreter certification by statute. According to Pousada, twenty-four states have some provision for appointment of court interpreters, but the majority of these provisions depend on administrative or judicial regulation, not statutes.[26] Therefore, in many states and municipal courts the use of interpreters is an arbitrary determination.

At present, several states are revising or otherwise evaluating their court interpreter services. New Jersey, for example, heads a nationally recognized pioneering effort in this area. The New Jersey Task Force on Translation and Interpretation Services has carried out an in-depth, detailed, study at the state level. The Florida legislature is currently considering legislation calling for certification and uniform standards for interpreters in the state courts.[27] Other states, among them Hawaii[28] and Colorado, are considering measures to upgrade the quality of the interpreting services available in their courts.

Of the steps taken to implement the Court Interpreters Act of 1978, perhaps of greatest significance for the profession of court interpreting has been the design of the federal court interpreter certification examination. The federal examination was developed by a multidisciplinary panel of consultants which included court interpreters, international conference interpreters, language specialists from various universities, and test construction experts.[29] The result was a two-part test consisting of an oral and a written examination. This format, developed for the first Spanish/English certification examination, is still used to date.

The written portion of the federal examination is a screening device to determine whether individuals can demonstrate, at least in a written format, that they could perform at the level of language used in the courts. It consists of a multiple choice test which treats the following in English and Spanish: 1) antonyms; 2) synonyms; 3) sentence completion; 4) reading comprehension; and 5) language use. The latter refers to the grammatical errors that native speakers make in their own language, not the errors that foreigners tend to make in the second language. The second portion of the certification exam (the oral) may be taken only after a person has passed both parts of the written portion of the test. This generally consists of three parts: sight translation, consecutive interpretation, and simultaneous interpretation. Candidates are expected to sight translate texts which are written in language that may be characterized as highly colloquial and highly formal. The consecutive interpretation portion may consist of a cross-examination, and the simultaneous portion may comprise an attorney's opening or closing argument or a judge's instructions to the jury. In each mode that is tested, colloquial and formal language in English and the language to be tested are employed, and candidates are evaluated on their ability to preserve the tone, style, intent, and language level of the speaker(s).[30]

Upon passing the oral examination, candidates are certified and can work in the U.S. district courts. The Administrative Office of the U.S. Courts provides the courts with a roster of certified court interpreters who have successfully completed these written language proficiency and oral interpreting skills examinations. Successful completion of these examinations does not constitute an offer of employment by the United States Courts, however, successful candidates are placed on the eligibility list from which court interpreters may be selected.

There are no formal educational requirements for federal certification, however, the difficulty of the bilingual examination is at the college degree level of proficiency, and successful completion of the oral skills portion would normally require prior training or experience in simultaneous and consecutive interpretation and sight translation. Candidates may take the examinations as many times as they wish. The examinations are presently administered by the University of Arizona under contract with the Administrative Office of the U.S. Courts, but are held in various localities in the contiguous United States as well as Alaska, Hawaii, and Puerto Rico.

In 1980, for the first administration of the test, 7.7 percent of the 1,370 persons who took the two-part test were certified. During the second administration of the test in 1980/1981, 13.2 percent were certified.[31] In 1989, 24 percent of those who took the test were certified. This increase in the passing rate over nearly a decade may be attributable to better preparation on the part of candidates since, as reported by Edward Baca, the examination was tested psychometrically and found to be of comparable difficulty to previous examinations.[32]

As of this writing, the federal standards for court interpreter certification have not been adopted by any of the states, although there is some interest in doing so.

Concluding Remarks

In summary, unlike practitioners in the legal, medical, accounting, and many other professions, translators and interpreters in the United States may offer their services in private business or to the general public without prior licensing or certification. The major exception, as we have discussed, is the federal district court system, which has developed certification for Spanish, Haitian Creole, and Navajo. States are now more aware of the role court interpreters play in their judicial systems and of the disadvantage that non-English speakers have in legal proceedings.

Court interpreting has made significant gains toward professionalization as a direct result of federal legislation. The Court Interpreters Act of 1978 and its subsequent amendments have, among other improvements: helped to make the judiciary and other courtroom personnel more keenly aware of the importance of qualified and professional interpreters; created the mechanism by which certification examinations may be developed and administered; provided for the use of simultaneous interpretation equipment when interpretation is required at multidefendant trials; and authorized the Director of the Administrative Office of the United States Courts to prescribe a schedule of fees for services rendered by certified and otherwise qualified interpreters. As pointed out by Arjona, "the impact of the examination and the legislation that mandated it has been immediate and rapidly felt within the court interpreting profession."[33] Standards and the certification of professionals are now established facts.

Due process[34] must be ensured for everyone. In addition to rigorous academic preparation, a certification examination modeled after the federal program and adequate remuneration, are the best way to fill the need for competent interpretation services in all our courts in the United States. Society will accord status to professionals whose competence, achieved through formal education, has been objectively validated by a community of his peers.

The future of court interpreting is promising. It appears that the rapid changes in demographics over the past decade will continue, thus necessitating a greater number of interpreters to fill the needs of courts in multilingual communitities throughout the United States. Foreign language educators have become aware of court interpreting as an alternative career for language majors. To what extent states will adopt legislative measures modeled on the federal law is unknowable. However, federal measures, the increasing recognition by the legal community of the role played by interpreters in the administration of justice, and the efforts of individuals who are working actively to pass laws to regulate and thus improve court interpretation services at the state level, augur the coming of age of court interpreting as a profession.

PART II

PRACTICE

PREFACE

Part II contains authentic texts which have been adapted for the practice of sight translation, consecutive interpretation, and simultaneous interpretation. Although these materials are taken from actual court cases, all identifying data (e.g., proper names, dates, addresses, case numbers, geographic location of courts, etc.) have been changed to protect the identity of all parties involved in these legal proceedings.

The practice materials are presented in four sections: 1) sight translation; 2) consecutive interpretation; 3) consecutive and simultaneous interpretation; and 4) simultaneous interpretation. The inclusion of a substantial amount of practice materials will give instructors greater flexibility and freedom of choice in tailoring the book to the needs of their classes. Instructors are encouraged to be selective. Students with prior training or experience in consecutive interpretation, for example, may not need to perform the note-taking exercises. Instructors may supplement this component of the book with additional texts such as birth certificates, newspaper articles, dialogues prepared by the students themselves, or recordings of televised courtroom proceedings. Thus, Part II is easily adapted to class needs.

What follows are general suggestions for using the materials in Part II to teach court interpreting. I emphasize that these are suggestions and that instructional methods will be conditioned, in part, by the students' background in interpretation and by the duration of the course.

Sight Translation. Students should prepare the first sight translation exercises in advance using dictionaries. These will then be read in class, but without the benefit of notes. Subsequent sight translations should be done in class, without prior preparation.

In performing sight translations, students should perform at a speaker's podium, facing the class. Attention must be paid to public speaking quality, presentation, poise, speed, clarity, and accuracy of the rendition.

Consecutive Interpretation. Memory exercises initiate consecutive interpretation training. In the beginning, students practice with rather simple material. The length and difficulty of the exercises is gradually increased. These first exercises involve retention and subsequent repetition of utterances in the same language without taking notes.

After students have had sufficient practice with memory exercises, note-taking is introduced. Students should be encouraged to take notes from memory (i.e., after the speaker has finished). They should refrain from taking down too much information. Before attempting to interpret legal material, beginners should practice interpreting simple dialogues. Videotaping the students' performance of both sight translation and consecutive interpretation is strongly recommended.

Simultaneous Interpretation. Students should first have the opportunity to hear a simultaneous interpretation. Prior to interpreting in the simultaneous mode, beginners should practice shadowing: students repeat everything they hear word-for-word, simultaneously and in the same language. Students practice shadowing in both of their working languages. The material to be used at this stage of instruction includes short, speeches prepared by the students and delivered in class or tape-recorded for practice in the language laboratory. If the exercise is done in class, the "speaker" stands at the front of the room, facing the class. In this way, the shadowing exercise is also useful for practice in public speaking. Suggested topics for these speeches include a visit to the courthouse, current events and controversial issues. The speeches should be presented in ascending degree of difficulty. For instance, an oral presentation on the individual's career goals will be simpler to shadow than one on a technical subject.

Once students are comfortable listening and speaking simultaneously, the difficulty of switching from the source to the target language is introduced.

Although the recommended sequence of instruction is sight translation, consecutive interpretation, and simultaneous interpretation, all three modes should be practiced throughout the course. After all, in a court of law, interpreters often use all three modes within a short period of time, as determined by the situation and the nature of the proceedings. For example, in a pretrial detention hearing (see section 3), an interpreter may be required to sight translate a foreign language document introduced as evidence, interpret the proceedings simultaneously for the non-English-speaking defendants, and interpret in the consecutive mode for non-English-speaking witnesses.

Section 1

SIGHT TRANSLATION PRACTICE

UNITED STATES DISTRICT COURT
CENTRAL DISTRICT OF CALIFORNIA

CASE NO. 89-438

UNITED STATES OF AMERICA,

Plaintiff,

vs.

VERDICT

Defendant.

Mario Gasco
____________________________/

WE, THE JURY, find the Defendant, Mario Gasco:
as to Count One: guilty ;
as to Count Two: guilty .

SO SAY WE ALL.

February 3, 1991
DATE

Mary Johnson
FOREPERSON

UNITED STATES DISTRICT COURT
CENTRAL DISTRICT OF FLORIDA

CASE NO. 90-151

UNITED STATES OF AMERICA,)

v.)

Ermenegildo Loma)

This cause came before the Court for preliminary hearing pursuant to Fed.R.Crim.P. 5.1 and the government having established probable cause to believe that the offense(s) charged in the complaint has been committed by the above-named defendant(s), it is thereupon

ORDERED that the above-named defendant(s) is held to answer in the District Court.

DONE AND ORDERED at Orlando, Florida this 8 day of 1990.

Peter Melton
UNITED STATES MAGISTRATE

cc: United States Attorney
Defense Counsel

INTERROGATION: ADVICE OF RIGHTS

YOUR RIGHTS

Place Chicago, Illinois
Date 3-11-88
Time 5:25 pm

Before we ask you any questions, you must understand your rights.

You have the right to remain silent.

Anything you say can be used against you in court.

You have the right to talk to a lawyer for advice before we ask you any questions and to have a lawyer with you during questioning.

If you cannot afford a lawyer, one will be appointed for you before any questioning if you wish.

If you decide to answer questions now without a lawyer present, you will still have the right to stop answering at any time. You also have the right to stop answering at any time until you talk to a lawyer.

WAIVER OF RIGHTS

I have read this statement of my rights and I understand what my rights are. I am willing to make a statement and answer questions. I do not want a lawyer at this time. I understand and know what I am doing. No promises or threats have been made to me and no pressure or coercion of any kind has been used against me.

Signed ____________________

Witness: Jack Orr
Witness: Marla Irving
Time: 6:55 pm

UNITED STATES DISTRICT COURT
WESTERN DISTRICT OF VIRGINIA

CASE NO. 90-532

UNITED STATES OF AMERICA, :
v. : ORDER ON BOND MOTION
:

Carmen Ortiz-Mena

This Cause came before the Court upon motion of the (defendant) (government) to (reduce) (increase) (modify) the bond. Upon consideration, it is

ORDERED AND ADJUDGED as follows:

_x_ The motion is denied; bond remains at $50,000 .

___ The motion is granted; bond is set at ________ .

___ Personal Surety, unsecured, in the amount of $________ .

___ Personal Surety in the amount of $________ . with 10% posted with Clerk of Court.

___ Personal Surety in the amount of $________ . secured by the following collateral: ________

____

________ .

___ Full Cash in the amount of $________ .

___ Corporate Surety in the amount of $________ .

___ Full Cash or Corporate Surety in the amount of $________ .

In addition to the standard conditions of bond, the following special conditions are hereby imposed:

If bond is changed from that set in another District, the reason pursuant to rule 40(f) is:

DONE AND ORDERED at Willow, Virginia this 3 day of May ,199 0 .

Eleanor James
UNITED STATES MAGISTRATE

cc: Defense counsel
U.S. Attorney
U.S. Marshal

PROMISSORY NOTE

$ 4,000.00

January 16, 1991

For value received, I promise to pay to the order of Steven Marlow the sum of four thousand dollars and No/100 Dollars ($ 4,000.00), plus interest at the rate of 10.5 % in equal monthly installments of one hundred Dollars ($ 100.00) beginning January 30, 1991, and continuing on the same day of each month thereafter until this Note is fully paid.

This maker agrees to waive demand, notice of non-payment and protest, and in case suit shall be brought for the collection hereof, or the same has to be collected upon demand of an attorney, to pay reasonable attorney's fees for making such collection.

UNITED STATES DISTRICT COURT
NORTHERN DISTRICT OF FLORIDA

CASE NO. 89-593

UNITED STATES OF AMERICA, :

v. : NOTICE OF TEMPORARY APPEARANCE AS COUNSEL

Teodoro Juan Rodríguez :

COMES NOW Leopoldo Arnett, Esquire and files this temporary appearance as counsel for the above named defendant(s) at initial appearance. This appearance is made with the understanding that the undersigned counsel will fulfill any obligations imposed by the Court such as preparing and filing documents necessary to collaterize any personal surety bond which may be set.

Counsel's Name (Printed) Leopoldo Arnett
Counsel's Signature ____________
Address 5201 North Franklin Drive, Suite 2235B
Ft. Wakuka, FL Zip Code: 33051
Telephone 721-5013 ext. 2215

UNITED STATES DISTRICT COURT
CENTRAL DISTRICT OF NEW YORK

CASE NO. 87-235

UNITED STATES OF AMERICA, :

v. :

Hiram T. Casal :

NOTICE OF PERMANENT APPEARANCE AS COUNSEL OF RECORD

COMES NOW Ana Marta Sales, and files this appearance as counsel for the above named defendant(s). Counsel agrees to represent the defendant(s) for all proceedings arising out of the transaction with which the defendant is presently charged in the United States District Court in and for the Central District of New York.

Counsel hereby states that this appearance is unconditional and in conformity with the requirements of Local General Rule 16 and the Special Rules Governing the Admission and Practice of Attorneys.

Counsel acknowledges responsibility to advise the defendant(s) of the right of appeal, to file a timely notice of appeal if requested to do so by the defendant(s), and to pursue that appeal unless relieved by Court order.

FEE DISPUTES BETWEEN COUNSEL AND CLIENT SHALL NOT BE A BASIS FOR WITHDRAWAL FROM THIS REPRESENTATION.

DATED: 2/10/87

Attorney Ana Marta Sales
Address 5412 Linsey Lane
City Bay Village
Telephone 453-8890

The undersigned defendant(s) hereby consent(s) to the representation of the above counsel.

____

UNITED STATES DISTRICT COURT
WESTERN DISTRICT OF TEXAS

CASE NO. 88-15

UNITED STATES OF AMERICA

v.

ARRAIGNMENT INFORMATION SHEET

Defendant
John Leonardo Martin /

The above-named Defendant appeared before Magistrate Lorraine Wholsum, where the Defendant was arraigned and a plea of not guilty was entered. Defendant and court-appointed/retained counsel of record will be noticed for trial by the District Judge assigned to this case. The following information is current as of this date:

Defendant: Address: 75 West Boulevard Apt. 3-H
Austin, Texas
Tel. No: 328-7612

Defense Counsel: Name: Anthony Walters
Address: 319 Maple Rd.
Austin, Texas
Tel. No: 344-5903

Bond Set/Continued: $ 25,000 PSB

DATED this 5 day of September, 1988.

Maria Josephs, CLERK
By________________________
Deputy Clerk

cc: Clerk for Judge
U.S. Attorney
Defense Counsel
PreTrial Services

UNITED STATES DISTRICT COURT
SOUTHERN DISTRICT OF FLORIDA

CASE NO. 87-698

U. S. A.

v.

Mario Pérez-Ortiz /

WAIVER

I, Mario Pérez-Ortiz, the above-named defendant, being advised of the nature of the charge(s) pending against me in the U.S. District Court, Southern District of Florida, hereby acknowledge the following facts to be true:

1) I have been fully advised of my rights, specifically my right to counsel.
2) I possess full knowledge and understanding of the charges pending against me in this case.
3) Of my own free will, I do hereby refuse and waive in open court on 17 April, 1987 __________, my right to a preliminary hearing.

____
Defendant

____
Counsel for Defendant

MAGISTRATE CERTIFICATE

The undersigned United States Magistrate certifies that the defendant, having been advised of his constitutional rights, has refused and waived his/her right to a preliminary hearing.

DATED this 17 day of April, 1987, at ________________ Southern District of Florida.

____
UNITED STATES MAGISTRATE

UNITED STATES DISTRICT COURT
EASTERN DISTRICT OF TEXAS

CASE NO. 89-041

UNITED STATES OF AMERICA,
Plaintiff,
v. INDICTMENT
Javier Olivo Fuentes,
Defendant.

THE GRAND JURY CHARGES:

COUNT ONE

One or about February 3, 1989, in the Western District of Texas, Defendant, Javier Olivo Fuentes did knowingly and intentionally and by means of a dangerous weapon, to-wit: a pistol, did forcibly assault, resist, oppose, impede, intimidate and interfere with Martin Douglass, a United States Border Patrol agent while he was engaged in the performance of his official duties, in violation of Title 18, United States Code, Section 111.

A TRUE BILL.

Osvaldo Martin
FOREMAN

United States Attorney
BY:
Mary Jo Kornovich
Assistant United States
Attorney

UNITED STATES DISTRICT COURT
EASTERN DISTRICT OF LOUISIANA

CASE NO. 88-532

UNITED STATES OF AMERICA,)

v.) ORDER FOR DISTRIBUTION OF AVAILABLE FUNDS

Carmelo Mesa)

Counsel or other services having been ordered for the above named defendant pursuant to the Criminal Justice Act, and the Court having found that private funds are available for payment by the defendant for partial reimbursement for the cost of such services, it is thereupon

ORDERED AND ADJUDGED that the above named defendant shall pay the sum of $ 25,000 to the Court for deposit in the Treasury as a reimbursement to the appropriation current at the time of payment, pursuant to 18 U.S.C. Section 3006A.(f).

DONE AND ORDERED at Baton Rouge, Louisiana this 7th day of October, 1988.

Janice P. Greene
UNITED STATES MAGISTRATE

cc: Defense counsel
Administrative Office

UNITED STATES DISTRICT COURT
WESTERN DISTRICT OF WASHINGTON

CASE NO. 91-736

UNITED STATES OF AMERICA,)
v. José Domingo)
Defendant)

PLEA AGREEMENT

The United States of America and José Domingo (hereinafter referred to as the "defendant") enter into the following agreement:

1. The defendant agrees to plead guilty to Count Two of the Indictment, which count charges the defendant with knowingly and intentionally possessing with the intent to distribute a Schedule II narcotic controlled substance, that is, at least five hundred (500) grams of a mixture and substance containing a detectable amount of cocaine and its salt, cocaine hydrochloride, in violation of Title 21, United States Code, Section 841(a)(1) and Title 18, United States Code, Section 2. Specifically, defendant agrees to plead guilty to possession of two (2) kilograms of cocaine.

2. The United States agrees to dismiss count One of the indictment, with respect to the defendant, after sentencing.

3. The United States and the defendant understand and agree that the court may impose any sentence authorized by law and that the defendant may not withdraw his plea solely as a result of the sentence imposed. The defendant understands and agrees that the court must impose a minimum term of imprisonment of 5 years and may impose a statutory maximum term of imprisonment of up to 40 years, followed by a term of supervised release. In addition to a term of imprisonment and supervised release, the court may impose a fine of up to $4,000,000.

4. The defendant further understands and agrees that, in addition to any sentence imposed under paragraph 3 of this agreement, a special assessment in the amount of $50.00 will be imposed on the defendant.

5. The United States makes no agreement with respect to sentencing.

6. This is the entire agreement and understanding between the United States and the defendant. There are no other agreements, promises, representations, or understandings.

Respectfully submitted,

Date: 3-7-91 By: Janet Goodman
ASSISTANT U.S. ATTORNEY

Date: 3-7-91 By: Robert Jones
ATTORNEY FOR DEFENDANT

Date: 3-7-91 By: José Domingo
DEFENDANT

STATEMENT

NOTE: This is an actual written statement given by a Spanish-speaking defendant. Names have been changed, but the language of the original, including spelling errors, has been retained.[1]

Yo Pedro Martínez estoy dispuesto ha decir la verdad. Yo y otros tres hicimos un escape el dia sabado 28 enero a las 7:30 en el condado de Zapata.

La historia empezo cuando ingreso al condado con nosotros Jose DeLeon, el cual al momento nos conto que una puerta trasera de tuberias de plomeria se habria de un tiron fuerte y nos comprobo al momento, y despues de varios dias empezo ha ser el escape. De palabras despues nos invito a salirnos, y nosotros no quisimos. Cuando trajeron otros compañeros, empezo ha invitarlos Jose, pero se negaron casi todos; nomas uno si acepto, no se el nombre de el, que el dia 20 mas o menos entro con nosotros, y al ver Jose que estaba apoyado por el, cambiaron las cosas.

Yo sabia que habia una segueta que estaba escondida, pero no sabia donde. Yo supe esto por un compañero que salio antes, y despues supe que el chino Pepe, que asi lo llamabamos, que el sabia donde estaba y se lo dijo a Jose, y se la presto ha Jose para que el hiciera lo que tenia que hacer.

Momentos despues, Jose empezo ha cortar la rendija que estaba detras de la puerta de tuberias, y hizo el agugero ese dia, que fue el viernes 27 de enero. Despues oi decir que mejor el sabado 28 despues de la cena. Ese dia se hizo el escape como a las 7:30. Yo ya tenia 3 meses una semana de estar aqui en el mismo lugar y estaba desesperao porque yo nunca habia estado en la carcel, y ademas me presionaban los problemas que estaba cruzando mi esposa por la posision economica, ya que tengo tres hijas, dos de ellas las mas chicas usan pampers y leche y ella no habia podido conseguir trabajo, y cuando se comunicaba conmigo me dijo que estaba batallando mucho. Yo nunca me habia separado de ella tanto tiempo; es por eso que lo ise.

Yo cuando llego el dia sabado en la mañana pasaron unos compañeros y Jose rapido los invito y uno de ellos acepto. Ya llego la hora de hacer el escape, y cuando yo vi que estaban saliendo, me dije aqui esta mi libertad para estar con mi esposa y mis hijas, pero en ese momento mi desesperacion no me dejo pensar lo que despues venia a suceder. Ya salimos por el agugero y despues corrimos agarrar el monte. Corrimos como unas 10 calles y se quedo uno atras que no se su nombre. Despues seguimos corriendo asta llegar al monte y ayi caminamos mucho, casi toda la noche. Pero Jose que iba de guia se vorteo y le estubimos dando vueltas a Crystal.

Ya amanecido nos dormimos todo el dia, y cuando volvio a escurecer volvimos ha caminar y habiamos caminado 2 horas cuando llegamos a una casa ha pedir agua y comida. Pero nos toco que ayi vivia un agente de migracion, y hasi fue como llegamos hacer aprendidos como a las 8:30 o 9:00.

UNITED STATES DEPARTMENT OF JUSTICE
EXECUTIVE OFFICE FOR IMMIGRATION REVIEW
OFFICE OF THE IMMIGRATION JUDGE

RECORD OF MASTER CALENDAR APPEARANCE

IN THE MATTER OF: HEARING DATE January 6 19 90
Margarita Valito) File No. A 5971286

RESPONDENT

IN DEPORTATION PROCEEDINGS)

Respondent, through counsel of record, stipulates to the following:

1. All factual allegations in the Order to Show Cause are admitted, with the exception(s) of ______________.
2. The issue of deportability is conceded X, contested ______.
3. Designation of Country of Deportation, if necessary: Nicaragua.
4. Relief sought: hearing.
5. Relief application to be filed with the Immigration Court, Miami, FL, no later than: February 16, 1990. If not timely filed, claimed relief will be considered abandoned.
6. If the sole form of relief sought is in the form of voluntary departure, it is stipulated that voluntary departure be granted until ______, 19 ______.
7. A hearing on the merits is scheduled for ______ on ______, 19 ___, at: ______.
Respondent's failure to appear may result in an order of abandonment.
8. If Respondent does not sufficiently understand and speak English an interpreter in the Spanish language is needed.

Through this document, Respondent's counsel acknowledges proper service of the Order to Show Cause, and that Respondent has been apprised of the nature of these proceedings, including items 1 through 8 of this record.

Counsel of record and the Immigration Service, through its General Attorney, accept this Record of Master Calendar Appearance as Notice of Hearing and of all other matters set forth hereinabove.

______________________________ ______________________________

General Attorney for the Immigration and Naturalization Service | Respondent's Attorney or Representative

NOTE: The following letter was written to a U.S. district court judge. Names, case number, etc., have been changed, but the language of the original, including spelling errors, has been retained.

Institution: Martin, C.I. Cell/Dorm & Rank: H-H-C-13
Name: Macondo, Paco Number: 486342

Por favor yo estoy pidiendo de urgent un dertetibe un investigador para ablar mi problema que yo tengo en esta prision por 2 official y el prole es de muerte es muy serio ok, lla ellos trataron de aserme dano ami y ami family porque ellos estaban asiendo negosio de droga con migo en esta prision y ellos quieren que yo le page toda la droga que el me dio ami, y yo tengo testigo de todo ok, y me estan botando todas mis carta asta los carta legal y no medegan escribil, tengo que estar usando el nombre de otra persona para yo podel escribil ok, por favor yo estoy en Guerga, guerga de andre y ase 5 dia que no Como y no boy a comer asta que yo no able con ustedes urgent porque esta coriendo peligro mi vida en esta prision y yo lo reporte pero ellos aqui no me asen caso y yo tengo en los reco medico que el official me gorpio y me pincho con una pluma, pluma de escribil.

Por favor yo tan bien boy a reportal esto a la federal urgent please, espero por un envestigador federal y por su contesta ok, urgent please coro peligro aqui ok thank so much, me contestan ami, nombre de Paco Macondo 486342 ok

NOTA: Por favor llo quiero sabel como esta el caso mio en corte el numero del Caso #90-1129 Civil por favor mandame adesir como esta porque llono a resibir notisias demada ok, y yono tengo dinero ni abogado ok aquí en esta prision me estan botando las carta no me lasdan ami ok y yo quiero sabel como esta los demando llo estoy mandando nota el sobre, con el ombre del amigo porque ami no medegan escribil carta porque mis carta melas botan las estan votando aqui en la prision pero me contestan con el nombre mio de Paco Macondo ok y yo espero que usted pueda ayudarme pronto en mi caso ok.

Phoenix, Noviembre 21, 1990

Honorable Señor Juez:

El motivo de la presente es para pedirle en nombre de Dios, que tenga compasión el día de mi sentencia la cual está fijada para el 30 de noviembre del presente año.

Yo sé que cometí un error el cual estoy pagando separada de mis dos hijos menores de edad y de mi esposo, como Ud. sabe la situación económica en nuestros países es crítica y yo creyendo que encontraría una solución rápida a los múltiples problemas que nos agobiaban me dejé utilizar y por esto me he visto envuelta en tan triste situación.

Señor Juez a la presente le adjunto copias de mis certificados de trabajo y antecedentes como persona de bien en mi país de origen Bolivia. También le pido si es posible tomar en cuenta el tratado Bilateral de Extradición que existe con mi país, para que de esta forma Ud. me permitiera en nombre de Dios y de la Justicia pagar el tiempo al que he de ser condenada en Bolivia. Esto me permitiría estár cerca de mis hijos y mi madre de 89 años quien está sola y delicada de salud.

Al tiempo de presentarle una vez más mis disculpas lo saludo con todo el respeto que se merece.

Marta Pastrano #41165

REPUBLICA DE BOLIVIA
POLICIA NACIONAL
DEPARTAMENTO NACIONAL FINANCIERO

CERTIFICADO DE ANTECEDENTES

EL DEPARTAMENTO DE REGISTROS DE SANTA CRUZ - BOLIVIA Certifica que el Sr. (Sra.) Dña. Marta Pastrano con CEDULA DE IDENTIDAD No. 2341569 expedida por el Gabinete de Identidad de SANTA CRUZ DE LA SIERRA, domiciliado en C/Parada No. 1, cuya firma e impresión dígito pulgar figuran al pie, registra los antecedentes ANOTADOS A LA VUELTA.

____
Firma del Interesado

____
Jefe Departamento Registros

INDV. DACTILOSCOPICA STA CRUZ 18 de Agosto

Serie: 5131.-
Seccion: 4111.-
Confecc. por: S.C.
Revisado por: S.C.

____
Sub-Cmdte U. de Criminal y Policia Judicial

NOTA: El poseedor de este certificado debe acompañar su CEDULA DE IDENTIDAD, sin cuyo requisito no tiene ningún valor.

ESTADO LIBRE ASOCIADO DE PUERTO RICO
INSTITUTO DE CIENCIAS FORENSES
SAN JUAN, PUERTO RICO

INFORME DE TOXICOLOGIA

NUM. DE AUTOPSIA 0123-89 NUM. DE LAB 1234-89
NOMBRE Teodoro Santos Quiros FECHA DE RECIBO 7-1-89
PATOLOGO Dr. C.M. Mariana PROCEDENCIA ____
MUESTRAS SOMETIDAS Sangre (15cc + 25cc) (descompuesta). Hisopo Nasal (1). Bilis (10cc).
ANALISIS REQUERIDOS Alcohol y Narcóticos.

VENENOS VOLATILES (Alcoholes)
Sangre: Contiene 0.18% de alcohol/peso. Negativo para Metanol, Isopropanol y Acetona.

RASTREO ACIDO (Barbitúricos-Salicilatos)
RASTREO BASICO (Fenotiazinas, Estricina, Librium)
METALES PESADOS (Arsénico, Mercurio, Antimonio, Bismuto)
MONOXIDO DE CARBONO
PROCESOS ESPECIALES (Narcóticos y Otros)
Bilis: Positivo para Cocaína.
Negativo para Morfina, Heroína, Quinina, Codeína, Metadona, Talwin y Anfetaminas.

Hisopo Nasal: Positivo para Cocaína.

____
ANALISIS TOXICOLOGICO EFECTUADO POR

6 de julio de 1989
FECHA

CAPARRA HEIGHTS STATION
SAN JUAN, P.R.

INFORME MEDICO - FORENSE

Autopsia Núm. 0123-89

Nombre del Occiso: ______

Domicilio en: Se ignora

Edad: 32 años Sexo: Varón Raza: Blanca

Lugar de muerte: San Juan, P.R.

Fecha de muerte: 30 de junio de 1989

Fecha de autopsia: 1 de julio de 1989

Identificado por: No fue identificado por sus familiares

Domicilio en: ______

Relación: ______

Fiscal: ______

Distrito Judicial: San Juan, P.R.

Causa de muerte: Severo trauma corporal.

Manera de muerte: Explosión de Bomba. (Pendiente de Investigación).

DR. C.M. MARIANA
Patólogo Forense

Fecha del Informe: 4 de noviembre de 1989

NOTE: The original language of the following letter, including spelling errors, has been preserved.

HONORABLE JUEZ
E. S. D.

Ref Case: YOUR FILE No 11123
CASE No 87-426

Su Senoria, es para mi un privilegio saludarlo en el nombre de CRISTO JESUS, esperando que al recivir la presente DIOS nuestro SENOR, haya puesto paz en su corazón y haya coronado de sus mas ricas bendiciones a su familia.

Senor Juez, yo me dirijo a ud en estas tres letras y antes le pido me gaste tres minutos de su tiempo y me excuche. O.K. Senor Juez como ud sabe cuando fuimos a juicio, el Abogado que me puso la Corte no me represento ami y no fue al juicio. Mis companeros salieron libres y fueron deportados a su pais. O.K. Y yo ya tengo (36) meses y estoy aqui sin saber nada de mi caso o que es lo que van hacer conmigo. Yo entiendo Su Senoria que el que comete su delito tiene que pagarlo, pero, tambien entiendo que la ley debe de ser justa con todos. O.K. Usted sabe que you fui mal representado, y estuve (16) meses sin Abogado. El (20) Febrero del año pasado vino el Senor Winston, hablar conmigo, que vino de parte suya, tanto le agradezco a usted por ser tan amable; pero voy a cumplir (12) meses y no he vuelto a verlo y mientras yo estoy aqui sin saber nada. Yo le suplico en nombre de CRISTO JESUS que tome conciencia de mi y me den una oportunidad de llegar yo tambien al lado de mis hijos a darles el calor que ellos se merecen de su padre. Usted sabe su Senoria el deber y la responsabilidad que tiene un padre en un hogar, yo tengo tres hijos varones y hoy se estan criando solos sin el calor de su padre. Que vienen aser ellos manana? Unos gamines porque no han conocido calor de padre ni un colegio Senor JUEZ, yo soy un Colombiano que no tengo ni cama donde tender, solo me lucho la vida trabajando para sobrevivir con mi pobre familia y yo sali de mis casa no a buscar este problema sino a buscar el pan para mis hijos. Su Senoria usted sabe la tristeza mas grande que hay en un hombre es estar sin trabajo sin poder darle la alimentacion a sus hijos. Hoy llego ante usted a pedirle que tenga compacion de mi familia, vemos la compacion que tiene DIOS para con nosotros y el dice en su palabra: AMAOS UNOS A OTROS COMO YO LO HE AMADO O.K. Yo soy un ser humano como cualquiera que puede cometer errores y si DIOS nos perdona porque nosotros no podemos perdonar a otro que nos ofenda. O.K. Yo he entregado mi vida al SENOR y le prometo no cometer un error mas ni a este pais ni a otro porque cuando uno conoce que CRISTO es instituto Salvador la GRACIA de DIOS cae sobre la persona y llega a hacer nueva criatura en CRISTO JESUS. Y eso es lo que soy yo hoy dia O.K. porque todos somos lavados con esa sagrada sangre porque la BIBLIA nos dice cuan grande es el AMOR de DIOS para todos los que en EL creen O.K.

Yo le pido, Sr. JUEZ, a ud si esta carta tiene algun error sepame disculpar O.K. por mi idioma que no me puedo expresar directamente a usted. Que DIOS lo colme de sus mas ricas bendiciones y yo estare orando dia y noche por su hogar. Gracias por escucharme y la PAZ de DIOS sea a su vida y deme por favor una respuesta, ya son diez cartas que le he escrito y no me ha contestado ni una.

Sin otro particular me suscribo atentamente de usted con admiracion y respeto:

ATENTAMENTE

____

STATEMENT OF __Jack Linares__ TAKEN IN WACO, TEXAS ON MAY 14, 1988, RELATIVE TO THE INVESTIGATION OF CASE NUMBER 90-1213[2]

My name is __Jack Linares__, I am 33 years old and I live at 1449 2nd Street in Waco, Texas. I have lived in Waco for the last 17 years.

On or about January 31, 1990, I was at my place of business The Blue Bird Lounge in Waco, Texas, where I met a person by the name of Ricardo, whom I know now as being Sergeant of the Laredo Police Department, working with the DEA in Laredo, Texas. Ricardo and another guy came into the bar and they wanted to buy some heroin, I told them that the man with the heroin was there and told Ricardo and his friend that the man with the heroin was supposed to contact me later and deliver some heroin to me. Ricardo and his friend left the bar and agreed to return later to see if I had received the heroin. Later that afternoon I again met with Ricardo and his friend and told them that the man with the heroin had not been able to deliver but that I had a man that had plenty of cocaine.

Ricardo told me that he would wait a little bit longer for the heroin and if he couldn't get the heroin he would buy the cocaine from me. Ricardo and his friend said they would wait for me at the Purple Parrot Restaurant parking lot.

I had talked to __Oscar Jiménez__ earlier about the possibility of selling some cocaine to Ricardo and he said that he would sell the cocaine to them. At approximately 7:00 p.m., Oscar Jiménez came by the Blue Bird Bar and he and I went to the Purple Parrot where I met with Ricardo and his friend. I asked him if he was still interested in buying the cocaine. Ricardo told me that he would buy 1/4 ounce as a sample and it if was any good he would come back at a later date and buy larger quantities. Oscar and I went back to the bar where Oscar gave me the cocaine, and I went back to the Purple Parrot and delivered the cocaine to Ricardo and his friend. I returned to the bar where Oscar was waiting for me and I gave Oscar $500.00 of the $600.00 that Ricardo had given me for the cocaine.

About two or three weeks later, Ricardo and another guy came back and told me that they wanted to buy one ounce of cocaine. I went to Oscar's house, on Yota Street in Waco, and told Oscar that the guy was in town and wanted to buy one ounce of cocaine. I remained in the living room of Oscar's house and I believe he went into the bedroom and got one ounce of cocaine and gave it to me. I left Oscar's house and went to the mall where Ricardo was waiting for me and we drove back behind the mall area in the residential part and I delivered the cocaine to Ricardo. I took the money that Ricardo had paid me for the cocaine and took it back to Oscar but I don't remember if I gave him the money at his house or at the bar.

On or about April 6, 1990, I had made arrangements to deliver seven ounces of heroin to Ricardo. When the guy with the heroin got there I had talked to Oscar and he told me that he wanted to buy two ounces of heroin of the seven ounces that I was supposed to deliver Ricardo. I owed Oscar about $1,200.00 from loans and cocaine that he had given me and I was supposed to give Oscar the two ounces of heroin for $5,000.00 each and at the same time liquidate my $1,200.00 debt. Sometime about mid-day I met Oscar at his house and gave him the two ounces of heroin and Oscar said that he would pay me the $10,000.00 later that day. I left Oscar's house and I didn't see him anymore until later that day when we were both arrested by the Drug Enforcement Administration.

This statement is true and correct to the best of my memory and ability and I have not been coerced or intimidated in giving this statement.

____

____
Angela Arca
Special Agent - DEA

____
Tomás Rodríguez
Sergeant DPS Narcotics

____
Lorenza Machado
Waco Police Department

Section 2

CONSECUTIVE INTERPRETATION PRACTICE

SELF-EVALUATION OF VIDEOTAPED CONSECUTIVE INTERPRETATION

Demeanor	Body Language	Voice	Accuracy
Additional Observations:			

Consider the four categories above as you view and evaluate your videotaped performance. *Demeanor* includes poise and professional behavior; *body language* refers to posture and to distracting mannerisms or gestures on the part of the interpreter; *voice* includes appropriate volume and intonation, hesitation, stammering, and mumbling on the part of the interpreter; and *accuracy* refers to changes such as omissions, additions to the original testimony, use of deceptive cognates by the interpreter, use of filler words (e.g., "you know", "este", "uh") not uttered by the source language speaker, and other changes in the original message (e.g., 2 kilos is changed to 12 kilos).

PRELIMINARY EXERCISES

I. MEMORY EXERCISES

A. Listen to each statement as it is read to you. Do not take notes as you listen. Then repeat each statement verbatim (word-for-word).

1. Please state your full name and your age for the record. Both your home and business addresses and spell your last name.

2. *No recuerdo exactamente si estaba oscuro o no. Lo que sí vi fue que el objeto estaba sobre la mesa.*

3. After crossing the border illegally, were you greeted by officials of the Immigration and Naturalization Service?

4. *Yo me metí en el revolú este de las drogas por casualidad, porque cuando yo salí con Hector esa noche fue con la intención de ayudarlo a limpiar el restaurante.*

5. Is it your intention to set the stage for offering evidence that the defendant was not in the area at the time of the transaction?

6. *Yo diría . . . en total fueron unos $150,000 en cinco años. No estoy seguro porque a veces me pagaban $2,000, a veces $3,000. Además yo me ganaba la vida en construcción.*

7. On Monday evening, October 6, 1989, at approximately 9 p.m., where were you and what were you doing?

8. *Me arrestaron a mi y a unos tres más. Habíamos terminando de cargar tres carros con toda la hierba que habían traído las embarcaciones de pesca al muelle. Habíamos metido unas veinte libras en cada carro cuando llegaron los agentes.*

9. During this whole trial opposing counsel has done nothing more than put up a smoke screen because she knows she doesn't have a case.

10. *Yo vendo piezas de repuesto para electrodomésticos. Vendo repuestos para batidoras, aspiradoras, lavadoras de ropa y lavaplatos. También vendo televisores, radios, grabadoras y cámaras fotográficas.*

11. I proceeded with asking the applicant's full name, his date of birth, his address, the manner by which he entered into the United States, and the last day of his arrival in the United States.

12. *Bueno, lo que dije fue que el agente examinó unas cajas y luego le dijo al undercover que la mercancía no estaba en buenas condiciones porque a algunas de las armas les faltaba el cerrojo. Esa es la parte del arma que contiene la aguja de percusión.*

13. The work life expectancy of somebody who was 65, well, actually 64 at the time of his accident is 2.3 years and his work life expectancy at the present time, aged 68, is 1.2 years.

14. *Me dijo que tenía que pagarle treinta dólares por la cama y la comida y que cada uno de nosotros tenía que pagarle además de lo que ya le habíamos dado, doscientos dólares para que nos llevara a un sitio llamado Jomsted o algo así.*

15. Your Honor, I'm going to object to the question. She has testified that she didn't go there until at least a half hour after the accident. She couldn't say she knows the condition at the time of the accident.

16. *El problema es que aquí dizque ponen fianzas exageradísimas y si me ponen una fianza exagerada, ¿de dónde voy a sacar yo pa' poner fianza? Hay gente que se especializa en poner fianzas y esa vaina, pero necesitan*

que uno les pague un porcentaje y no sé qué vaina de la fianza que van a poner. Y eso es lo que está difícil.

17. Did you think it was at all unusual that if this guy is trying to bribe you that he would come up to your office with all of these people around in broad daylight with no disguises and present the bribery note? Did you think that was strange in any way? Did it seem a bit unusual to you?

B. Repeat completely and in the same language, a short story or tale told by another speaker. Gradually increase the length and complexity of the story.

Note that the additional difficulty of interpreting from one language to another is introduced only after considerable practice in repeating English texts in English and Spanish texts in Spanish (or other language combinations).

II. NOTE-TAKING EXERCISES

A. Listen to each statement as it is read to you, taking notes as you listen. Then repeat the statement verbatim.

1. Is it true, Mr. Moller, that when you returned to work that day, there was $2,100 missing from the safe deposit box as well as several dozen gold watches, twenty rings, and fifty-nine pearl necklaces?

2. *Dile que yo no tengo, que como ella sabe, nunca he tenido nada que ver con drogas ni tenga nada que ver, ni nunca he tenido antecedentes, ni tengo dinero, ni nada de esas cosas; que yo no tengo problema.*

3. Yeah, that's how it works. They didn't design the airplane just to go from here to Cayo Tirol, you know, they designed the airplanes to go — to be versatile. To go, ah, maybe eight hundred miles with all the seats filled, or

something like that, you know, or, or, you know, four hundred miles.

4. *Yo fui una vez con Franklin, yo fui a ver si había llegado un avión de él. Después fui a verlo; estaba él diciendo a unos tipos ahí cómo debían llegar acá esas cosas, y qué es lo que iban a hacer en Cayo Tirol, que a dónde debía llegar a Cayo Tirol . . . Pero yo nunca supe ni qué era lo que iban a buscar ni que era lo que iban a traer, . . . tú sabes que nunca he, nunca hemos tenido dinero para nada, así que no sé cómo van a poder vincularme a mí en eso.*

B. Use the Memory Exercises above (I.A.) to practice note-taking. Listen to each statement as it is read, taking notes as you listen. Then repeat the statement verbatim.

C. Practice repeating passages that contain many numbers, such as the one below. This exercise is useful for learning to take down figures.

EXAMPLE: On each of the dates as indicated, as we went through the number of applications presented by the defendant, Dennis Forest was paid by the defendant the following sums of money: April 6th, 1988, one application, $400; April 7th, 1988, two applications, $980; April 21st, 1988, two applications, $1,000; April 22nd, 1988, two applications, $700; April 27th, 1988, nine applications, $4,500.

D. Interpret from the source to the target language (e.g., English to Spanish) a short story or speech told by another speaker. Be sure to take notes as you listen to the source language speaker.

NOTE: When using the texts in this section to interpret in the consecutive mode, students should take turns playing different roles (e.g., attorney, judge, defendant, interpreter, etc.), thus simulating a court proceeding. The performances may be audio or videotaped.

INITIAL APPEARANCE

JUDGE: All defendants appearing for the first time in this court are advised that you have the right to remain silent. You are not obliged to make any statement here in court, but if you do make a statement the content of that statement may be used against you in future proceedings. You have the right to an attorney and the right to have that attorney present with you during all court proceedings.

You also have the right to have that attorney present with you anytime that you are questioned by an agent of the government. If you do not have the money to hire your own attorney this court will appoint an attorney for you after you have shown that you do not have the funds to hire your own attorney. In order to show that you do not have the money to hire your own attorney, I will require that you fill out a financial affidavit. That financial affidavit is made under penalty of perjury. If you make any false statements in the financial affidavit you could subject yourself to further prosecution.

You are here for an initial appearance before the United States Magistrate. The purpose of this appearance is for you to be told what the charges are against you and to have the court set conditions for your pretrial release. You have the right to a preliminary hearing to determine if there is probable cause to believe that you committed the crime which is alleged against you in the complaint. That hearing must be within ten days of today's date should you be in custody, or within twenty days of today's date if you are not in custody. If at any time before the end of the ten or twenty day period of time you are indicted by the federal grand jury, then you no longer would have the right to a preliminary hearing.

You also have the right to be released on reasonable bail. If you cannot make the bail which the court sets for you here today in this hearing, you have the right to come back to this court at some later time to have the court again consider whether the bail that was set in your case was the proper bail for your case after considering the facts and circumstances of your case and your particular, individual situation.

JUDGE'S OPENING STATEMENTS TO DEFENDANTS IN ARRAIGNMENT CALENDAR

Good morning, ladies and gentlemen. You are here this morning for your arraignments. You have been charged with either a misdemeanor or a county ordinance violation, and as such you face a fine, a jail sentence or both if you are found guilty today.

You can enter a plea of guilty, not guilty or no contest. Before I explain each of these pleas to you I want to advise you that you have the right to be represented by an attorney, but must hire your own attorney unless certain conditions are met which are: one, the state is seeking jail time against you in the event you are found guilty, and you do not have adequate funds of your own to hire your own lawyer.

Today, if you enter a plea of not guilty your case will be set for trial and you will receive another notice in the mail telling you when to return to court, but if you plead guilty or no contest we will not fight or contest that charge.

ARRAIGNMENT

JUDGE: Ladies and Gentlemen, you are appearing in County Court, Criminal Division.

You will be advised of the charges against you and you may enter your plea of not guilty, guilty or no contest.

Your name will be called and you will come up one at a time.

You have the following choices:

Guilty: If you plead guilty, you are admitting the charges against you.

No contest: If you plead no contest, you are not contesting the charges against you.

Not guilty: If you plead not guilty, your case will be set for trial in approximately six weeks.

Before you enter your plea, I want to advise you of your rights, as guaranteed by the constitution. You have the right:

- To remain silent and not have that fact considered by the judge or jury at trial.
- To an attorney, and the right to have an attorney appointed if you cannot afford one if the court is considering a jail sentence on this charge.
- To a trial before a judge or a judge and jury.
- To a presumption of innocence until the state proves you guilty beyond a reasonable doubt.
- To question witnesses at trial.
- To call witnesses of your own at trial and have those witnesses subpoenaed by the court.
- To testify at trial and have your testimony considered by the same standards as the other witnesses.
- To have a reporter make a complete record of the proceedings.
- To appeal any harmful error to a higher court.

OPENING REMARKS, PRE-TRIAL SESSION

JUDGE: Good morning, Ladies and Gentlemen:

This is a pre-trial session of the Civil Division of the County Court. It's called a pre-trial because your case will not be tried today. Certain preliminary matters will be taken care of today so that your case will be ready on the trial date. For those of you who are unfamiliar with Civil Court, I am going to take a few minutes to explain how civil cases are handled. In a few minutes you will be before the Court individually, if you have any questions concerning the procedures, feel free to inquire.

The person who files a civil law suit is called the Plaintiff. The person being sued is called the Defendant. In order for the Plaintiff to win, the Plaintiff must prove two things: First, the Plaintiff must prove that the Defendant owes something to the Plaintiff, that's called proving liability. Second, the Plaintiff must prove the amount owed by the Defendant, that is called proving damages. In order to win, the Plaintiff must prove both liability and damages.

It's possible for both sides to agree and for the case to be settled right here today. It's also possible for the parties to agree on part of the case, and to go to trial only on areas of the disagreement. It's important for you all to try to agree on at least part of your case. It will reduce the amount of time it will take to try your case and may save you some witness fees. In addition, it saves precious time so that those who cannot agree on anything will have plenty of time to tell their side to the Court. Of course, if you cannot agree, rest assured that you will have ample opportunity to explain your side of the case.

The judge will discuss the case with you to try to help you settle your dispute. If that is not possible, the judge will make an estimate of the amount of time your case will take to try. You will be receiving your trial date from the Clerk's Office in the mail. This is the only notice you will get. If you are the Plaintiff and you fail to appear on time at the time of trial, your case will be dismissed. If you are the Defendant and you fail to appear on time, a judgment will be entered against you. So you can see, it is important that you be in court, on time.

It is also important for you to be prepared to go to trial. Whatever witnesses or physical evidence such as maps, photos, diagrams you wish the Court to see or hear must be brought with you on the day of trial. The Court ordinarily will not grant a continuance during the trial to allow the parties to bring in more evidence.

Certain cases present special problems of proof. If you are a Plaintiff suing someone for damages to your automobile you should bring an expert witness to court on the trial date. The expert should be someone who has examined your car and who is in a position to tell the Court the cost of repairs. If you are a Defendant in an automobile case you have a right for you and your expert to examine the Plaintiff's car. If you have a construction case in which you are suing someone for plumbing, electrical, or similar work which you say was not done properly, you will need an expert who has examined the work and can tell the Court what is wrong with it and how much it will cost to make it right.

DEPORTATION HEARING

JUDGE FOR THE RECORD

This is a deportation hearing at Los Angeles, California, on May 5, 1988, before Immigration Judge Angela Menendez, in the matter of Marta Josefina Mendoza, file No. 44-567 and her minor child, Alberto Rodríguez-Mendoza, file No. 44-568. On behalf of the government, General Attorney Jack Barrister. The official Spanish interpreter is Josefina Ceballos. To the respondent, adult respondent:

JUDGE TO MS. MENDOZA

Q. What language do you speak and understand best?

A. *El español.*

Q. How old is your child?

A. *Tiene seis años de edad.*

Q. Would you please stand and raise your right hand. Do you solemnly swear to tell the truth, the whole truth and nothing but the truth, so help you God?

A. *Sí, lo juro.*

Q. Please be seated. State your full and correct name for the record.

A. *Marta Josefina Mendoza.*

Q. And your child's name?

A. *Alberto Rodríguez-Mendoza.*

Q. Now Miss Mendoza, at this hearing, excuse me, this hearing is to decide whether you must leave the United States. Do you understand that?

A. *Sí. La fianza se va a pagar.*

Q. At this hearing, you have the right to an attorney or someone here to represent you at your own expense. The interpreter is providing you a form I-618, notice of your rights, as well as a legal aid list of organizations in the Los Angeles area that may represent you for little or no money. You have requested a bond hearing and a deportation hearing. Do you wish to proceed, at this time, without an attorney, or do you want an opportunity to get an attorney?

A. *Quiero un abogado.*

Q. I'll reset your case then to June 1, 19 88 at 1 p.m. to give you an opportunity to get an attorney and to bond out, as you've indicated you desire to do so. At that time, however, if you are not bonded out and do not have an attorney, I expect you to be here ready to represent yourself and your child. Do you understand that?

A. *Sí.*

JUDGE FOR THE RECORD

This hearing then is adjourned.

JUDGE FOR THE RECORD

Continued deportation hearing at Los Angeles, California, June 1, 19 88. On behalf of the respondents, no one. On behalf of the government, General Attorney Jack Barrister. The official Spanish interpreter, Josefina Ceballos.

JUDGE TO MS. MENDOZA

Q. Now Ms. Mendoza, an attorney, Mr. Bryan, did appear earlier today, although he was not available to represent you and your child this afternoon. He has indicated, however, that he requests a one week continuance in order that he may discuss this case with you before he proceeds further. Do you have any objection to your case being reset to next week?

A. *No, me parece bien.*

JUDGE FOR THE RECORD

This hearing is adjourned to June 8, 19 88 at 1 p.m.

DEPORTATION HEARING

JUDGE FOR THE RECORD

The proceeding will come to order. It is one in deportation which is being conducted on the 21st day of January 1989. This is Immigration Judge Joseph Wright . With me at the Immigration Court, Phoenix, Arizona, on this date is Ms. Thimas. She's the trial attorney. She represents the Immigration Service. Also present are the respondents. By respondents I'm referring to individuals. The mother and her minor daughter. They are the subjects of case 88-715 . In that file the respondent's name is Hortensia María Martínez. The related file of the daughter is case 88-715 , Rogelia Antonia Lemos-Martínez.

This proceeding will be conducted in part in Spanish through the interpreter of the court, Mirta Paredes .

JUDGE TO MS. MARTINEZ

Q. Ms., for the record, would you please state your full name?

A. *Hortensia María Martínez.*

Q. And seated next to you is your daughter, is that correct?

A. *Sí.*

Q. And what is her full name?

A. *Rogelia Antonia Lemos-Martínez.*

Q. How old is she?

A. *Tiene cinco años.*

Q. Your case was transferred to this court from the Immigration Court in San Francisco, California, do you recall that?

A. *Sí.*

Q. And the issue of deportability has been resolved in your case. By that I mean that the Immigration Judge has previously determined that you are a native and citizen of the country of El Salvador that you entered the United States without inspection. And that you are subject to deportation for the reason that you entered the United States without inspection and that is in violation of Section 241(a)(2) of the Immigration and Nationality Act. Now, you have filed as a form of relief from deportation an application for asylum, do you still wish to request asylum from this court?

A. *Sí.*

Q. Court in considering your application for asylum will consider asylum under Section 208 of the Immigration and Nationality Act as a form of relief and also withholding of deportation under Section 243(h) of the Act. Now we are required by regulation to receive an advisory opinion from the State Department and we have received that. It is dated January 19, 1989. Have you received a copy of that document?

A. *No.*

Q. We will get you a copy of that copy. And do you have a copy of your application for asylum which was filed with the court?

A. *Creo que sí. Sí, la tengo.*

Q. All right. Your attorney in San Francisco furnished you with copies of documents?

A. *Sí, me los dio.*

Q. All right. I'm going to advise you at this time, that in this proceeding, and your hearing in reference to your application for asylum, you do have the right to be represented by your counsel. Now, you must retain counsel at your own expense. If, for whatever reason, you cannot afford to retain counsel, I will provide you, this date, with a legal aid list which contains organizations which may represent you at little or no cost. I'm going to reset her case . . .

JUDGE TO MS. MARTINEZ

Q. Ms., I'm going to reset your case for April the 4th, 1989, at 1 o'clock in the afternoon. This is the only notice that you will receive. This is April the 4th, 1989, at 1 o'clock. On that date we will take up for consideration your request for asylum. I want you to bring with you, on that date, any witnesses that you may have to testify in reference to your case. Also any documents or papers that you may have to support your case for asylum. If these documents are in Spanish or in a language other than English, they must be interpreted into the English language, and they must be certified as a true and correct interpretation. And on that, April the 4th, 1989, you need not bring your daughter, inasmuch as she is five years of age. But you are expected to appear and I strongly suggest that you have counsel with you on that date. And if you will wait, we will give you your copy of the advisory opinion. I'll have you wait in court for a while. Return April the 4th, 1989, at 1 o'clock.

MISDEMEANOR OFFENSE

JUDGE TO MR. PEREZ

Q. Mr. Perez, the government says that you tried to run away after your arrest. Is that true, and if so, why did you do it?

A. *Sí, no, es cierto. La razón porque lo hice fue lo siguiente: cuando el de la migra nos pescó a todos los compañeros que veníamos juntos desde Matehuala, nos habló de forma . . . muy áspera, dura. Nos gritaba que qué pensábamos hacer, que nos calláramos, que no hiciéramos borlote porque nos iba a ir muy mal. Yo me fijé que el migra traía pistola, y con los nervios que tenía, pensé que tal vez nos disparara, porque lo vi bien enojado. A mí me habló de mala forma, diciéndome "Pinchi mojado, no abras la boca. Quédate allí, quieto." Bueno, Sr. Juez, como le digo, estaba yo bien nervioso por la situación y por la manera de hablar y de actuar del oficial. Por eso fue que me eché a correr pa'l monte, sin pensarlo siquiera.*

JUDGE TO AGENT

Q. Do you have anything further in your report on this?

A. Yes, Your Honor. The agent making the report says that the defendant was cursing, using abusive language and being totally uncooperative.

MR. PEREZ

A. *Tal vez yo haiga dicho algo malo, porque con el susto ni sabía lo que decía. Si fue así, les pido disculpas a los señores oficiales. Yo no quería portarme mal con ellos, pero es que la forma en que le tratan a uno pues tampoco es muy respetuoso. Uno es humano también, y no quiere que le traten como animal.*

JUDGE

Q. It says here that after you all got into the van you took off at a high rate of speed. Where were you going?

A. *Pos yo no sé a dónde irían los demás. Yo me iba a Dallas porque un concuño mio dijo que me conseguía chamba allí.*

Q. Who was driving?

A. *Un vato que ni sé su nombre, nomás le dicen el "Tuerto."*

Q. Were you paying for the trip?

A. *Sí, todos pagábamos los gastos entre todos. Y al comenzar a trabajar, le íbamos a pagar $100 cada uno al que hizo los arreglos. No sé su nombre, nomás la dirección donde había que mandar el dinero. O sea, se me figura que él es el coyote, pero no sé cómo se llamará.*[3]

DEPOSITION

Q. Please state your name for the record.

A. *Me llamo Ramón Abelardo Jiménez.*

Q. Mr. Jiménez, how long have lived in this country?

A. *Quince años.*

Q. Can you please tell us about your accident?

A. *Sí, como no. Ocurrió cuando entraba yo a trabajar en el baño de la casa del señor Waterman. Yo tenía que reparar la cabeza de la ducha, que estaba tupida, no dejaba pasar el agua—y al colocar el ladder me resbalé y me caí para atrás, di con el lavamanos, la pila, y me lastimé la espalda . . . pues se me dañaron dos discos de la columna vertebral, no pude levantarme . . . y ¡que dolor! por Dios.*

Q. How do you know two verterbral discs were damaged?

A. *Bueno, salió en la radiografía. Claro, yo no sabía en esos momentos qué me había pasado. Sólo sentía ese gran dolor y no podía levantarme. ¡Qué iba a saber yo lo que tenía! Já.*

Q. When was the X-Ray taken, who ordered it to be done, and where was it done?

A. *La radiografía se hizo a los dos o tres días. Fue después de que salí del emergency . . . a los dos o tres días si mal no recuerdo. Creo que se hizo porque lo pidió el insurance, no sé. El médico me dijo que fuera pallá . . . no sé.*

Q. Which doctor? When did he see you? Was that the emergency room at General Hospital?

A. *Sí, del General. El doctor era el doctor Valdivieso, de Hialeah. El me atendió después de salir del General, al día siguiente, o a los dos días. El insurance me lo recomendó.*

Q. How long were you at General Hospital?

A. *Sólo hasta esa noche. Ahí me atendieron, como no podía caminar ni jorobarme ni nada, me pusieron unas inyecciones y luego descansar sí pude y me mandaron unas pastillas para el dolor además.*

Q. Thank you, Mr. Jimenez. I have no further questions.[4]

SENTENCING

NOTE: The following is the testimony of a witness, the mother of defendant Edward Lasuna, at his sentencing.

CLERK: Do you swear to tell the truth, the whole truth, and nothing but the truth, so help you God? [oath is interpreted]

A. *Sí, lo juro.*

Q. Mrs. Lasuna, tell us your name and age, please.

A. *Magdalena Jaramillo de Lasuna.*

Q. Edward Lasuna is one of your sons?

A. *Sí.*

Q. Where are you from?

A. *De Ecuador.*

Q. How many children do you have?

A. *Siete.*

Q. How old was Edward when he first went to work?

A. *El empezó a trabajar a la edad de unos nueve años. El iba a la escuela y después de que terminaba la escuela ayudaba al padre en el taller. Así terminó la elemental.*

Q. Did there come a time when your husband left Ecuador to come to the United States?

A. *Desde el momento en que se vino mi esposo a los Estados Unidos, yo trabajaba como ayudante de enfermería en un hospital en Quito y en ese tiempo los salarios eran pocos. Entonces viendo Edward la necesidad que yo tenía con el resto de sus hermanos, para reponder del mortgage que yo tenía de una casita allá que el gobierno nos había dado, él abandonó sus estudios y se puso a trabajar.*

Q. How old was he when he started working to support the family?

A. *Diez años.*

Q. What kind of work did he do?

A. *El fue a una construcción y allá él lavaba el granito del piso, pasaba el ladrillo de mano a mano hasta la obra. Me partía el alma cuando llegaba con sus manos todas sangrando.*

Q. Did he finally come to the United States himself?

A. *Sí, pero antes . . . después consiguió otro empleo en La Barca, un restaurante internacional que había en Quito. Allá él limpiaba el pescado . . . sus manos también eran todas llenas de las punzadas del pescado y ganaba cincuenta pesos semanales, o sea un dólar. Y eso me lo llevaba para sustento de la familia.*

Q. How old was he when he finally came to the United States?

A. *Quince años.*

Q. Did he work here to help bring the other members of the family here?

A. *Sí, él vino para ayudarle al padre que había establecido un garaje de mecánica en Nueva Jersey.*

Q. What happened with the garage?

A. *Hubo un robo muy grande y no dejaron ni una sola herramienta, hasta los carros se los llevaron. Mi esposo quedó sin nada. Entonces, Edward siguió trabajando para ayudar a traer a su familia que habíamos quedado en Ecuador.*

Q. Was he going to work in a factory after the robbery in the garage?

A. *Sí, nos trasladamos para una familia a Massachusetts. Allá nos ayudaron a conseguir un apartamento. Y un señor que vivía en el bilding, yo fui y le hablé, le conté mi situación. Yo no lo conocía—y él me dijo que le iba a hablar en la factoría, pero él problema era que era demasiado niño y no lo recibían. Entonces él se empezó a dejar bigote para representar más edad y lo lograron entrar. El trabajaba overtime sábados y domingos donde hacen todas esas casas grandísimas de inflar de lona. Entonces los que cosían ese material . . . él los jalaba y llegaba con esos dedos sangrando y ampollados hasta que a lo largo se le hicieron callos. Se sacaba quinientos pesos a la semana y a veces seiscientos.*

Q. What would he do with the money?

A. *Todo el cheque nos lo pasaba completico. Así fue todo el tiempo hasta que ahorramos un dinerito y se compró un garaje con dos mil pesos en la ciudad de Boston. Y ya cuando el padre se organizó con el garaje se salió de la factoría a trabajar con el padre. Así que él fue un tiempo de día al high school pero al ver que el padre no podía solo con el garaje—él ayudaba a vender gasolina—se retiró y terminó su high school con la equivalencia de noche. En ese bilding donde nosotros vivíamos, ahí conoció a su esposa. El día que cumplió veinte años se casaron y después resolvió ya hacer su vida yendo para el Army de los Estados Unidos. Estuvo en Alemania, allá nació su primer niño. Duró cinco años, saliendo con los mejores honores, con las medallas más grandes. Se vino para Boston nuevamente y ya su hermano, Jorge, se había venido para la ciudad de Los Angeles para trabajar para el Ayuntamiento. Ya él le abrió paso para venir a entrar aquí. Ahí fuimos viniendo todos poco a poco y todos empezaban a entrar en el Ayuntamiento.*

Q. Mrs. Lasuna, could you describe your feelings for your son, what kind of man he is. Tell the Court what you think of him, what kind of man he is.

A. *Señor, Ud. pensará qué como madre voy a decir lo mejor de los hijos. Pero yo sé que tengo en cada uno de ellos. Edward es una de las personas . . . Ud. ha oído de su niñez, ha sido el support, la columna de la familia. Mi esposo es una persona enferma, sufre del corazón, de la columna. Edward es el que me ha ayudado en las batallas duras. Hasta cuando sucedió el problema, me ayudaba a pagar el mortgage. Iba a la casA. «¿Mamá, qué necesitas? ¿Por qué no me dices que estás atrasada en una deuda?» Es imposible que con tantos problemas yo le pida ayuda. Como hijo no lo puedo describir. El para sus hermanos siempre tiene algo. Dinero les da cuando necesitan. No solamente con los hermanos, sino con todas las personas. Edward es una persona que tiene mucho carisma, es una persona que cree en Dios y él le sirve a las personas sin interés ninguno ni esperando que le den. No lo digo porque yo como madre . . . sino que lo dicen todas las personas que lo conocen desde niño.*

Yo como madre le pido al Señor Juez, que se habrá dado cuenta que nosotros somos una familia decente, que no nos gusta el alboroto, que nos gusta la honestidad, porque así acostumbré a mis hijos, a ser unas personas responsables, que no tomaran, que no fumaran, que no estuvieran en la droga, sino solo en el trabajo.

Nunca a mí me ofrecieron welfare para que me quedara cuidando a mis hijos en mi casa. Nunca hemos sido carga pública ni del gobierno. Todos mis hijos han trabajado desde pequeños y han estudiado y han compartido el cheque para los gastos de casa. Ud. se habrá dado cuenta que no somos personas de destruir, sino de unir las comunidades. Por lo tanto, le pido por favor que me deje a mi hijo libre hasta que llegue su apelación. No solamente en nombre de mi hijo, sino en nombre mio, se lo ruego. Gracias.

ATTORNEY: Our next witness is David Lasuna, Your Honor. The defendant's father.
Witness takes oath: Do you swear to tell the truth, the whole truth, and nothing but the truth, so help you God? [oath is interpreted]

A. *Sí.*

Q. Mr. Lasuna, could you tell us your name, please?

A. *Yo soy David Lasuna.*

Q. Could you tell us your relationship to the defendant?

A. *Yo soy el padre de Edward Lasuna.*

Q. When did you come to the United States?

A. *Yo vine a los Estados Unidos hace aproximadamente veinte años.*

Q. How old was Edward when he came to the United States?

A. *El tenía cuando yo, cuando él vino a los Estados Unidos unos trece o catorce años.*

Q. When he came here, did you have a business?

A. *Sí, yo tenía un negocio.*

Q. What business was that?

A. *Yo tenía un garaje pequeño donde trabajaba reparando carros porque esa ha sido mi profesión toda mi vida.*

Q. When Edward came here, did he go to work for you?

A. *Sí, como no.*

Q. What hours did he work at the garage?

A. *Bueno, el trabajaba distintas horas porque él estudiaba, nos ayudaba a un part time que teníamos en Nueva York, en Brooklyn, pues nos íbamos todos a hacer un part time de limpieza.*

Q. And you would clean office buildings late at night, would you not?

A. *Sí, como no.*

Q. Between what hours would the family clean office buildings?

A. *Bueno, los limpiábamos . . . después de las siete de la noche teníamos que llegar allá.*

Q. That was in addition to the other job that you had during the day?

A. *Sí, como no.*

Q. How many days a week did Edward work at the garage?

A. *El trabajaba toda la semana. Eh, usted sabe que cuando teníamos un trabajo que entregar, él pues, eh, muchas veces se iba a jugar con los amigos por las tardes un rato, pero regresaba nuevamente al garaje para continuar trabajando. Y le daban las dos, tres, cuatro de la mañana terminando los trabajos.*

Q. After you lost the garage, did Edward go to work in a factory?

A. *Sí, como no.*

Q. How many hours did he work at the factory?

A. *Bueno, ellos tenían varios horarios. Ellos tenían un horario desde las seis de la mañana. Trabajaba hasta las once, doce, de la noche . . . eran diferentes horarios en referencia a ese trabajo.*

Q. What age was he when he went to work at this factory?

A. *Tenía quince, dies y seis años, más o menos.*

Q. When Edward came here, did he try to learn English? Well, let me withdraw that for a minute. When Edward first arrived here, could he speak any English?

A. *No, no podía hablar inglés. No sabía nada.*

Q. Did he study to learn English?

A. *Sí, él estudió por las noches y fue como lo pudo ir aprendiendo, ¿no?*

Q. Is there anything that you would like to say to the Judge about your son?

A. *Sí. Yo le pido al Sr. Juez que nos tenga en cuenta pues en este sentido, puesto que necesitamos a Edward Lasuna, eh, en libertad, mientras haga el proceso de apelación para este juicio. Así que de todo corazón le pido, Sr. Juez, que deje a mi hijo Edward Lasuna en libertad bajo palabra y le doy mis más sinceros agradecimientos. Gracias.*

Section 3

CONSECUTIVE AND SIMULTANEOUS INTERPRETATION PRACTICE

TRANSCRIPT OF PRETRIAL DETENTION HEARING

NOTE: Instructors are encouraged to use the transcript below to simulate a courtroom proceeding in the classroom. Students take turns playing the various roles that appear in the "script" including, of course, that of interpreter.

The testimony of non-English-speaking witnesses must be interpreted in the consecutive mode. The simultaneous mode is used to interpret the rest of the transcript.

UNITED STATES OF AMERICA,
Plaintiff

vs. Leopoldo Suárez
and Manuel López

Defendants.

THE COURT: United States vs. Leopoldo Suárez and Manuel López. We are here for a pretrial detention hearing. Let's have each defendant state his name and age and then we'll have appearances.

DEFENDANT: *Leopoldo Suárez, treinta y tres.*

DEFENDANT: *Manuel López, treinta y tres.*

THE COURT: Okay. Counsel, if you'll announce your appearances.

MR. HARRISON: Mr. Harrison on behalf of the government.

MR. SULLIVAN: Mr. Sullivan on behalf of Mr. López.

MR. WHITE: Mr. White on behalf of Mr. Suárez as well as—

MR. TAYLOR: John Taylor.

THE COURT: Good morning, counsel. What's the government's recommendation in this case?

MR. HARRISON: Judge, I believe on this case we're asking for pretrial detention.

THE COURT: Okay, on the basis?

MR. HARRISON: Bringing in drugs. The defendants are each facing over ten years possible sentence. They have no fixed ties to the community. We suggest, Your Honor, that they are a flight risk as well as a danger to the community.

THE COURT: Counsel, you are ready to proceed? The defendants can be seated with their counsel at the table. All right, the government can proceed.

MR. HARRISON: Call Mr. Bester, Your Honor.

(Robert Bester, Plaintiff's witness, sworn.)

THE CLERK: Please be seated. State your full name, spell your last name for the record and if you'll please pull the mike towards you.

THE WITNESS: Robert Bester. B-E-S-T-E-R

DIRECT EXAMINATION

BY MR. HARRISON:

Q. Mr. Bester, are you employed, sir?

A. Yes, I am.

Q. By whom are you employed?

A. U.S. Customs.

Q. In your official capacity, sir, did you have the occasion to meet the two men who are currently before the Court?

A. Yes, I did.

Q. When did you first meet them, sir?

A. I first met them on the evening of the 4th of this month when they were placed under arrest for smuggling cocaine into the United States.

Q. Where were they when they were arrested, sir?

A. New Orleans, Louisiana.

Q. Where in New Orleans?

A. They were arrested at the customs house on the Mississippi River.

Q. All right, sir. Were they in a vessel at the time?

A. Yes, they were.

Q. Was this vessel searched, sir?

A. The vessel was listing to the starboard side as it went up the river and looked suspicious. The Customs Patrol brought the vessel back to the customs house and conducted a search. When they opened the hatch, they could smell fresh paint and/or fiberglass and the paint was still wet, so they opened the area and there were 350 packages of cocaine concealed in a hidden compartment. The weight of the cocaine was 881 pounds and has a value of approximately $10 million.

Q. Sir, have you had an occasion to check into the—

THE COURT: $10 million?

THE WITNESS: Yes, sir.

BY MR. HARRISON:

Q. Have you had an occasion, sir, to check into the background of these two men?

A. I haven't had time as yet to do a thorough background, but based on their own statements at the time of arrest, they indicated—one gentleman indicated he has no ties to the community.

Q. Which is this? Which is this gentleman?

A. Manuel López.

Q. All right, sir, and he said what?

A. He stated he was a citizen, a Dominican, was not a citizen of the United States and he has no ties to the community. The other defendant, Leopoldo Suárez, stated that he had only lived in New Orleans two years. He did have some relatives, but no significant ties to the community.

Q. Have you been able to establish whether or not this man is employed on any regular basis in New Orleans?

A. Manuel López stated he was not employed and Leopoldo Suárez said he, I believe, was a carpenter and did not indicate whether he's steadily employed.

Q. Thank you.

MR. HARRISON: Pass the witness, Your Honor.

CROSS EXAMINATION

BY MR. WHITE:

Q. Mr. Bester, it is true, isn't it, that Mr. Suárez has no prior criminal record? Is that correct?

A. I haven't received information back yet, but he made a statement to us that he had a prior criminal record. He stated he was arrested in 1985 in Orchid City for possession of cocaine.

Q. All right. Did Mr. Suárez tell you at the time of the arrest that he had come from Cuba via Panama two years ago?

A. No, he did not make that statement to me.

Q. Has your somewhat thorough investigation revealed that, in fact, he came from Panama via Cuba?

A. I stated there has been no thorough investigation as of this date.

Q. Has your investigation shown that he has come from Cuba?

A. The investigation hasn't, no.

Q. Now, with respect to the cocaine, is it true that it was hidden in a compartment, is that correct?

A. Concealed compartment, yes, on the boat.

Q. That means that anyone on board cannot readily detect that there was cocaine on the boat, isn't that true?

A. If you are asking could a person look through the wood and see, the answer is no.

MR. WHITE: Thank you.

No further questions.

THE COURT: Thank you, counsel.

BY MR. SULLIVAN:

Q. Along the same lines, Agent, you didn't make the search of this vessel in this case, did you?

A. No, I didn't, not the initial search.

Q. Also, you were not the individual who signed the affidavit forming the basis of the initial complaint in this case, correct?

A. That's correct.

Q. It was Agent Vitier?

A. That's correct.

Q. Are you familiar with his affidavit or were you privy to the information provided to him that formed this affidavit?

A. That's correct. I provided the information.

Q. And you've read the affidavit, I assume?

A. Yes.

Q. And on the affidavit it says the "officer smelled fresh paint and fiberglass," that's the only statement it contains regarding—

A. That's correct.

Q. It doesn't say that they smelled it only as a result of opening up the hatch into a secret compartment.

A. That's correct.

Q. So, which is more accurate: that they smelled it or they smelled it as a result of opening the hatch in a secret compartment —leading to a secret compartment—as what you stated on direct?

A. I'm stating my experience. I was there at the dock. I went on board the vessel. I smelled the fresh paint and fiberglass. I witnessed the fresh paint. It was still wet to the touch and the officers who had opened up the compartment actually got it on their hands and on their clothing—the wet paint.

Q. When they opened the compartment?

A. That's correct.

Q. Okay, so now—I'm just trying to establish your testimony. Your direct was they opened up the compartment and as a result of that, they were able to determine the freshness of the paint or the smell of the paint.

A. That's correct.

Q. Okay. And then you are saying subsequently, you went on the boat to the same area which had already been opened and smelled the same paint odor and the freshness of the material?

A. That's correct.

Q. Did you ever determine who was the captain of the boat?

A. Yes, Manuel López stated that he was the captain.

Q. Oh, so he's made more . . . now, all of a sudden, he's made more statements.

MR. HARRISON: I'll object to—

THE WITNESS: Not all of a sudden. I said he—

THE COURT: Objection sustained.

BY MR. SULLIVAN:

Q. Why don't you tell me about the statements that Mr. López ostensibly made to you?

A. Why am I telling you?

Q. No, why don't you tell me at this point. Let me ask you more specifically. What statements did Mr. López ostensibly make to you upon his being seized?

A. The statements he made to me were that he was the captain of the vessel. He had taken the vessel at six o'clock the previous morning, left with Leopoldo Suárez, went to the Bahamas, picked up the cocaine—it was loaded by four Bahamians—returned to New Orleans, and upon coming up the river was stopped by Customs, brought back to the customs house where they located the cocaine on board.

Q. And he made these statements in what you consider a free and voluntary manner?

A. He was advised of his—

MR. HARRISON: Objection, Your Honor. This is not a suppression hearing.

THE COURT: Overruled. You can answer the question. Would you like it repeated?

THE WITNESS: Yes. I heard the question. He was advised of his rights and it was made very clear to him what his rights were before he made those statements.

BY MR. SULLIVAN:

Q. So I assume you got these statements in writing as well as verbally to preserve your notes and records?

A. Are you—

Q. Did you—I'll rephrase the question. Did you then take a written confession?

A. No, I didn't take a written confession. He made a verbal statement and notes were taken.

Q. Did you ever determine or bother—did you ever bother to determine who owned the vessel?

A. I have the registration with the owner's name on it.

Q. May I see the registration, please?

A. I would rather not give this information if I don't have to.

MR. HARRISON: I would object, it's irrelevant.

THE COURT: You have an objection?

MR. HARRISON: I object, Your Honor.

THE COURT: Sustained.

MR. SULLIVAN: Well, I'd like to have argument, Your Honor, at this time, on the point of the relevancy of who owns the boat in a bond hearing. I think it's totally relevant.

THE COURT: I think for limited purposes you can get into the strength of the government's case, that's why I allowed an answer to the previous question, but I've sustained the objection.

MR. SULLIVAN: Your Honor—the last thing that I'm going to say—I hate to be argumentative, but one more point. The government opened up the door by saying $10 million worth of cocaine. I think at the least, I should be able to ascertain who they feel the owner of the boat is in regard to the statement of $10 million worth of cocaine.

THE COURT: I've sustained the objection.

MR. SULLIVAN: Thank you.

BY MR. SULLIVAN:

Q. Without divulging the name of the owner of the boat, is my client deemed by you to be the owner of the vessel?

A. The name on the paperwork is not the name of your client.

Q. Okay. Thank you. Number two—or should I say I'm getting down to my last few questions. What evidence, at this particular time, do you possess other than what you stated in terms of the facts of the case, that my client is a risk of flight?

A. There are no ties to the community—

Q. No, I understand. Let me rephrase my question. Your direct testimony was already that he has no ties to the community, that's something the Court can consider or will consider that. What specific facts or what specific knowledge do you have that the defendant will not appear in court at all times as required to appear in court?

A. I have no specific information.

Q. Okay. Thank you very much.

MR. SULLIVAN: Your Honor, I would move at this time to have the agent preserve his rough notes and other notes that he's taken in this case.

THE COURT: Okay, I will enter such an order. I'm sure the government has no objection to that. Any further questions?

MR. HARRISON: That is the standard in any case, Your Honor. I suppose you've already entered the standing discovery—

MR. SULLIVAN: No, we haven't gotten that. That's why I wanted early on...

MR. HARRISON: I think the agents are well educated in that regard.

THE COURT: Okay. Thank you. Does the government have any further testimony?

MR. HARRISON: No, Your Honor.

THE COURT: Counsel? Any evidence as opposed to argument?

MR. WHITE: Your Honor, I've got four family members here and I'll proffer to this Court they'll come in and they tell the Court that my client came from Cuba—

THE COURT: This is on behalf of your client who is?

MR. WHITE: Mr. Suárez.

THE COURT: Okay.

MR. WHITE: And they'll come in and basically tell you that they're willing to supervise the defendant in the event that the Court places my client on bond. That they consider him not a dangerous person to the community and they will tell you a little bit about their background. Namely, they lived in the United States since they came from Cuba, fifteen, seventeen years ago. In fact, one of the brothers is currently going to the police academy in Tallahassee, which will show to the Court a certain amount of pro-police attitude in the family. If the Court would like to hear the testimony, I got the mother, one of the brothers and a sister-in-law.

THE COURT: Okay. Why don't you ask them to step up to the podium and you could have the—we'll swear them, have them identify their relationship to the defendant. I see two witnesses coming up.

MR. WHITE: Yes, Your Honor.

THE COURT: All right, let us swear them, please.

MR. WHITE: They need interpreters.

THE COURT: We do not have an interpreter?

THE CLERK: She's with the defendants.

THE COURT: Okay. Ms. Interpreter, you're going to have to speak up loud enough for—you have to do this in stereo, okay? So the defendants can hear it and the witness can hear.

NOTE: The following section is interpreted in the consecutive mode.

THE CLERK: Do you swear to tell the truth, the whole truth, and nothing but the truth, so help you God?

[oath is interpreted]

WITNESS: *Lo juro.*

THE COURT: Okay. Let's start first with the lady there.

BY THE COURT:

Q. Ma'am, would you state your name.

A. *Jesusa.*

Q. Okay. Don't be nervous. You just have to speak up loud enough for me to hear you and so that we could record your testimony.

A. *Jesusa.*

Q. What is your relationship to the defendant, Leopoldo?

A. *Es mi hijo.*

Q. **THE COURT:** Okay counsel, I'll let you ask some limited questions.

MR. WHITE: Sure.

DIRECT EXAMINATION

BY MR. WHITE:

Q. Do you have any other sons?

A. *Sí, tengo uno en Washington y dos en Nueva York.*

Q. And the one right next to you is one of your sons, correct?

A. *El es hijo mío.*

Q. Where was your son Leopoldo five years ago?

A. *Hace cinco años . . . yo lo traje de Cuba por Panamá.*

Q. Exactly how did you do that?

A. *Cuando yo llegué él tenía un permiso de entrada.*

Q. To your knowledge, is he a lawful resident?

A. *Sí, él vino con la residencia.*

Q. Okay, now tell the Court all the family members of your son who live here in New Orleans.

A. *Aquí, dos hijos míos, hermanos de él.*

Q. Okay, what about any other family members in the United States?

A. *Mis otros dos hijos en Nueva York y uno en Washington.*

Q. Any family back in Cuba?

A. *No, sólo un hermano mío.*

Q. Any other family members, immediate family members outside the United States?

A. *No.*

Q. Where does he live?

A. *¿Leopoldo? Vive conmigo.*

Q. And what is your address, please?

A. *2052 Maplewood.*

Q. How long have you lived there?

A. *Un año y medio.*

Q. How long have you lived here in the United States yourself?

A. *Veinte años. Yo llevo 20 años aquí.*

Q. Okay. Thank you.

MR. WHITE: I have no further questions, Your Honor.

BY THE COURT:

Q. Ma'am, has your son ever been arrested before?

A. *No, nunca.*

THE COURT: Does the government have any questions?

CROSS EXAMINATION

BY MR. HARRISON:

Q. Ma'am, where was your son living in December of 1985?

A. *Yo no me acuerdo si ya él estaba aquí en esa época.*

Q. How long has your son been living in the United States?

A. *Creo que lo traje de Panamá hace dos o tres años, pero no me acuerdo muy bien. El siempre vivió conmigo.*

Q. He has always lived with you since he's been in the United States?

A. *Sí, conmigo.*

Q. How long did he live in Panamá?

A. *Unos ocho meses.*

Q. What did he do for a living in Panamá?

A. *No, él no hacía nada.*

Q. What does he do for a living in the United States?

A. *Es carpintero, él hace algunos trabajitos por aquí, por allá . . . lo que se vaya presentando.*

Q. Does he work for a company?

A. *No, trabaja por su cuenta.*

Q. How many days a week on average will he work?

A. *Cuando tiene trabajo.*

Q. How often does he have a job?

A. *El pinta y hace distintos trabajitos cada semana. Hace de esto, de lo otro.*

Q. On an average, how many days a week does he have an odd job?

A. *Como cinco días, si tiene trabajo.*

Q. Do you have any knowledge of your son being arrested for possession of one gram of cocaine in December of 1985?

A. *No.*

MR. HARRISON: Thank you, Your Honor.

THE COURT: Let's have the young man step to the microphone, please.

BY THE COURT:

Q. Sir, would you state your name?

A. *Alberto, 23 años de edad.*

Q. And you are the defendant's brother?

A. *Sí.*

THE COURT: All right, counsel.

MR. WHITE: Your Honor, essentially he will say the same thing. If you want me to, I'll go through the testimony, but I don't know that he's going to add anything other than what the mother already said.

THE COURT: Okay. Does the government have any questions?

CROSS EXAMINATION

BY MR. HARRISON:

Q. Sir, are you aware that your brother was arrested for possession of cocaine in December of 1985?

A. *No.*

Q. Do you know where your brother was residing in December of 1985?

A. *Estaba viviendo con mi mamá.*

Q. Do you know when he came to the United States?

A. *Hace como tres años. No estoy seguro de la fecha. No lo tengo escrito.*

MR. HARRISON: Thank you, Your Honor.

THE COURT: Thank you.

NOTE: The following section in interpreted in the simultaneous mode.

THE COURT: Okay, you may be seated. Thank you for coming in. Any further testimony, counsel, as opposed to legal argument?

MR. WHITE: None, Your Honor.

THE COURT: Okay.

MR. SULLIVAN: Thank you, Your Honor. First, we'd call Customs Agent Bester back to the stand.

THE COURT: Okay, now this testimony is on behalf of the defendant Manuel López.

MR. SULLIVAN: Yes. Thank you, Your Honor.

DIRECT EXAMINATION

BY MR. SULLIVAN:

Q. Mr. Bester, at the time were you acting in your official capacity? At the time of the arrest.

A. Yes, I was.

Q. In your official capacity, did you have the opportunity, either you or someone in your care, custody or control, or an associate, to search defendant Manuel López?

A. Yes.

Q. Did you remove from his person or the boat his immigration papers, visas or passport?

A. Yes, we did.

Q. Would you tell this Court, please, did he have a valid visa or permission to enter into the United States?

A. He was here legally, yes.

Q. Legally?

A. Yes.

Q. Now, if he would be released today, if he would be released today, he would still be in the United States legally, correct?

A. Yes, he's here legally.

Q. And he would be here legally until the expiration of his visa, would that not be correct?

A. That's correct.

Q. And how long a period, sir, would that be? May I make it simple? He has a B-1 and B-2 visa with a expiration date in 1987 or 1988?

A. November 1988.

Q. Did you have any conversation with Mr. López about his source of income from Santo Domingo?

A. No, I didn't.

Q. Did he tell you about the business that he and his family own in Santo Domingo which provides an income?

A. No, we didn't get into that discussion.

Q. Did he also tell you about the family members of his mother's family that reside here in New Orleans?

A. No, he didn't.

Q. Did he tell you about the friends that he has here, in New Orleans?

A. He wasn't asked about his friends.

Q. He told you, sir, that he had an apartment at the Hotel Ambassador?

A. Yes, he did.

Q. And he lived and resided in the Hotel Ambassador for approximately six months? Approximately, I don't remember exactly what he told me. I'm not trying to tie you down to a date certain.

A. I'm aware that he lived in the Hotel Ambassador, yes.

Q. And that he lived under a lease agreement, a contract between himself and the Hotel Ambassador?

A. I didn't check into his lease.

Q. He has been incarcerated for seven days?

A. Correct.

Q. And the purpose of your testimony today is to suggest to this Court that they should enter an order of pretrial detention for this gentleman right here?

A. That's correct.

Q. And there was no investigation by the government, to your knowledge, of his ties to the community other than what he said?

A. Limited.

Q. Limited. Now, can you tell this Court, please, what evidence the government has or what you have, specifically, or what you have through your associates, evidence that this man will flee if released today by this Court? I only say if released.

A. I don't have specific evidence, clear cut evidence that he will leave.

Q. What you're telling this Court is that, because there is 400 kilos of cocaine and he is on the boat, and he is a citizen of Santo Domingo, this Court should enter an order of pretrial detention—that's the sum and total of your testimony.

A. Well, no, I believe that he is a threat to the community. Anyone bringing in that quantity of cocaine—

Q. All right, sir.

A. And I have other reasons which I don't want to divulge to the Court, because it is related to this and other investigations—

Q. All right, sir. Let me ask you this question. Would you treat this gentleman the same way as if he was the owner of the cocaine rather than the transporter of the cocaine?

A. I don't know that he is not the owner at this point.

Q. Do you have any evidence, sir, that he is the owner of the cocaine? And also, sir, the second part of that question, do you have any evidence to show the potential of being an owner of the cocaine?

MR. HARRISON: Your Honor, I'm going to object to that. I think it is getting in the realm of speculation. We've shown that he was certainly in possession of it when he was arrested and that's the basis upon which we are asking the Court to make its decision.

THE COURT: Restate the question, Mr. Sullivan, if you don't mind.

MR. SULLIVAN: Thank you, Your Honor.

BY MR. SULLIVAN:

Q. Do you have any evidence, sir, that this gentleman is a potential owner of the cocaine? Any evidence. Hard evidence. Hard facts.

MR. HARRISON: Again, Your Honor—

THE COURT: I'll sustain the objection. I think that should be reserved for a legal argument.

MR. SULLIVAN: Most respectfully, Your Honor, we can't have legal argument of something that's not an issue or something that's not a fact. I understand that the government has not proven that fact, nor have they have alluded to that fact other than the fact that he is in the possession, as captain, of the vessel that contained the cocaine. I understand that, but—

THE COURT: Let me ask the witness so that the record is clear. You've testified that the defendant admitted he was the captain of the boat?

THE WITNESS: Yes, he did.

THE COURT: You found him on the boat at the time that the alleged contraband was seized, is that correct?

THE WITNESS: That's correct.

THE COURT: And you found ownership papers that were not in either defendant's name, is that correct?

THE WITNESS: That's correct.

MR. SULLIVAN: Your Honor, There is no question about that and we stipulate to that because those are the facts of this case.

BY MR. SULLIVAN:

Q. Did this defendant offer any resistance at the time of his first stopping?

A. No, he did not.

Q. Is it a fact, sir, that the defendant, along with the codefendant, took the boat in question to the customs dock upon request?

A. That's correct.

Q. And could you tell this Court, please, the number of weapons found aboard that vessel?

A. There were no weapons.

Q. So, to summarize your testimony for the purposes of this bond hearing, we have both of these defendants in the care, custody and control of the vessel—

MR. HARRISON: Excuse me. I object to the form of the question. The witness is here to give his own testimony. I think it's improper at this time for counsel to be making his summations.

THE COURT: I think he's just laying the predicate for a question, so I'll overrule your objection.

BY MR. SULLIVAN:

Q. Again, to summarize your testimony, sir, the evidence that you presented to this Court is that these two gentlemen were in the care, custody and control of the vessel in question which contained the cocaine?

A. That's correct.

Q. You really have nothing more than that, do you?

MR. HARRISON: Your Honor, I'm going to object. That's the basis upon which we wish Your Honor to make your decision.

THE COURT: I'll sustain the objection.

MR. SULLIVAN: Your Honor, I'm not arguing with the Court. I'm only suggesting to the Court that this witness has been most candid with the Court and he has certainly had the ability to answer the question whether or not they have any evidence, in addition to what's been testified to. Evidence relating to bond. I'm not asking about their guilt or innocence.

THE COURT: I think he's been very candid in his testimony and we have the facts on the record. If the government does not have the facts, then you'll prevail.

MR. SULLIVAN: I have no further questions of this witness. Thank you.

THE COURT: Thank you.

MR. SULLIVAN: Your Honor, most respectfully, we would call the following witnesses. We have five witnesses before the Court. I'd rather avoid going through their individual testimony, Your Honor. It will be lengthy and an interpreter is necessary. I can proffer—

THE COURT: Surely.

MR. SULLIVAN: —their relationship and what they would testify to.

THE COURT: You want to introduce them all at once and then proffer all at once?

MR. SULLIVAN: Well, Judge, how about if I just have them stand in tandem. It will be a lot easier.

THE COURT: Fine. Identify them by name and their relationship to the defendant.

MR. SULLIVAN: If the record will reflect that standing before the Court are—one, two three, four, five, six, seven, eight, nine—nine people, all of which are friends and/or relatives. I'm only going to bother with five at the moment. The other four are purely friends of longstanding.

MR. HARRISON: Excuse me, Your Honor. I don't wish to place any undue burden on the Court, but ordinarily when we do a proffer, we at least have the witness, after the lawyer makes the proffer, say is that what your testimony would be and the witness could say yes or no—

MR. SULLIVAN: I have no difficulty.

MR. HARRISON: If counsel says that these people need an interpreter in order to do that, I'd ask that they come up where the interpreter—

MR. SULLIVAN: No, we have no problem with that.

MR. HARRISON: —so that they can—

THE COURT: We'll proceed this way, counsel. I always give the government an opportunity when there is a proffer to see if they have questions.

MR. SULLIVAN: No problem.

THE COURT: You can state their names, you can make the proffer and then, if the government would like to ask any questions of these people, the government will have that privilege.

MR. SULLIVAN: Your Honor, the first witness we would have called would be Carmen, who is the aunt of the defendant in question. She is the half sister of the defendant's mother. She is a resident alien of the United States and has been in that immigration capacity for the past eight years.

She owns no property in Louisiana. She actually owns no property in the United States, period, but what she does own is a vehicle along with her son and the defendant could reside with them if the Court wishes. Although the defendant does have a—I guess the best term is a wife, although they are not legally married—who does live and reside in New Orleans, Louisiana.

She is willing to pledge her passport and she is willing to pledge her resident alien card which are her two most valuable assets. Although it really doesn't mean too much to us, Your Honor, to a foreigner living in the United States, Your Honor, sometimes that resident alien—if I might give the Court an example. I know we've been through this times before, the crosses and the chains that they wear that there are sentimental attachments to those items, are far more important than $100,000 cash in the pocket or the house. To these people, Your Honor, their resident alien card and their passport is probably the most valuable asset that they have.

I have explained to the lady and to her son that, if this Court permits a bond, and as part of that bond it's conditioned upon either the defendant residing with them or them guaranteeing their appearance, that they could be held in contempt of this Court and subjecting themselves to a sentence of imprisonment if, in fact, he does fail to appear. The next witness we could call would be Victor José—

MR. HARRISON: That's just not stating the law and to suspect that this Court is going to perpetrate a fraud upon people who are going to give security for this man if Your Honor releases him I think is a—

THE COURT: What is a fraud of the Court? What specifically?

MR. HARRISON: Well Your Honor, to suggest that these people can put up these documents which they do not own—the documents are the property of the United States—for whatever property value they have in them which is minimal, but to suggest that they are subject to deportation based upon what somebody else does, is just not the state of the law.

THE COURT: Okay, counsel, I'll let you make appropriate argument at the appropriate time.

MR. SULLIVAN: I have nothing to say, Judge. Victor, who's the son of the aunt, Carmen. The only asset that he has of any value is a Chevrolet Nova, the year is 1977. Now again, Judge, it means nothing, but to a man who has nothing, that is a Cadillac 1987. And the value to him, of course, is not—you can't count that in money.

The next two individuals we would have, Your Honor, are Pedro and Antonia. That's a husband and wife. Now they are friends of Manuel. They've known him approximately—they've known him and his—again we'll use the term "wife"—for approximately eighteen months. They also own no property. They can only pledge their word that this man will appear before this Court.

We have Francisca Llanos. Now that is the—what we call the wife of the defendant. If the Court is reviewing the Pretrial Services report, the defendant has two children by two other ladies, both in Santo Domingo. This wife and this defendant contribute and support both of those children. The only thing that this lady has of any value is the furniture in her apartment and her passport and her vehicle which is a 1983 Chevy Celebrity.

Again, Your Honor, these are the type of things that to us maybe seem insignificant, but to them it's everything they own and everything they own is the most important thing that they have. And she'd be willing to pledge that. She would also be willing to give her passport up to Pretrial Services or the U.S. Attorney's office and do whatever the Court would require her to do to insure and assure the defendant's presence.

Now we do have one long time friend, Juan Vicente. Now, Mr. Vicente has known the defendant for between eight and ten years. His mother and father know the defendant's mother and father. I didn't get too deeply into that relationship, Your Honor, but he and his family live at 4715 Captiva Street in Gretna. They own their own home. It's in his name alone, he's discussed it with his wife. They would be willing to pledge their home on behalf of the defendant. Although they don't have an awful lot of equity in the house, I believe they have somewhere in the neighborhood of about $10,000.00 equity in the house. The house was purchased approximately three years ago. He lives there with his wife and children. Your Honor, this is the sum total of the evidence to be presented before the Court on behalf of defendant Manuel López. Most respectfully, I think we have two hurdles to reach in this case—

THE COURT: Let me first inquire whether the government would like to question any of the witnesses?

MR. HARRISON: Your Honor, is it Mr. Juan Vicente who owns a home?

THE COURT: Yes.

MR. HARRISON: We would ask specifically when he purchased the home and how long a mortgage he has on the home.

THE COURT: Okay. Let's ask him to step up, Mr. Sullivan.

NOTE: This section is interpreted in the consecutive mode.

THE CLERK: [to the interpreter] Please have the witness raise his right hand to be sworn. Do you swear to tell the truth, the whole truth, and nothing but the truth, so help you God? [oath is interpreted]

MR. SULLIVAN: [to the interpreter] Have him state his name, age, and residence.

THE WITNESS: *Juan Vicente, treinta años de edad, 4715 Captiva Street, Gretna.*

THE COURT: Okay. Mr. Harrison, do you have any questions?

CROSS EXAMINATION

BY MR. HARRISON:

Q. Mr. Vicente, how long have you owned the house on 4715 Captiva Street?

A. *Dos, tres años, más o menos.*

Q. Do you not recall the date you purchased the home?

A. *Ahora, así de repente, no.*

Q. What type of a residence is that, sir?

A. *Es una casa normal. Es una casa normal de familia. No es muy grande.*

Q. How much is the amount of the mortgage?

A. *El dueño anterior dejó una hipoteca de $40,000 y yo asumí la hipoteca que tenía por $8,000 o $9,000 en ese momento.*

Q. So there are currently two mortgages on the house, is that correct?

A. *Sí.*

Q. How long do you have to pay on those two mortgages?

A. *Creo que son treinta años. No recuerdo exactamente, pero creo que son treinta.*

Q. On both mortgages?

A. *Sí.*

Q. Sir, is this house owned by both you and your wife?

A. *Está a nombre mío porque cuando la compré ella todavía no estaba aquí.*

Q. So as far as the technical legal title is concerned, is it your house only?

A. *¿La escritura? Tiene la hipoteca que tiene con el dueño anterior. Pero está a nombre mío.*

Q. Do you personally know Mr. López?

A. *Personalmente, sí.*

Q. How long have you known him, sir?

A. *Sus padres y los míos eran amigos allá en Santo Domingo. Yo, en realidad, no tuve contacto con él allá, pero llegué a conocerlo después de llegar a este país.*

Q. How long has that been, sir?

A. *Hace como tres años y medio, cuatro años. Conocimiento humano, contacto humano.*

Q. So you consider him a good friend of yours?

A. *Sí.*

Q. How long have your parents known his parents, if you know?

A. *Como diez años o más. Más o menos, no sé exactamente.*

MR. HARRISON: Thank you, sir. Thank you, Your Honor.

THE COURT: Thank you.

MR. SULLIVAN: We have no further questions, Your Honor.

NOTE: The rest of the transcript is interpreted in the simultaneous mode.

THE COURT: Thank you. Okay. Let's hear first from the government, then we'll hear from the counsel. Mr. Harrison, why should the Court impose pretrial detention in this case?

MR. HARRISON: If Your Honor, please, as to the defendant Mr. López. He is here legally, but his contacts to this community are very limited. I would suggest, Your Honor, based upon the fact that he has two children living in Santo Domingo and only a leased apartment in the United States, that his contacts to the United States are very minimal and very tenuous, that his contacts to his country of origin are much stronger. I would suggest to Your Honor that the fact that he was in control of the boat with that amount of dope on it, in and of itself shows that he is a danger to the community. Again, we relied upon the presumption of a risk of flight in addition to the fact that he has very little, if any contacts to this community. The things that he suggests that he would pledge if Your Honor decided to let him out on bond, are of no material value, regardless of the sentimental value that these people place on them. Counsel is, in essence, asking us to hold these people hostage in a manner that is totally contrary to the law. Basically, there's no amount of bond that would assure that this man would appear as required.

As to Mr. Suárez, his contacts to the community are a little better, although counsel suggests that his family has a pro-law enforcement sentiment, one would have to believe, based upon the fact that this man was taken off of a boat with 800 pounds of cocaine, that is a sentiment that he certainly does not share. He has a mother and some family here, but he has no wife. He has no children. He has no residence of his own. He has no regular employment. And there's just nothing to hold him here.

THE COURT: Thank you, counsel.

MR. WHITE: Well, Your Honor, I tend to disagree with the government in this particular instance. This man—

THE COURT: That came as no surprise.

MR. WHITE: This man came from Cuba two, three years ago. He's not going back to Cuba. Whatever family ties he's got in this world, he's got them here in Louisiana or in the United States. He's legally in the United States, so I just don't see where he will be a risk of flight. If he flees, he's going to have to come to back. There's no one else in this world to shelter him. All the family has indicated that this is out of character for Mr. Suárez. The government makes a big show of that particular instance where he was arrested for cocaine, but I'm sure if the Court investigates, it will find out that the case was not prosecuted at all. I've spoken to my client and I've received that information. I haven't been able to verify that for the Court.

Overall, Your Honor, the fact that he was on the boat, he was not the captain of the boat. The government is only relying on the amount of cocaine obtained and the fact that he was on the boat to hold him in pretrial detention. I don't think that's fair. He's entitled to the Eighth Amendment reasonable bail in this case because he's got substantial ties to the community and being under the circumstances—I've spoken to my client and he's prepared to meet a $15,000.00 bail in this case, which I suggest to the Court to enter a $15,000.00 bail amount.

THE COURT: Thank you very much, counsel.

MR. TAYLOR: Your Honor, I think the Court in requesting of the government that they furnish what facts and evidence they have to meet the threshold question of whether or not the government is entitled to pretrial detention in this case is an important one and probably the crux of the testimony offered by both the government and the defendants in this case.

The first question that must be answered by this Court is whether or not the government has, by clear and convincing evidence, established to this Court's satisfaction that this or any defendant stands in a position where his freedom should be taken away from him. And, of course, we must accept at all times that every defendant, whether it be this or any other defendant, has an Eighth Amendment right to bail that has not been alleviated by the Bail Reform Act. What the Bail Reform Act does is set certain requirements for the government to follow in order to alleviate the Eighth Amendment.

In this particular case, Your Honor, the evidence is very clear. What the government has said in more words than one is that these people were in the care, custody and control of a boat containing 400 kilos of cocaine. Those facts are insufficient as a matter of law, either to establish risk of flight or danger to the community.

Going backwards for a moment, the Eleventh, Ninth and Second Circuit have already stated that everybody who is a criminal, so to speak, or violates the laws of the United States, is a danger to the community. That factor, in and of itself, should not be considered by any court in reviewing and taking away from any defendant his right to bond. The issue is whether or not he's a risk of flight. Now, the government has presented—

THE COURT: Let me stop you there, sir, so you're not misled by what you perceive to be my thinking. It's very clear from the legislative intent that the court is required to consider the fact that a defendant is charged with a narcotics violation—

MR. TAYLOR: Yes.

THE COURT: —in terms of whether or not that person is a danger to the community. Now, there are narcotics charges and there are narcotics charges. I'm required by law to make that consideration and that determination. And certainly the quantity of cocaine involved in this case is something I'm required to consider.

MR. TAYLOR: Yes, sir. As well as the sentence that can be imposed, which could be at least forty years in this particular case.

THE COURT: In terms of quote, danger to the community, unquote.

MR. TAYLOR: Yes. There's no question about that, Your Honor, that's why I'm not making any issue about it because I think that all of us here are old enough to understand that problem, and understand the problems that face this and every other community in the United States. There's no question about it. There's no question under the Uniform Bail Act what this court must do.

I'm suggesting to the Court two things: Number one, that the Eleventh Circuit, the Ninth Circuit, and the Second Circuit, have already agreed that the mere fact that someone is a danger to the community, in and on itself, is insufficient as a matter of law to deny him bail.

Now, what the Court is saying is that there are other factors under the Uniform Bail Act. We agree with that. And probably a danger to the community should be considered by this Court just like any other condition. What I'm suggesting to the Court is that the government has the burden of proving to this Court with clear and convincing evidence, something less than beyond a reasonable doubt, that this person is both a risk of flight and a danger to the community.

The evidence offered by the government of the United States is that these two, again, were in possession of a vessel containing 400 kilos of cocaine. Well, those acts, in and of themselves, may be a crime, but they don't evidence the requirements under the Uniform Bail Act. Everyone, as an example, who commits an armed bank robbery is in possession of a weapon in the commission of a felony. That, again, doesn't make them a danger to the community, nor does it evidence their flight.

The evidence of flight is an area entirely different than the crime itself. The crime itself may show certain things, and we admit that and we'll stipulate that a crime was committed and that—I'm not going to stipulate that these people committed the crime, obviously, but these people were in a position where their circumstances are something less than tenable. But that doesn't mean, because they're involved in something, that they should be denied bond. We're not talking about whether or not they committed the act or whether or not they should be sentenced for that act. We're only talking about bond.

Along these lines, if we accept the government's position and we take a chain—we take Mr. A, who's the owner of the cocaine, the purchaser of the cocaine and the one who negotiated the deal and the one who distributes the cocaine, and then you take the man on the bottom who, let's say is hired to take a boat and go to the Bahamas and bring the cocaine back, and you treat them equally, that's certainly not what's intended by the Act either. What's intended by the Act is the person who has the ability to flee, the person who is the danger to the community because he has the ability to buy, sell and distribute. Now, we don't have those factors by the government's evidence before this Court and that's the point I'm trying to make.

If you take the government's case at its best, at this juncture, we show that these two men were in control of the vessel at the time of the arrest of the vessel and the arrest of the two men. That's the evidence at best. The next evidence at best is that one individual is a resident alien or some such immigration status and the other individual is here in the United States legally with a B-1 and B-2 visas. His passport is in the care, custody and control of the United States government.

So the government is not saying that Mr. López came here specifically to make a cocaine transaction and go back to Santo Domingo. They're not saying any such thing. Of course, in the direct case, the government failed to mention to this Court that he was here legally and responsibly, but the inference was that he was a citizen and resident of Santo Domingo and he was going to just get off the boat and go right back to Santo Domingo. But now we find out something different than that.

We also find out that he has a family both here and he has a family in Santo Domingo. There's nothing wrong with that. That doesn't evidence flight either. It does evidence, if the government can show that there are people in Santo Domingo that may have bank accounts for him and have businesses for him, which in this particular instance they may have. But it doesn't mean that he is going to leave this community.

Everybody, Your Honor, is a potential bond jumper. We don't question that. Anyone that comes before this Court—I don't care who it is—has that potential. I think we recognize that. If we don't recognize that, it's foolish not to. What we do is we have to take the best shot we have in every given case. In this particular case, Your Honor, I would suggest that maybe bond alone is insufficient, but we can come up with a plan where this defendant is—for example—could report on a daily basis to the agent in question. We have no problem with that. In person, seven days a week, five days a week, whatever the Court would order. The Court could so order that the government take possession of his passport and his travel documents. We have no difficulty with that. We have no difficulty with this defendant in the morning calling this customs officer or Pretrial Services by telephone and in the afternoon or early evening hours, meeting with this customs officer or Pretrial Services on a daily basis, seven days a week. We have no difficulty with that either. We have no difficulty, Your Honor, with the people who proffered their testimony, with providing this Court with their travel documents and their passports and their visas and their resident alien cards. It's their life, so to speak. It's their life's blood. It's everything they have because they don't have an existence in the United States, in their mind, Your Honor, without these documents. That's why they're so important.

It's like sometimes we have the Haitians come before this Court and when they say they're a resident alien, even though they are here in trouble and they are here with a problem and they are here violating the laws of the United States, when they say they are resident aliens, you can just see their chests swell up because that is the most important thing that they own in their life and they may have a million dollars, that doesn't mean anything. It's an attitude that they have and that attitude will carry with them the rest of their life. It's an accepted fact, and that's what we have in this case here. We have people who are just normal, everyday, dollar, you know, week to week people. That's what they are. That's what we have to contend with and we have to accept that and whatever they have in the way of material things, whatever they have in the way of emotional and documents, they're willing to provide this Court with to assure their presence. I don't think we could ask for anything more. But there is certainly a combination of factors that this Court can order to require and assure that Manuel will present himself each time he's required to.

Thank you, Your Honor.

THE COURT: Thank you very much. I want to thank you, counsel, for your very helpful presentation of evidence and argument in this case. I'm impressed by the fact that both defendants have family and friends who are willing to come to Court and stand by them.

Nevertheless, there's no getting around the fact that this case involves an excess of 800 pounds of cocaine. And there's no getting around the fact that to somewhat different degrees these defendants have limited ties to this community. There are additional factors that I have considered and which I will incorporate into my written order which will follow today. But based upon the evidence before me, I find that there are not conditions of release that will reasonably assure the appearance of the defendants as required and the safety of any other person and the community, therefore, I will enter orders of detention pending trial as to both defendants and I will prepare and file my written order sometime today. Again, thank you all very much.

MR. TAYLOR: Your Honor, before we recess, this matter is scheduled for a hearing tomorrow at ten o'clock—I think it's ten o'clock, I'm not sure of the time—for arraignment, I believe. I wonder if the government knows at this time whether or not an indictment has been returned and, if there is an indictment, maybe we can do the arraignment now.

THE COURT: Maybe that's why Mr. Harrison was late this morning.

MR. HARRISON: I was late because of another one that had been scheduled this morning. I am advised that there may be, but it hasn't been returned as yet, Your Honor.

MR. TAYLOR: Does the government wish to hear it tomorrow is really what I'm saying, Your Honor.

THE COURT: You're correct, Mr. Taylor, this matter is on for arraignment tomorrow at ten o'clock.

MR. TAYLOR: I think it's on for something other than arraignment tomorrow at ten o'clock.

THE COURT: Preliminary examination or arraignment. I ask the government, as a courtesy, if an indictment is going to be returned today, that you let counsel know.

MR. HARRISON: I don't know, Your Honor.

THE COURT: Okay. That's the best I could do.

MR. HARRISON: I'm advised by the case agent that the grand jury was scheduled to hear the case this morning.

(Whereupon the pretrial detention hearing in the matter of U.S.A. v. Manuel López and Leopoldo Suárez was concluded.)

Section 4

SIMULTANEOUS INTERPRETATION PRACTICE

OPENING STATEMENT

NOTE: This is the opening statement of a defense attorney whose client is accused of bribing a public official.

DEFENSE ATTORNEY:

Jury members, good morning. As His Honor told you, we are at the time that we call opening statement. What an opening statement is, in reality, is a road map to a place you haven't been before. If you were taking a motor car trip with your family you would want an accurate set of directions to get from A to B to C to D, your destination, without getting lost. To begin to understand what really happened in this case, you have to begin by taking a look at the person, Marie Michel, born in Haiti, grew up in Haiti under the Duvalier regime, thirty-two years old, came here to New York in March of 1981 illegally. And then turned herself in, presented herself to the Immigration Service and then was released with temporary work permits and temporary visas to remain here, in New York.

From March of 1981 till now, about nine years, Ms. Michel has never been convicted of any kind of crime. Ms. Michel has two kids that were born here in New York, U.S. born, New York born children: a two-year old, Danielle, a little girl, and a six-year old, a little boy, James. She has a first grade education, a first grade education from Haiti. She didn't actually complete the first grade, cannot read, cannot write in any language and can only print her name, not even scripting together like writing, but printing, Marie Michel.

How she met Danny Montes is that in December of 1987, Ms. Michel was going to the main immigration office in New York. She went there for herself to apply for her permanent residency. She wanted to become a permanent resident here, and came with her own papers. Danny Montes was working in December of 1987 at the immigration office in New York as an officer and he was the one who was processing her. She went up to him in front of the line and started speaking to him, and they started getting in a conversation as he's reviewing her documents. This is in December of '87. He starts. He starts saying things to her, things like, "Oh, well, I'm Haitian also, I'm originally from Haiti. Isn't it a terrible thing what's going on here with the Haitians in this country, with Immigration in this country. The lines go around the building, it takes forever to get people processed." It's a very bad situation, especially for Haitians. Ms. Michel is sitting there listening and speaking to him because he is the government representative who is handling her permanent residency application. He then says that because he is Haitian and because he wants to try to help her and the United States government also wants to try to help in processing people quicker, he says to her the following. This is in December of 1987.

That if she goes to these immigration offices . . . there are about a thousand of these immigration offices, little storefront immigration offices in the Little Haiti area, which is roughly from 48th Street in the North end to 9th Street between NE 27nd Avenue and NW 17th Avenue in that Little Haiti area, there are roughly about a thousand immigration offices where people set up store fronts and help immigrants process immigration applications. He said that if she would like, Ms. Michel, if she was interested, and if she was getting other people to go to these immigration offices, and to contact the people in all of these immigration offices and tell them that the government is going to be attempting to process Haitians and other people in a quicker fashion. He was going to be the person who was going to be receiving the application and that the fee, the government fee, the fee that he was accepting was going to be $300 per Haitian and $500 for anyone else other than Haitians, and that normally for immigrants trying to get their papers approved, these immigration, these individual immigration offices would make anywhere from between two thousand and thirty-five hundred dollars per immigrant to prepare the papers and the documents and get everything all prepared. He said to Marie that what you're going to get out of this is that you're going to transport the people. In other words, you're going to go to these offices, tell them about the situation, they are going to get people, they are going to find people who need their documents prepared, those people are going to meet at the various immigration offices in Little Haiti. We'll let you know when they're going to be there. You show up with your little station wagon. We will give you all the documents, all the folders, all the documents. We'll give you the three hundred or five hundred dollars per person that you have to give to Mr. Montes, the immigration agent. You drive all the Haitians or other immigrants in your station wagon to the immigration place.

At that point he was changing the place where he was working. It was not going to be 80th Street, it was going to be in Park South, way down in the Hilldale area. You go down there, you see Mr. Montes, you bring him the file with all the papers, you bring him the money, and he will take it, and then you leave and he will interview the various people. And that's how it was going to work.

There was absolutely no mention to Marie about anything illegal, any kind of bribe, her getting anything other than transportation money, because Danny Montes said these people will pay you in these various immigration offices in Little Haiti. If they are getting two thousand to thirty-five hundred dollars per head to do all the paper work and gather all the documents together, and I'm going to be getting, on behalf of the Immigration Service, three to five hundred dollars per head on my end, they will probably pay you fifty to a hundred bucks a piece to come to the immigration offices in Little Haiti, put them in your station wagon, drive them down to Hilldale, drop off the documents and the money with Mr. Montes, wait for them to be interviewed—because there may be six or seven people packed into the station wagon or maybe more—wait for them to be interviewed and then drive them back to the immigration offices in Little Haiti from Hilldale. And you will get fifty to one hundred bucks per head for transportation, period. Over and out. That is it.

Danny Montes relocates in December of '87 from the 80th Street Office down to the Hilldale office. At about the end of March or beginning of April, Marie Michel, in the meantime, has started going around to these thousand or so little immigration storefronts in Little Haiti, telling them about Danny Montes and what he has said. And they said, "Fine, we'll gather up these people, we'll prepare these documents, you are not involved in the preparation of documents, you are not gathering documents. You check in with us, we'll let you know when we have enough people on a given day where we have enough files prepared and their papers are prepared, we'll have them gather in our office, you come and pick them up. You take the three hundred to five hundred dollars per person that Danny Montes is going to get, plus the files, and drive them down and give them to Danny Montes. Wait for them to be interviewed and then take them back, drive them down to Little Haiti. That is what's going to happen."

That is what started to happen in April and May of '88. And yes, she was making fifty to a hundred dollars per person to do exactly that: pick them up, bring them down to Hilldale from Little Haiti, wait for them and bring the documents in, give the three to five hundred dollars per person to Danny Montes, and bring them back. No kickbacks, no bribes, no nothing. And I do want you to pay very close attention to this little movie you are going to see here. You will be seeing videotapes because they had like a camera in Danny Montes's office so you could see this bribery. You want to see what the briber looks like, you know. She is kind of hiding and secretive and you can hear the audio tapes, you know, whispering and being very cautious about everything. See if you see that on the tapes. See if you hear that on the tapes. If a person is doing a bribe—an illegal activity—for thirty to plus thousand dollars, what would be the mentality of the briber? Is she going to sit out there, like a casual person in front of everybody and just pass money and talk openly about things?

You have to understand also you are not going to see on the tapes exactly how the immigration office in Hilldale is set up. It's a one-story building, king of long, and you walk in and there is like a waiting area and some counters up at the front. And Danny Montes has like a little cubicle, basically. They are temporary cubicles, little two by four cubicles with a little desk in it, and temporary partitions that go up about six feet with a cut-out for a door, no door, it is open and there is airspace above the partition so you could hear across the partition from one to the other. And there are maybe four or five of these where the various officers like Danny Montes who sat and worked and interviewed people. And what Ms. Michel would do . . . Was she paying bribes on the street and meeting people in parking lots? No. She brought the people repeatedly the same way: picked them up from these offices in Little Haiti, brought them to Hilldale, brought them to the office, brought in the documents and the money she got from these immigration offices, went up to the front counter in the Hilldale Office, asked for Danny Montes, he came out, she walked into his little cubicle with the open door and the open top, sat there and gave him the money and gave him the documents and told him—you are going to hear this on the tape—told him specifically, "I'm here to do transportation. I get paid fifty to a hundred bucks per person to transport these people. I don't have any involvement in preparing documents. I don't have any involvement in any other money. I don't want any problems. I'm not doing anything, absolutely nothing wrong. I have kids in this country. I am here . . . I'm trying to become a permanent resident." It is all there and there is nothing in her conduct. Look at the woman when she's supposed to be doing these bribes and then think to yourselves, is this the kind of woman who is committing a bribe? I mean, is this the conduct of a person who is committing a bribe? Listen to the tapes. Is this the kind of conversation, in the setting that she was doing it in, that's the kind of setting that the person would be bribing somebody? Listen. Pay attention. The key here is not . . . obviously, she presented the money to Danny Montes—three to five hundred dollars per person—obviously she presented the papers. That is not contested, that is not the issue. The issue here, is, did she have a specific, willfull, corrupt, criminal intent to bribe Danny Montes? Her state of mind is the issue, not passing the money. If that was the issue, we'd have no trial. Of course she gave the money, she gave the documents, but the issue was: was she bribing Danny Montes? Was she criminally intending to bribe Danny Montes? Period. One issue. And that is the issue that you all have to decide.

You are the collective wisdom of this community. The twelve of you are going to sit and decide that issue. Did Marie Michel from these tapes and from the audio tapes, the videotapes, from the testimony . . . Did the government meet their burden of proof beyond every reasonable doubt that she had a corrupt, criminal intent to bribe somebody? That she was a briber? Has it been proved? If that is the case, she's guilty. If that is not the case, she is not.

I will have a chance to come back at the end of the trial and just kind of sum up, you know, what you heard. And suggest to you what I believe from the evidence the only verdict that I believe speaks the truth, and that is: not guilty. Thank you.

EXCERPTS OF TRIAL TRANSCRIPT

UNITED STATES OF AMERICA
Plaintiff,

vs.

CARLOS SANTIAGO, CIRO MONTORO,
HAROLD RED, JACK MARTIN, JOE COX

APPEARANCES:
For the Government: THEODORE THOMAS
THERESA JONES
Assistant United States Attorneys

For the Defense: MICHAEL DUNNELL
JEAN BRUCKER
WILLIAM WESTON

(Ricardo Sandoval, Government's witness, sworn.)

THE COURT: State your full name for the record.

THE WITNESS: Ricardo Sandoval.

DIRECT EXAMINATION

BY MR. THOMAS:

Q. Mr. Sandoval, how old are you?
A. Forty-nine.
Q. Where were you born?
A. Havana, Cuba.
Q. When did you come to this country?
A. January 5, 1963.
Q. Where do you live?
A. Right now?
Q. Yes, sir.
A. Panama City, Fort White.
Q. What do you do for a living?
A. I have a business. I have a dump truck to carry rock and fill for construction.
Q. How long have you been in that business?
A. Since December of last year.

Q. Did you have some other business prior to that one?

A. Prior to that, yes.

Q. What was that?

A. Franchise for Ridewell Tire Company back in 1974 to 1977 in Key Largo.

Q. During the time you had the tire business to the present time with the trucking business, did you have some other form of business?

A. Yes.

Q. What was that?

A. I was engaged in the illegal sale of cocaine.

Q. When did that business end?

A. It ended September 10, 1983.

Q. What happened?

A. I was picked up on a federal warrant here at the airport.

Q. Who arrested you?

A. Agent Petrelas from the Sheriff's Department.

Q. What were you charged with?

A. I was charged with continuing criminal enterprise and conspiracy for distribution and sale of cocaine.

Q. Did you have discussions with the government concerning the disposition of federal charges against you?

A. Yes.

Q. Did you come to some agreement with the government?

A. Yes.

Q. What is your understanding of that agreement?

A. That I will plead guilty to the conspiracy charge and that I will cooperate with the government in anything that will be necessary.

Q. Have you plead guilty to some charge?

A. Yes.

Q. When did you do that?

A. January 3rd, 1984.

Q. What was the charge?

A. Conspiracy.

Q. You have some agreement with the government concerning the maximum punishment that you face under that plea of guilty?

A. Yes.

Q. What is that?

A. They put a cap of five years.

Q. Is there a possible fine as well?

A. Yes.

Q. What is that?

A. I think it is up to fifty thousand.

Q. Have you been sentenced yet?

A. No.

Q. What on your part are you supposed to do?

A. Give information to the government on people that were around and come to court like I am coming today to testify.

Q. Do you own a home in the Panama City area?

A. Yes, sir.

Q. When did you get the house?

A. When I got it? In September 1980.

Q. Do you recall the address?

A. 202 Rosevine Lane.

Q. What is the phone number?

A. 261-0404 and 261-0074.

Q. Give us the date you were arrested by the United States government.

A. September 10, 1983.

Q. When was the last time prior to that date you saw Carlos Santiago?

A. I think it was at the end of August.

Q. Where and what circumstances?

A. Where? I picked up one kilo of coke at his house.

Q. When in relation to the date of your arrest, when was the last time you saw Ciro Montoro?

A. I didn't see Ciro at least seven, eight months prior to that.

Q. When was the last time?

A. I would say maybe at the beginning of 1983, January.

Q. Where was he?

A. Well, I saw him at Carlos Santiago's house.

MR. THOMAS: I am at a point now that requires further discussion with the Court.

THE COURT: All right, ladies and gentlemen, you may retire to the jury room.

(Proceedings adjourned at 5:00 p.m.)

(Call to order of the court.)
(Jury present.)
(Ricardo Sandoval, Government's witness, sworn.)

THE COURT: State your full name for the record.

THE WITNESS: Ricardo Sandoval.

DIRECT EXAMINATION (Continued)

BY MR. THOMAS:

Q. Mr. Sandoval, you are still under oath from last Friday.
Mr. Sandoval, give us again the date that you were arrested by federal authorities.

A. September 10, 1983.

Q. When did you come to an agreement with the government to cooperate?

A. September 15th.

Q. Subsequent then, after September 15th—by the way, were you in jail at any point in time between your arrest and your agreement to cooperate?

A. September 10th to September 15th.

Q. What happened on September 15th?

A. I was released on bond.

Q. Was that part of your agreement with the government?

A. Yes.

Q. Did you have any further contact with any other persons that you have testified about last Friday?

A. Yes.

MR. DUNNELL: Objection for the reasons previously stated.

THE COURT: Overruled.

BY MR. THOMAS:

Q. Who was that?

A. I had contact with Mr. Carlos Santiago.

Q. When did you initiate or how did those contacts get started?

A. On September 16th I went to his house with surveillance of the FBI.

Q. Where was his house?

A. 23rd Court.

Q. Was that an appointment or you just came on your own?

A. No, I just came on my own.

MR. DUNNELL: Objection.

THE COURT: Overruled.

BY MR. THOMAS:

Q. What happened when you went there?

A. When I went there I found his wife in the yard.

Q. Did you see Mr. Santiago?

A. No, he wasn't there. She called him on the beeper but he never answered back.

Q. Did you make any further contact or attempts?

A. The next, the following week I contacted him.

Q. When and where was that contact?

A. I contacted him I think about October 4th or 5th approximately.

Q. Where?

A. I saw him at Joe's Restaurant at the end of 67th Avenue. I think it is on 1st Street.

Q. What happened at Joe's Restaurant?

A. I explained to him what happened. I gave him a copy of the charges that were brought against me.

Q. What did he say if anything?

A. He said that he was going to check with a friend of his and see what he could do.

Q. Do about what?

A. About solving his problem.

Q. What was his problem?

A. The problem—

MR. DUNNELL: Objection. May I have a continuing objection?

THE COURT: You may.

BY MR. THOMAS:

Q. You can answer.

A. He has a friend named Fred Stone who he had already told me was working with him and another Customs agent, Nathan Hart, and he told me maybe he could solve the problem with Fred Stone like he already did on another occasion.

THE COURT: Ladies and gentlemen, any statements made by Mr. Santiago relating to solving the problem is admitted against him alone. You may not consider it as evidence against anyone else.

MR. DUNNELL: May we have a sidebar?

(Sidebar conference reported but not transcribed.)

THE COURT: Mr. Sandoval, please just answer the question asked and answer yes or no and if you need to explain you can do that.

BY MR. THOMAS:

Q. Were you supposed to do anything with this person Fred Stone?

A. Yes.

Q. What was that?

A. Originally Mr. Santiago asked me to cooperate with him in an investigation.

Q. Wait a minute, you are not answering the question. With reference to your problem that you were discussing at Joe's Restaurant about what you could do with this person Fred Stone.

A. This person could work something out with the Department of Justice in Washington.

Q. How would that benefit you?

A. That would benefit me because I would probably walk out on probation in this case.

Q. Would you have to do anything for that assistance?

A. Yes, pay him $75,000.

Q. Was that discussed with Mr. Santiago?

A. Yes.

Q. Did you agree or disagree with that?

A. I agreed to that.

THE COURT: Again I remind you, ladies and gentlemen, any statement relating to such payment is limited only as to Mr. Santiago and not as to any other defendant.

BY MR. THOMAS:

Q. Who was to receive the $75,000?

A. Carlos Santiago and then transfer to Mr. Fred Stone.

Q. When would have been your next contact with Mr. Santiago?

A. When it would have been?

Q. When?

A. After October, probably in the next couple of weeks.

Q. Did that occur?

A. An October 21st on the phone.

Q. Where were you phoning from?

A. I called originally from my house.

Q. What was the reason for making that phone call?

A. The reason was to explain to him that I was supposed to appear in the office of Magistrate Peter Nagosoni.

Q. Who is Peter Nagosoni?

A. He is a magistrate.

Q. What were you to do?

A. I had to do that because I have been indicted by the grand jury.

Q. What did you tell Mr. Santiago about that?

A. I told Mr. Santiago that I was indicted and supposed to be in front of the magistrate and the time was getting short so he better talk to his friend and try to do something by that time.

Q. Who are you referring to by the friend?

A. Fred Stone.

Q. I would like to have this marked as Exhibit 20-A. Mr. Sandoval, I am going to show you what I have marked here as Government's Exhibit 20-A and ask you to identify it if you can.

A. Yes, this is a tape with my signature on it.

Q. Do you know where that tape was made?

A. In my cassette recorder.

Q. Where were you at the time?

A. At my house.

Q. Where is that?

A. At the time in Baja Mar.

Q. Who were you calling when you made that tape?

A. Carlos Santiago.

Q. What did you do with that tape after you made it?

A. I turned it over to the authorities, the FBI.

Q. Did you ever listen to that tape after you made it?

A. Yes.

Q. When did you first listen to it after first making it?

A. When I first listened to the tape was the same day, on the 21st.

Q. What did you do with it?

A. I cued the tape, signed it, put the date on it and held it until I turned it over to the authorities.

Q. Did you tape something?

A. Yes, sir.

Q. What did you tape?

A. Conversation with me and Mr. Carlos Santiago.

Q. When is the next time that you listened to that tape?

A. The next time that I listened to this tape was last week.

Q. Is what you heard on Exhibit 20-A an accurate recording of the conversation you had on October 21, 1983?

A. Correct.

Q. I would also show you Government's Exhibit 20 and 21 and ask you to identify those.

A. Yes.

Q. What are those?

A. These are the transcripts of the phone conversation taped on this date.

Q. Did you have anything to do with creating Exhibit 20 and 21?

A. I went over the translation on most of the transcripts and checked whatever was on there.

Q. Are those two transcripts accurate renditions of what was on the tape 20-A?

A. Yes.

Q. Do they conform with your memory of the conversation that you had on October 21st?

A. Correct.

MR. THOMAS: At this time the Government moves for permission to play Exhibit 20-A.

THE COURT: In what language was the conversation?

BY MR. THOMAS:

Q. What language was the conversation that you had on October 21st?

A. In Spanish.

Q. Are you fluent in Spanish?

A. Yes.

Q. Where are you from?

A. Cuba.

Q. The transcripts are in what language?

A. The transcripts are made in English.

Q. Are they an accurate translation?

A. To the best of my knowledge and my English language, yes.

Q. How long have you lived in this country?

A. Twenty-one, twenty-two years, twenty-three to be exact.

MR. THOMAS: I would move into evidence subject to being connected up 20, 21 and the tape, 20-A and request permission to play it.

MR. DUNNELL: May I voir dire on this?

THE COURT: You may voir dire.

VOIR DIRE EXAMINATION

BY MR. DUNNELL:

Q Mr. Sandoval, are there two separate conversations on that one small micro-cassette tape?

A. Yes.

Q. And your testimony is that you made that tape while on the telephone from your house in Baja Mar?

A. The first phone call was made from my house in Baja Mar.

Q. And the second one?

A. The second one is the answer back from Mr. Santiago calling back at the public phone at the Village Shopping Center.

Q. Did you bring the machine with you that you used to make those recordings?

A. Yes.

Q. Do you have it?

A. I gave it to Mr. Fortrel.

Q. When did you turn that over to the government agents, what date?

A. What date? I don't recall the exact date.

Q. Was it the same day or the next day?

A. The date—

Q. Let me finish my question. Was it the same day or the next day after making that recording?

A. It wasn't the same day or the next day.

Q. Was it the next week?

A. Probably.

Q. Probably? Was it the next week?

A. Yes.

Q. So now we are talking about the first week of November 1983?

A. Correct.

Q. In other words, is it your testimony that you did not keep that tape in your possession very long, a week at the most?

A. As far as I can recall.

Q. Who did you give the tape to, what agent of the government?

A. I don't recall exactly.

Q. Were any of the agents of the government with you when you made that tape recording?

A. No.

Q. Were you not being surveilled by any agents at the time?

A. No.

Q. No one was listening in on an extension?

A. No.

Q. So it was you and your little recorder on one end and Mr. Santiago on the other. Is that your testimony?

A. Yes.

Q. How do you know that the date of the conversation was October 21, 1983?

A. After I finished the tape I proceeded to cue the tape so it could not be erased or taped over and I wrote the date on it.

Q. So it is your word and your word alone that that was the date when that conversation was made?

A. Correct.

MR. DUNNELL: Thank you, your Honor.

THE COURT: All right. You are offering Exhibit 20-A and 21 as an aid to the jury only?

MR. THOMAS: I am offering Exhibit 21 and I move to play 20-A.

THE COURT: Ladies and gentlemen, I will admit the exhibit proffered. Exhibit 21 has been identified as a typewritten transcript reflecting translations of Spanish into English of the oral conversation which can be heard on the tape recording received in evidence as Exhibit 20-A. The transcript also purports to identify the speakers engaged in such conversation. I have admitted the transcript for the limited and secondary purpose in aiding and following the content of the conversation as you listen to the tape recording which was spoken in Spanish and also to aid you in identifying the speakers. However, you are specifically instructed that where the transcript correctly or incorrectly reflects the content of the conversation or the identity of the speakers is entirely for you to determine based upon your own evaluation of the testimony you have heard concerning the preparation of the transcript in relation to your hearing of the tape recording. The tape recording is the primary evidence. If you determine that the transcript is in any respect incorrect or unreliable you should disregard it to that extent.

MR. THOMAS: The government has prepared Xerox copies of the transcript.

THE COURT: Marked as Exhibit 21 and they will be passed out to the jury at this time. When the tape has been played and completed then you are to retrieve the transcripts.

MS. BRUCKER: I would like to reserve an objection at this time.

THE COURT: You may. I would ask that the jurors not read the transcript until the tape has been played.

MR. THOMAS: Your Honor, I have asked the agent who is fluent in Spanish to announce as the tape is played when the page should be turned to correspond where the transcript is to the tape, if that is all right.

THE COURT: You may do that.

MR. DUNNELL: Objection.

THE COURT: Overruled.

(Government's Exhibit Nos. 20, 20-A and 21 were received in evidence.)

(Tape played.)

DIRECT EXAMINATION (Continued)

BY MR. THOMAS:

Q. Mr. Sandoval, do you recognize that conversation and the voices of the people speaking?

A. Yes.

Q. Who were they?

A. The voices are myself and Mr. Carlos Santiago.

Q. On what day?

A. October 21, 1983.

Q. Is that tape recording an accurate rendition of the conversation you had on that date?

A. Correct.

Q. Did you ever come up with any money for this person Stone?

A. No. I couldn't come up with any money. The Department of Justice never came up with the money.

Q. Did you have any further discussions about it with Mr. Santiago?

A. Yes.

Q. When would have been then next time?

A. Probably in the next couple of months I talked to him about it. I even told him I was willing to give one boat as a guarantee.

Q. Did you yourself ever meet Stone?

A. No.

Q. Did you have any further discussion with Mr. Santiago about narcotics?

A. Yes.

MR. DUNNELL: Objection, leading.

THE COURT: Sustained.

BY MR. THOMAS:

Q. Did you discuss any other matters other than the Stone matter with Mr. Santiago?

MR. DUNNELL: Same objection.

THE COURT: Overruled.

THE WITNESS: On several occasions, yes.

BY MR. THOMAS:

Q. When did that start?

A. I went to see Mr. Santiago about seven or eight times.

Q. Over what period of time?

A. Over the period of time I figure since October to June.

Q. What year?

A. 1984.

Q. What did you discuss on those occasions?

A. In most of the cases when I went he asked me how I was feeling and if I knew anything else about the case. Every time I came from the court or I got any information I called him up and let him know about it. I gave him a copy of the indictment.

Q. Did you discuss any other people—

MR. DUNNELL: Objection, leading.

THE COURT: Overruled.

THE WITNESS: Can you repeat the question?

BY MR. THOMAS:

Q. Did you discuss any other people?

A. People, persons?

Q. Yes.

A. No.

Q. During this period of time did you engage in any narcotics discussions?

MR. DUNNELL: Objection, leading.

MR. THOMAS: I am trying to go into a new area and it is a transitional question.

THE COURT: Overruled.

BY MR. THOMAS:

Q. You can answer the question.

A. Yes.

Q. Can you recall the first time that you had such a conversation?

A. Such a conversation happened to be at his place of work R&R Enterprises, something like that in Westport.

Q. Who did you speak with?

A. I talked to Mr. Carlos Santiago.

Q. Did he want to do anything?

A. He asked me—

MR. DUNNELL: Objection, calls for a subjective conclusion and it is also misleading.

THE COURT: Sustained.

BY MR. THOMAS:

Q. What did you say and what did Mr. Santiago say?

A. I told Mr. Santiago that I was getting into a position that I probably would have to do something in the future. What I mean by something is deal in coke because I was instructed by you to keep in contact with him for eventually obtaining some cocaine with him.

Q. Did you discuss that with him?

A. Yes.

Q. What did he say?

A. On the occasion I was mentioning at his place of work in Westport he was mounting a radio on a red 450SL Mercedes Benz.

MR. DUNNELL: I am going to object for clarification. Does Mr. Thomas mean that Mr. Sandoval told Mr. Santiago to get some cocaine? It is misleading and I would move to strike it.

THE COURT: I will strike it.

BY MR. THOMAS:

Q. What was it that you said to Mr. Santiago?

A. I said that eventually I was going to have to get involved in some cocaine dealings.

Q. What did he say to that?

A. He said as soon as you are ready to let me know.

Q. Did you ever let him know anything further?

A. Yes, that same day he went to the trunk of his car and pulled out a kilo of cocaine and showed it to me.

Q. What did he say?

A. He said, "I am getting top quality cocaine."

Q. What did you say?

A. I told him that it looks good and whenever I am ready I will let him know.

Q. Did you ever contact him again for that purpose?

A. Yes.

Q. Where was that and what discussions did you have?

A. That was at his apartment on 26th Street. I think it is on 1st Street.

Q. What happened there?

A. I went on June 4th and told him that I was ready to start again in business.

Q. What year was this?

A. 1984.

Q. Was anyone else present?

A. His girl friend.

Q. What is her name?

A. Her first name is Valkiria. I don't know her last name.

Q. Was she present when you had conversations with Mr. Santiago?

A. Probably.

Q. What did you say to Mr. Santiago?

A. I told Mr. Santiago I was ready to start getting on with the business.

Q. What did he say?

A. He told me that Ciro stopped giving him credit and he didn't have too much merchandise and he proceeded to come down with approximately half an ounce of coke. That's what he told me.

Q. What did he do with it?

A. He turned it over to me.

Q. Did you examine it, look at it?

A. Yes.

Q. Was it coke?

A. It looked like it was coke.

MR. DUNNELL: Objection, move to strike, not responsive.

THE COURT: Sustained.

BY MR. THOMAS:

Q. How long were you there in the apartment on the 4th?

A. That day approximately two, two and a half hours.

Q. Did anything else happen there in the apartment?

A. That day?

Q. Yes.

A. I talked to Carlos Santiago.

Q. Were you able to get in contact with Ciro Montoro?

A. Not on that day. I think June 9th.

Q. What did you do with the small amount of cocaine on June 4th?

A. I put in my pocket and when I proceeded to leave his apartment I put it in my trunk and I went across the street to Joe's Restaurant and called Danny Hernando from the Department of Law Enforcement.

Q. What did you tell Agent Hernando?

A. That I have obtained approximately half an ounce of cocaine from Mr. Santiago, what to do with it. He told me to wait by the phone.

MS. BRUCKER: Objection to what he said.

THE COURT: Sustained.

BY MR. THOMAS:

Q. Don't tell us what he said. Did you do anything in response to what he told you?

A. I waited at the phone until I received a phone call from Agent Ritter.

Q. Did you do anything after receiving that phone call?

MS. BRUCKER: Objection.

THE COURT: Sustained.

BY MR. THOMAS:

Q. Were you told to do anything by Agent Ritter?

MS. BRUCKER: Object to that.

THE COURT: Sustained.

BY MR. THOMAS:

Q. What did you do after speaking with Agent Ritter?

A. I drove from Sunrise Drive up to 17th Avenue.

Q. What happened there?

A. Across from the First City Bank I proceeded to turn over to Mr. Hernando the coke that I received from Santiago.

Q. I will show you now, sir, what has been previously marked as Goverment's Exhibit 22 and ask you if you recognize it?

A. Yes.

Q What is it?

A. That is a transcript from the tape that I made between me and Mr. Santiago.

Q. On what date?

A. On June 8, 1984.

Q. Let me show you Government's Exhibit 22-A and ask you to identify it.

A. Yeah, it has my signature on it.

Q. What is that object? What is that you have in your hand marked 22-A?

A. This is a transcript of this tape.

Q. This object here is 22-A. I am asking you what this is.

A. A cassette tape.

Q. Does it bear any identifying symbols on it?

A. It has my initials and date.

Q. What is the date?

A. 6-8-84.

Q. Do you recall having any kind of telephone conversation on that tape?

A. Yes.

Q. Where were you when you had it?

A. In Ft. Lauderhill.

Q. Who did you call?

A. I called Mr. Carlos Santiago.

Q. What did you do at the time you were making the phone call?

A. I recorded it?

Q. Using what?

A. Using the recording equipment.

Q. What did you do with the tape after you recorded the call?

A. I turned it over to the authorities.

Q. Have you ever listened to that tape since then?

A. Yes.

Q. When?

A. Last week.

Q. Is that the first time you have listened to the tape since actually making the phone call and making it?

A. No, I listened to the tape after making the phone call.

Q. When and where did you do that?

A. The same day in the car.

Q. On the first occasion when you listened to it, was it an accurate recording of the conversation that you had?

A. Correct.

Q. When you listened to it here that was last week?

A. Yes.

Q. When you listened to it last week was it an accurate recording of that conversation on June the 8th?

A. Yes.

Q. Sir, is the transcript marked as twenty-two an accurate translation and transcript of what is on the tape 22-A?

A. Yes.

Q. Is it an accurate translation and transcript of the call that you actually had on June the 8th?

A. Correct.

MR. THOMAS: At this time I would move into evidence twenty-two, the transcript and 22-A tape.

MS. BRUCKER: Same objection as previously noted.

MR. DUNNELL: May I voir dire?

THE COURT: You may.

VOIR DIRE EXAMINATION

BY MR. DUNNELL:

Q. When you turned over that tape to the agent when did you do that and to which agent?

A. I can't recall, maybe the next day.

Q. Which agent?

A. The particular agent?

Q. Yes.

A. It could have been Fortrel.

Q. It could have been another agent?

A. It could have been.

Q. You don't remember?

A. Maybe Ms. Luzzler.

Q. This is four months and you don't remember?

A. I don't recall which one. I have so many tapes I don't know which one belongs to which.

Q. The conversations, that is Government's Exhibit 20 and 22-A, were any government agents present when you made the recording?

A. No.

Q. Was anyone listening on the other end?

A. Not that I know of.

Q. So it is you and Mr. Santiago and your recorder?

A. Correct.

Q. So all we have is your word for the accuracy of that tape?

A. That's what you say.

MR. DUNNELL: No other questions.

MR. THOMAS: I renew the motion.

THE COURT: Exhibit 22-A will be admitted and 22 will be admitted for the limited purpose of aiding the jury inlistening to the tape as it is played. I remind you ladies and gentlemen that Exhibit 22 has been identified as a typewritten transcript reflecting the translation of Spanish into English of the oral conversation which can be heard on the tape recording received in evidence as Exhibit 22-A. The transcript also purports to identify the speakers engaged in such conversation. As I instructed you previously I have admitted the transcript for the limited and secondary purpose of aiding you in following the contents of the conversation as we listen to the tape recording which is spoken in Spanish and to aid you in identifying the speakers.

However, you are specifically instructed that whether the transcript correctly or incorrectly reflects the contents of the conversation or the identity of the speakers is entirely for you to determine based upon your own evaluation of the testimony you have heard concerning the preparation of the transcript and from your own examination in relation to the hearing of the tape recording which is the primary evidence of its own content. If you should determine that the transcript is in any respect incorrect or unreliable you should disregard it to that extent.

MS. BRUCKER: May I ask the jury be allowed to use the aid only contemporaneous with the playing of the tape?

THE COURT: I agree with you it should be done that way. Ladies and gentlemen, do not look at the transcript until the tape recording is played.

(Government's Exhibit Nos. 22 and 22-A were received in evidence.)

(Tape played.)

DIRECT EXAMINATION (Continued)

BY MR. THOMAS:

Q. Did you listen to the playing of the tape?

A. Yes.

Q. Is that an accurate recording of the conversation that you had with Mr. Santiago on June 8, 1984?

A. Correct.

Q. Did you hear a reference by yourself to someone called Ciro?

A. Yes.

Q. Who was that?

A. That is Mr. Ciro Montoro.

Q. Why were you making reference to him?

A. I was making reference to him because I was supposed to have a meeting with that gentleman.

Q. Did you go over to Mr. Santiago's house on the 8th?

A. Correct.

Q. What happened there?

A. When we were seated there he called Mr. Ciro Montoro and he finally proceeded to come out.

Q. Could you hear the conversation Mr. Santiago was having on the phone?

A. He just called Ciro Montoro and told him to come over that his sister was there.

Q. Did that happen?

A. Yes.

Q. About what time was this?

A. Approximately 8:30.

Q. Did Mr. Montoro come over?

A. That is the time when he came over.

Q. What happened when he came over?

A. He came over and I said hello to him.

Q. Did he say anything?

A. Yeah, I sat down with him and I talked over a lot of things. I told him since I always pay him before I need to get some merchandise, and that I knew he stopped the credit on Mr. Santiago.

Q. Did you discuss that?

A. Yes, I discussed that with him.

Q. What did Montoro say?

A. That he would agree to give me merchandise through Santiago.

Q. What was this merchandise?

A. Cocaine.

Q. Did you discuss price and quantity?

A. I didn't discuss the price because he said he didn't have anything at the time. He mentioned something in the area of thirty thousand for a kilo.

Q. Was any agreement reached?

A. Agreement was reached that as soon as he gets the merchandise-

MR. DUNNELL: Object to the conclusion. The proof is in the pudding.

MR. THOMAS: I object to counsel's statement and move to strike.

THE COURT: It will be stricken. You may not draw conclusions. In other words, you can only say what he said, Mr. Sandoval.

Q. Did Mr. Montoro say anything what he could do for you?

A. He told me he could give me merchandise, that he would call Mr. Santiago as soon as he gets the merchandise so that he can turn it over to me.

Q. When was your next contact with either Mr. Santiago or Mr. Montoro?

A. The next contact I think was on June 21st.

Q. With whom and where?

A. At his apartment again.

Q. With whom?

A. Mr. Carlos Santiago.

Q. Why had you gone there?

A. I had gone there in order to find out if Mr. Montoro already had received the merchandise.

Q. Did you ask him anything about that?

A. Yes.

Q. What did he tell you?

A. Well, there is a tape of the whole conversation while I was there.

Q. Let me show you, sir, twenty-three.

MS. BRUCKER: Objection, move to strike the reference to the whole tape as a tape of the whole conversation. That is incorrect.

THE COURT: You are offering a portion of the conversation, Mr. Thomas?

MR. THOMAS: Under the discussions we had, your Honor, only that portion which is offered is to be considered. Judge, if we may approach.

(Sidebar conference reported but not transcribed.)

BY MR. THOMAS:

Q. Mr. Sandoval, did you have any meetings with anyone on June 21, 1984?

A. Yes.

Q. With whom?

A. With Mr. Carlos Santiago.

Q. Where?

A. At Mr. Carlos Santiago's apartment.

Q. Was anyone else present?

A. Yes.

Q. Who was that?

A. His girl friend.

Q. How did you happen to be there on that day?

A. I happened to be there on that day because in a previous phone call I asked him if I could talk to Mr. Montoro.

Q. What time approximately did you get to his apartment?

A. I figure it was about 6:30.

Q. Did you bring anything with you?

A. Yes.

Q. What was that?

A. A tape recorder, a micro-cassette tape recorder.

Q. What did you do with it?

A. I inserted a cassette before I went to the apartment and put it on when I was right at the door.

Q. Where did you have the cassette recorder?

A. In the right-hand pocket.

Q. Of what?

A. My trousers.

Q. Did you use that recorder for any purpose while you were inside?

A. To tape the conversation with Mr. Santiago.

Q. Did you in fact tape it?

A. Yes.

Q. What did you do with the tape afterwards?

A. After the tape was all ready I figure gone—

Q. Let me ask you what did you do after leaving the apartment?

A. After leaving the apartment I took the tape out and cued it.

Q. What do you mean by cue it?

A. Punch the holes on the sides so it cannot be altered or erased.

Q. How do you know about that?

A. I knew about that because Mr. Fortrel gave me those instructions.

MR. DUNNELL: Object to what he was informed.

THE COURT: Sustained.

BY MR. THOMAS:

Q. After cuing what did you do with it?

A. After cuing it I proceeded to play it.

Q. Where?

A. In my car.

Q. Was what you heard then an accurate recording of what had been said and what you heard inside the apartment?

A. Yes.

Q. What did you do with the tape afterwards?

A. It was turned over to Mr. Fortrel.

Q. Have you listened to it since then?

A. Yes.

Q. When?

A. Last week, last night.

Q. What was the purpose of doing that?

A. To check the translation of the transcript.

Q. Was the tape still the same accurate recording of the conversations in the apartment on the 21st?

A. Yes.

MS. BRUCKER: Objection to the characterization by counsel.

THE COURT: Sustained as to form.

BY MR. THOMAS:

Q. Did you reach any conclusion as to its accuracy?

A. Yes.

MS. BRUCKER: Objection. He is not an expert.

THE COURT: Overruled.

THE WITNESS: Yes.

BY MR. THOMAS:

Q. What was it?

A. The conclusion is what is on the tape is exactly the conversation that went on between Santiago and me.

Q. Let me show you Government's Exhibit 23 and 23-A and ask you to identify them.

A. Yes.

Q. Tell us what 23-A is.

A. 23-A is a micro-cassette tape of the conversation, the taped conversation that I had with Mr. Santiago in his apartment on June 21, 1984.

Q. Are there any identifying writings on 23-A?

A. Yes, my signature and date on it.

Q. What it twenty-three?

A. Twenty-three is a transcript of that tape.

Q. Did you do anything with the preparation of twenty-three?

A. I helped on it.

Q. Is twenty-three an accurate transcription of what is on 23-A?

A. Correct.

MS. BRUCKER: I object and move to strike. He said he only helped with it.

BY MR. THOMAS:

Q. Did you examine the transcript?

THE COURT: Sustained.

THE WITNESS: I went through the whole conversation.

MS. BRUCKER: I would ask for a ruling.

THE COURT: I ruled. Sustained.

BY MR. THOMAS:

Q. What did you do with Government's 23?

A. I went through the tape. I tried to correct whatever I thought there was in the translation to the best of my knowledge.

Q. Did you go through all the pages of this exhibit?

A. Correct.

Q. Did you come to a conclusion as to its accuracy after going through it?

A. Correct.

Q. What was the conclusion?

MS. BRUCKER: Objection. It is different from the certified translation.

MR. THOMAS: I move to strike that.

THE COURT: Granted. Overruled.

BY MR. THOMAS:

Q. What conclusions did you come to as to accuracy?

A. I concluded that it is accurate according to the transcript and the conversation that was on the tape.

MR. THOMAS: At this time I would move into evidence 23-A and ask permission of the Court to play the tape with copies of twenty-three being distributed to the jurors.

MR. DUNNELL: Objection on all previously stated grounds and may I voir dire?

THE COURT: You may. I will overrule your objection.

VOIR DIRE EXAMINATION

BY MR. DUNNELL:

Q. You said you got to Santiago's house at about 6:30 on the 21st?

A. Yes.

Q. What time did you leave?

A. Approximately 8:20, 8:30.

Q. Where did you go then?

A. I went then to my house.

Q. Did you meet agents of the FBI that day?

A. No.

Q. Do you recall testifying on Friday in this courtroom that immediately after you left Mr. Santiago's house you went to see Agent Fortrell and you gave him custody of that tape?

A. I recall testifying when I said at the beginning I went to my house but I got confused with the statement from Mr. Thomas.

Q. Do you recall testifying that you turned this exhibit over to Agent Fortrell on that day? Do you recall saying that?

A. Yes.

Q. And you were wrong about that?

A. Correct.

Q. Were any agents present with you at the time that you made this tape?

A. No.

Q. Were any agents outside?

A. No, sir.

Q. Were you supposed to meet agents before going to Mr. Santiago's house?

A. Correct.

Q. You decided on your own not to wait for them?

A. I didn't decide on my own. They couldn't make it up there.

Q. So you went without them?

A. Without them—with their permission.

Q. Then you taped this conversation without anybody else listening to it or monitoring its accuracy?

A. Correct.

Q. Showing you what appears to be a Pearl recorder, I would like you to stand up and show me—

A. Sir, that is not my recorder.

Q. That is not the recorder?

A. No.

Q. Showing you this recorder can you explain the difference between this one and the one you used?

A. The one that I used doesn't have all these buttons on the front.

Q. How about the difference in size?

A. It is about the same size, maybe a little smaller and I think it is a little bit thinner.

Q. So you left Mr. Santiago's house at about 8:30?

A. Between 8:20 and 8:30, I figure.

Q. Did you make any telephone calls to any agents that night?

A. What?

Q. Did you make a telephone call to any government agent that night?

A. No.

Q. So your testimony Friday that you made a call was a lie, is that right?

A. I didn't say anything in testimony that I made a phone call. I said I got confused and like I said first that I was going on the way to my house.

Q. Are you disputing that your testimony Friday was that you went to a convenience store, bought a soda and you called the agents? Isn't that what you said?

A. I was confused.

Q. Isn't that what you said on Friday?

A. Yes.

Q. Now, you may explain.

A. That is the procedure that I used the day that I came out of Mr. Carlos Santiago's house on June the 8th when I talked to Mr. Ciro Montoro.

Q. But it was not the procedure on June 21st?

A. Correct.

Q. Let me show you a Realistic micro-cassette tape recorder and ask you if you can identify that?

A. Yes, sir.

Q. What is that?

A. A micro-cassette tape recorder that belongs to me.

Q. That is your tape recorder?

A. Yes.

Q. Is that the machine that you used in connection with making this tape on June 21, 1984?

A. Yes, sir.

Q. Would you stand up please and put that in your right-hand pocket. Please sit down. How were you dressed on June 21, 1984?

A. With a pair of pants and a shirt.

Q. Did you have a sports coat on that day?

A. No.

Q. Did you have a tie on?

A. No.

Q. What kind of pants did you have on?

A. What kind of pants?

Q. Yes.

A. Polyester pants, black in color.

Q. Long pants, short pants?

A. No, regular pants.

Q. What kind of shirt?

A. What kind of shirt?

Q. Yes.

A. A regular shirt.

Q. Where were you seated in Mr. Santiago's house?

A. I was seated in the sofa in the closest point to the door.

Q. That is a hard back sofa or a soft back?

A. It is a cushion sofa.

Q. Anything in your lap?

A. Was there anything in my lap?

Q. Yes.

A. Sometimes I had like a pillow.

Q. Were you seated straight up or reclining?

A. I was seated straight up.

Q. When did you turn that tape over to agents of the government?

A. When did I what, sir?

Q. You say you took it on June 21st. On what date did you turn it over?

A. June 25th.

Q. So that tape remained in your possession for four days?

A. Correct.

MR. DUNNELL: I have no further questions.

MS. BRUCKER: I have some voir dire, if I might?

THE COURT: All right.

VOIR DIRE EXAMINATION

BY MS. BRUCKER:

Q. Mr. Sandoval, have you ever been certified as a translator in any court of law?

A. No, sir.

Q. Have you compared your version of what this tape says with any other version of what this tape says?

A. Yes.

Q. And there are substantial differences in your version and the other version, are there not?

A. On certain occasions, yes.

Q. No further questions.

BY MR. WESTON:

Q. When you went to Key Largo you said it was in 1974?

A. Correct.

Q. Let's go backwards. In 1974 you opened a tire store, Ridewell Tire?

A. Yes.

Q. How many people did you employ at Ridewell Tire?

A. A total of about four.

Q. Where was Ridewell Tire located, your franchise?

A. My store was at 1124 West Maple Street.

Q. When did you finish with that business, in what year?

A. I think it was about 1977.

Q. From 1977 until 1980 how were you employed?

A. I was manager of Migrate Tire Company in Hollyville.

Q. Is that the actual name of the company?

A. Yes.

Q. When did you finish your employment with Migrate Tire

Company?

A. At the beginning of September of 1980.

Q. Now, from 1980 on that is when you began dealing in narcotics, am I right?

A. From 1980.

Q. Am I right?

A. Yes.

Q. So you just kind of rolled from tires into narcotics?

A. Correct.

Q. That would mean, sir, that for several years your sole source of income was from the distribution of illegal narcotics, am I right?

A. Correct.

Q. Then in 1983 you went back to legitimate work again, am I right?

A. No, September of 1983.

Q. You have a new company now, don't you?

A. What, sir?

Q. You have a new company now?

A. Yes.

Q. That is Morning Trucking Company?

A. No.

Q. What is Morning Trucking Company?

A. That is that company that I lease my trucks to.

Q. Which trucks would those be?

A. The construction trucks.

Q. What kind of trucks does that company own? Well, which trucks specifically do you lease to Morning Company?

A. Trucks owned by R & R Trucking Company?

Q. I honestly don't understand the letters you said.

A. R & R.

Q. What trucks does R&R Trucking Company own?

A. Three trucks.

Q. Please describe them.

A. They are dump trucks.

Q. What kind of dump trucks?

MR. THOMAS: There may be a point to this but I haven't seen it yet. I object on grounds of relevancy.

MR. WESTON: I will withdraw the last question and connect it up right now.

BY MR. WESTON:

Q. You purchased those trucks, am I right?

A. Correct.

Q. All three of them?

A. Correct.

Q. What is the total purchase price of those three trucks?

MR. THOMAS: I renew my objection.

MR. WESTON: I will connect it up.

THE COURT: Overruled.

THE WITNESS: The price that I paid altogether is about twenty thousand.

BY MR. WESTON:

Q. And the twenty thousand that you used to purchase those three trucks came from your narcotics business, am I right?

A. No, it came from the sale of assets like furniture.

Q. All of which you purchased with drug money, am I right?

A. Some have been purchased with drug money and some I had before.

Q. So you roll drug money into assets which you sold and converted into the truck company?

A. That's what you are saying.

Q. That's what I am saying and that is right, isn't it?
It is the truth?

MR. THOMAS: Objection, arguing with the witness.

THE COURT: Sustained.

BY MR. WESTON:

Q. The R of R&R Trucking is Roland Pazos?

A. He owns one truck of the business that I have.

Q. And he would be the R in R&R?

A. Correct.

Q. So he is your partner?

A. Yes.

Q. So you work with him on a daily basis?

A. He drives a truck and I drive another one.

Q. You are driving a truck?

A. Yes, until August of this year.

Q. Then in August you quit?

A. I didn't quit. I was told by the federal authorities to put a driver on it and get out of my house.

Q. So you did that?

A. Correct.

Q. Mr. Pazos is your partner in that business? Is that a corporation?

A. No, a partnership.

Q. This arrangement that you have with Morning Trucking Company, do you work for them also?

A. Look, the way it works is you lease the trucks to Morning through the broker.

Q. How long term is that contract?

A. You renew a contract every year.

Q. Now is it your testimony that you had to sell assets in order to get money to but these trucks?

A. Correct.

Q. During the years that you were a cocaine distributor how much money were you earning on an annualized basis gross?

A. I don't keep books so I can't give you an exact figure.

Q. Do you recall testifying before a federal grand jury in Fort Wayne on June 2, 1984?

A. Yes, and I recall saying when they asked me about $750,000, that that was the income. But I never finished saying that that includes bad debts that I have that are uncollected.

Q. In other words, you are telling us that you included bad debts which you did not collect in the sum of $750,000?

A. For the three years between 1980 and 1983.

Q. Now, in addition to all those other parts of your deal that you have testified about, the government has agreed to try to postpone your sentencing, haven't they?

A. Correct.

Q. In fact you have not yet been sentenced?

A. No.

Q. You plead guilty in January of 1984?

A. Correct, January the 30th I think it is.

Q. And you still have not been sentenced, is that right?

A. Yes.

Q. Has a pre-sentence investigation report been prepared on you yet?

A. Yes, sir.

Q. Where was that done?

A. In Fort White.

MR. WESTON: I would like leave of Court at the recess to make a motion concerning the production of that document.

THE COURT: Let's go forward with any remaining questions you have for the next few minutes and then we will adjourn for the evening.

BY MR. WESTON:

Q. Who is the probation officer that prepared that report?

A. I got the card here.

Q. Would you read it to me.

A. The name is Eddie Armad.

Q. And he is in Fort White?

A. 500 Oland Terrace, P.O. Box 32697 Station F, Fort White.

Q. In 1981 you knew a person named Harold Red, am I correct?

A. Yes.

Q. In 1980 you were the owner of a Jeep automobile, am I right?

A. Correct.

Q. And at the same time that you owned that Jeep in 1980 you were a partner in a cocaine business according to you with Mr. Harold Red?

A. Correct.

Q. There was no doubt in your mind in 1981 that Harold Red's business and his only business was in the cocaine business with you, right?

A. Correct.

Q. And you knew in 1981 that Harold Red frequently was a carrier of cocaine, didn't you?

A. Yes.

Q. You knew how he carried it, correct?

A. Can you repeat the question?

Q. Sure. You knew that he sometimes would carry cocaine in a briefcase or a suitcase, correct?

A. I don't know the way he carried it when he carried it on his own.

Q. Did you not discuss this with your 50-50 partner?

A. No, my 50-50 partner—the only way we discussed bringing cocaine to the Keys was in the air vents of the car.

Q. But you knew that Mr. Red frequently traveled with cocaine, correct?

A. Correct.

Q. And that he frequently traveled with money which came from the sale of cocaine?

A. Correct.

Q. And there came a time when you decided to loan this particular Jeep to Mr. Red for a little trip?

A. The time came when Mr. Red's car was broken down and left at the shop and he had to go with his wife and kids to Deerfield.

Q. The very Jeep that we are talking about is the one that Mr. Red was driving the day that he was arrested in Deerfield?

A. Correct.

Q. You later learned that in that Jeep was found a quantity of cocaine in a briefcase, is that correct?

A. That's correct. That's what I heard.

Q. Were you the owner of that Jeep?

A. Correct.

Q. You actually paid for it?

A. Correct.

Q. You paid cash for it?

A. Of course.

Q. You paid cash for all of your cars, didn't you?

A. Yes.

Q. Not just your own cars but the cars that you sometimes gave to friends as gifts?

A. Correct.

Q. It was too troublesome to have financing from the bank?

A. I could not obtain credit.

Q. So you just paid cash?

A. Correct.

Q. You were disturbed to learn that the police were going to keep the Jeep, weren't you?

A. Yes, because I never loaned a Jeep in my name to him to be used in my name to transport cocaine when we had three or four rental cars.

Q. You knew if the coke was in the car it was undoubtedly Harold's?

A. If I knew he was going to transport I would not give him my own car to use.

Q. So you decided to go to Deerfield to the State Attorney's Office and make a sworn statement in order to get the Jeep back, didn't you?

A. Correct, sir.

Q. In fact you appeared before an Assistant State Attorney and you swore that you yourself were not involved in coke dealing and you had no reason to believe that Harold Red was involved in coke dealing? You swore to that?

A. As far as I can remember I didn't know there was any coke in the Jeep.

Q. I am not asking you that question.

MR.THOMAS: I object to this grand finale in that tone of voice.

THE COURT: I think the tone does not need to be as high.

BY MR. WESTON:

Q. Did you swear that you were not involved in coke dealing and that you had no reason to believe that Harold Red was involved in coke dealing?

A. Sir, I don't recall the statement that I made. If you give it to me I can read it again and you can refresh my memory.

Q. Perhaps, sir, you can explain to the jury the size fifty-six jacket which was found in the Jeep? Do you recall trying to get that jacket back also?

A. A jacket?

Q. Yes, a size fifty-six jacket.

A. I guess so.

Q. you got the Jeep back, didn't you, Mr. Sandoval?

A. Yes.

MR. WESTON: This is a good place for us to break, your honor.

THE COURT: We will be in recess until 8:30 tomorrow morning. I do remind you not to discuss the case among yourselves or with each other or listen to a discussion of the case in your presence. You may read the newspapers only after we have had a chance to excise portions of those papers for you.

THE COURT: We are ready for the jury, are we not?

(Jury enters at 9:00 a.m.)

Ricardo Sandoval, Government's witness, resumed.

CROSS EXAMINATION (Continued)

BY MR. WESTON:

Q. Mr. Sandoval, when we left off yesterday we were discussing a

1980 Jeep which was seized by the Deerfield Police Department, I believe in May of 1981. Do you recall that conversation?

A. Yes, sir.

Q. Now, you actually hired counsel to represent you with regard to getting back this Jeep?

A. Yes, I hired Murray Keystone. That was my lawyer at the time.

Q. And you told Mr. Keystone that you wanted him to proceed to get back your Jeep, correct?

A. Correct.

Q. Now, you were advised by Mr. Keystone that the Jeep, that the State or the City of Deerfield was going to try to keep the Jeep because the Jeep was guilty of committing a crime, which is carrying narcotics, correct?

A. Yeah.

Q. And you were advised that the law of this state dealing with forfeiture or seizure of an automobile provides that if the owner can establish his innocence, his blamelessness, that then, under those circumstances you might be able to get it back, correct?

A. Correct.

Q. So you then went ahead and you specified to an assistant state attorney in the presence of your attorney that you were blameless, that you were innocent and therefore you should get back your Jeep. You did that, didn't you?

A. Correct, I didn't have any knowledge of any cocaine in that Jeep.

Q. You didn't just say you had no knowledge of that particular cocaine. You also tried to show the assistant state attorney that you yourself were not involved in narcotics dealing, didn't you?

A. I told you yesterday I didn't recall exactly my words.

Q. Do you have a memory problem that you want to tell us about?

A. No, I don't have any memory problem.

Q. Do you recall filing through your attorney a petition to get back the vehicle?

A. Probably I signed some papers for Mr. Keystone. He is the one who handled the whole situation.

Q. Do you recall specifying in that petition, sir, and I quote: "In accordance with Statute 713.184 petitioner Ricardo Sandoval . . . "

MR. THOMAS: Your Honor, he said he had no memory.

THE COURT: Why don't you show it to him?

MR. WESTON: May I approach the witness?

THE COURT: You may.

BY MR. WESTON:

Q. Showing you Paragraph 2 of this petition, I ask you to read Paragraph 2 and then I will question you.

A. "In accordance with Statute"—

MR. THOMAS: Your Honor, he should read it to himself.

THE COURT: Yes, read it to yourself.

BY MR. WESTON:

Q. Does that refresh your recollection?

A. It refreshes to me that I asked for my Jeep to be returned.

Q. And you said it was taken wrongfully, in other words, that you were blameless, you were innocent. You told the Court that in a petition?

A. That I am telling you personally here I did not have any knowledge of any cocaine inside that Jeep.

Q. And you had no way of knowing that your friend, Mr. Red, would be carrying cocaine?

A. Mr. Red was going to supposedly sign for a house. So he was carrying nineteen or $20,000. So of course I didn't have any idea he would be carrying any coke.

Q. Now, this occurred in April or May of 1981. You knew that Harold was carrying coke with him all the time?

A. Sir, Mr. Red had a lot that was going on with his wife. I wouldn't give him a car in my name for coke when we had four rental cars.

Q. Didn't you know Mr. Red was using cocaine on a daily basis?

A. On a daily basis?

Q. You didn't know Mr. Red was shooting cocaine into his arms at that time?

A. No, sir.

Q. Or snorting it?

A. Snorting it from time to time whenever I saw him.

Q. From time to time every day?

A. I didn't say every day. I said I have no knowledge of that. I didn't live with Mr. Red. I couldn't see him on a daily basis.

Q. What is your citizenship?

A. United States citizen.

Q. Now, you testified yesterday that approximately three months before you were arrested and indicted you began cooperating. Is that your testimony?

A. I said I was approached by the United States Attorney's Office and the DEA to cooperate in a corruption case to bring up the Communist involvement in drugs.

Q. Was it before or after you had made approximately three-quarters of one million dollars in the drug business yourself as you testified yesterday that you decided to cooperate with the government and to show this Communist conspiracy?

A. I decided to cooperate in any situation. Even Mr. Santiago advised me that he was working with Customs Agent Nathan Hart and Fred Stone and I offered my cooperation to him.

Q. Are you saying that the drug organization in which you were involved was Communist inspired?

A. No. If it was Communist inspired I wouldn't be here, sir.

Q. You yourself have testified in federal court against people who are anti-Communist, haven't you?

A. What?

Q. You have testified in a court of law against people who are anti-Communists, have you not?

MR. THOMAS: Object, irrelevant.

THE COURT: Sustained.

BY MR. WESTON:

Q. Back in 1977, sir, did you associate with the following people as your friends or political affiliates? Orlando "Scarface" Millares?

MR. THOMAS: Objection.

THE COURT: Sustained.

BY MR. WESTON:

Q. Have you ever been a member of a terrorist organization?

A. No.

MR. THOMAS: Your Honor—

THE COURT: Sustained.

BY MR. WESTON:

Q. Now, Mr. Sandoval, the sentencing that you were facing in this case was originally scheduled within about thirty days of your guilty plea in January of 1984, correct?

A. Yes, sir.

Q. Then it was again set for April 19, 1984, wasn't it?

A. Yes.

Q. Again on April 9th it was postponed, wasn't it?

A. Correct.

Q. And it has been postponed several times even since April hasn't it?

A. I understand at the request of the government.

Q. So the government has kept your sentencing hanging over your head so to speak until you have finished testifying, isn't that right?

A. Correct.

Q. Now, your deal with the government specifies that you will not be charged for those crimes which you admit that you have committed so long as you provide truthful cooperation? That is your deal, isn't it?

A. That is what was written on the agreement.

Q. Included with your deal that we were talking about yesterday is the fact that you will not be charged for the distribution of cocaine which you made to a large number of people, right?

A. I plead guilty to a conspiracy charge.

Q. Please answer my question. Have you been given immunity? That means that you will not be prosecuted for the deliveries of cocaine which you personally made to a large number of people?

A. In a technical way I understand I already have plead guilty to that if it is one charge or if it is a hundred.

Q. You plead guilty to the conspiracy charge?

A. Correct.

Q. I am asking you about actual distribution, whether it would be by way of a gift or by way of a sale to other people. You have been given immunity in all of those crimes, am I right?

A. Yes, sir.

Q. Now, included within the people that the government has said that we are not going to prosecute you for giving cocaine to, these people would be the following people. Tell me if I am wrong. Connie Fianas?

A. Correct.

Q. Karen Halls?

A. Correct.

Q. Janet Paine?

A. Correct?

Q. Bonnie Paulson?

A. Correct.

Q. Carrie Moin?

A. Correct.

Q. Marla Pedroso?

A. Correct.

Q. Evelio Peña?

A. No.

Q. You deny that?

A. Evelio? I don't know that person.

Q. Steve Hawk?

A. Correct.

Q. Mickey Forbes?

A. Correct.

Q. Clayton Hernandes?

A. Correct.

Q. Farah Hill?

A. Correct.

Q. Vivian Cole?

A. What is the name?

Q. Vivian.

A. Yes.

Q. Would it be fair to say that the average age of those people is sixteen years old?

MR. THOMAS: Your Honor, objection.

THE COURT: Sustained.

MS. JONES: May we ask that the jury be excused. The government needs to make a record.

THE COURT: We can make that at the appropriate time.

BY MR. WESTON:

Q. You are an intelligent person and you are kind of innovative?

A. Kind of what?

Q. Intelligent and innovative, forward thinking?

A. Well, I know that word, sir.

Q. Did you ever distribute cocaine to people by putting about seventy or seventy-one bottles inside of a piñata at a party?
Did you ever do that?

A. If you can call that distributing.

Q. Yes, I call it distributing. Did you put seventy or seventy-one gram vials in a piñata?

A. Not me by myself. A group of people who were there in a party.

Q. It was your idea?

A. I guess so.

Q. Was it at your house?

A. No.

Q. Whose house was it at?

A. As far as I know it was a hotel.

Q. A room rented by you?

A. No, I didn't rent the room, sir.

Q. Besides the cocaine, there was also pot in the piñata?

A. I don't recall.

Q. Quaaludes?

A. I don't recall that.

Q. Sometime during the party just like in a Mexican Christmas celebration somebody comes up and snaps the piñata and everybody kind of dives for it. Do you recall that party?

A. I recall it, but the way you said it everything is—

Q. Mr. Sandoval, was that piñata party what is called in the Latin community a sweet sixteen party?

A. No, sir.

MS. JONES: Your Honor—

THE COURT: Sustained.

MS. JONES: Again may I suggest to the Court that the jury be excused so I can make a record?

MR. WESTON: I will not respond to that.

MS. JONES: He cannot because it is not before the jury.

THE COURT: Let's proceed.

BY MR. WESTON:

Q. You were in the habit of ingratiating yourself to people by giving away cars?

A. Can you repeat the question?

Q. You tried to get people to like you by giving them cars?

A. I didn't try to make people like me by giving away anything.

Q. You just like to give things away?

A. I have been generous to the point that the defendant in this court knows that I loaned him $5,000 and he never paid me back and he is sitting in the defense bench there.

Q. Did you give away jewelry?

A. Yes.

Q. Electrical equipment, tape recorders, video equipment, and television sets?

A. Approximately between ten and twelve VCRs and probably four, five TVs.

Q. And an apartment? You have people that you would let stay in this apartment?

A. An apartment that I was paying the rent that people stayed at, yes.

Q. During this same period of time that you are talking about in addition to distributing cocaine among other people and the names that I have just read to you, you were quite a user of cocaine, weren't you?

A. No, I wouldn't consider myself quite a user of cocaine.

Q. Since you have been arrested and made this deal with the government, have your eating habits changed significantly?

A. No, of course not.

MS. JONES: Objection, irrelevant.

THE COURT: Sustained.

BY MR. WESTON:

Q. Did you before you were arrested use cocaine by actually taking a card or some other object or a spoon and eating it?

A. No, sir.

Q. You never ate cocaine?

A. I might have put it in my mouth.

Q. How did you use cocaine?

A. I snorted it.

Q. Are you denying, sir, that you ever actually picked it up with a card in a large quantity and ate it?

A. No, if I picked it up in a large quantity you might go and overdose. So I don't think that is possible.

Q. Another part of your deal is that you have to make daily phone calls to government agents, isn't that right?

A. Correct.

Q. You have been doing that?

A. Most of the time.

Q. Was there ever a time that Harold Red gave you or sold to you—and this is back in 1980 or 1981—a machine gun?

A. A machine gun? No, he never sold me a machine gun.

Q. Did he ever give you a machine gun?

A. I saw a machine gun. As a matter of fact he gave it to Mr. Jack

Martin.

Q. But in addition to the one you said you saw him give to Jack Martin, did he also give you one?

A. No, sir.

Q. So you emphatically deny under oath that Harold Red ever delivered to you a machine gun, am I right?

A. No, he never gave me a machine gun for my use. I never had any machine gun that belonged to Harold Red.

Q. Did Harold have a machine gun?

A. As far as I know—

MR. THOMAS: Objection, irrelevant.

THE COURT: Sustained.

BY MR. WESTON:

Q. Now, your partnership with Mr. Red began—as I understand your testimony from last week—in 1980 when he became actual partners with you?

A. Correct.

Q. Do you recall the exact date it began?

A. No, sir.

Q. Was if after Christmas?

A. No, I think it was before Christmas, right in that area.

Q. Right around Christmas? Was it in 1980 or 1981 that you have this recollection that you gave a small amount of personal use cocaine to Joe Cox?

A. I think it was in 1981. I gave an ounce at the Pizza King in Key Largo.

Q. That was just a gift? That is how you described it?

A. That's a gift.

Q. You didn't get paid for it?

A. No, I never requested to be paid for it.

Q. Now, you also testified that Harold Red told you that Joe was his customer at some point in time in 1980, 1981?

A. 1981.

Q. Or part of 1981.

A. The beginning of 1981.

Q. So whether that statement is true or not you don't know because you are just relying on Harold Red's word for that statement, am I right?

A. Of course.

Q. Just last week, did you speak with Mr. Ritter, investigator Tom Dantel and Rue Dodd?

A. Correct.

Q. Did you tell those men that in the course of your conversation with them that the United States government had proposed to you that they will recommend probation for you?

A. No, sir, is not the way it came, sir.

Q. Do you deny that you made that statement?

A. They asked me what are the conditions that I am going to get. I said I hope that they will recommend probation.

Q. Do you recall telling them and I quote "I only work for one side at a time and right now I am working for the government"?

A. I told him that I consider myself a case agent on the case.

Q. Sir, is your answer yes or no and then explain if you think it is necessary. Would you please answer whether you said that to those men?

A. Can you repeat it?

Q. Did you say and I quote, "I only work for one side at a time and right now I am working for the government"?

A. Not your precise words.

Q. Almost my precise words, Mr. Sandoval?

A. One word can change the whole meaning of the conversation, sir.

MR. WESTON: That's all I have.

UNITED STATES DISTRICT COURT
NORTHERN DISTRICT OF CALIFORNIA

UNITED STATES OF AMERICA

- vs - CASE NO. 90-643-CR-MONT

FRANCISCO LLANO
FLORENCIO CARRANTE
ANGEL BOSQUET
EMERIO PORTAL
and
JAIME JUNCO

JUDGE'S INSTRUCTIONS TO THE JURY

Members of the Jury:

It is now my duty to instruct you on the rules of law that you must follow and apply in deciding this case. When I have finished, you will go to the jury room and begin your discussions — what we call your deliberations.

It will be your duty to decide whether the Government has proved beyond a reasonable doubt the specific facts necessary to find the Defendant guilty of the crime charged in the indictment.

You must make your decision only on the basis of the testimony and other evidence presented here during the trial; and you must not be influenced in any way by either sympathy or prejudice for or against the Defendant or the Government.

You must also follow the law as I explain it to you whether you agree with that law or not; and you must follow all my instructions as a whole. You may not single out or disregard any of the Court's instructions on the law.

This indictment or formal charge against any Defendant is not evidence of guilt. Indeed, the Defendant is presumed by the law to be innocent. The law does not require a Defendant to prove his innocence or produce any evidence at all; and if a Defendant elects not to testify, you should not consider that in any way in your deliberations. The Government has the burden of proving a Defendant guilty beyond a reasonable doubt, and if it fails to do so, you must find the Defendant not guilty.

Thus, while the Government's burden of proof is a strict or heavy burden, it is not necessary that the Defendant's guilt be proved beyond all possible doubt. It is only required that the Government's proof exclude any "reasonable doubt" concerning the Defendant's guilt.

A "reasonable doubt" is a real doubt, based upon reason and common sense after careful and impartial consideration of all the evidence in the case.

Proof beyond a reasonable doubt, therefore, is proof of such a convincing character that you would be willing to rely and act upon it without hesitation in the most important of your own affairs. If you are convinced that the Defendant has been proved guilty beyond a reasonable doubt, say so. If you are not convinced, say so.

As stated earlier, you must consider only the evidence that I have admitted in the case. The term "evidence" includes the testimony of the witnesses and the exhibits admitted in the record. Remember that anything the lawyers say is no evidence in this case. It is your own recollection and interpretation of the evidence that controls. What the lawyers say is not binding upon you. Also, you should not assume from anything that I may have said that I have any opinion concerning any of the issues in this case. Except for my instructions to you on the law, you should disregard anything I may have said during the trial in arriving at your own decision concerning the facts.

In considering the evidence, you may make deductions and reach conclusions that reason and common sense lead you to make; and you should not be concerned about whether the evidence is direct or circumstantial. "Direct evidence" is the testimony of one who asserts actual knowledge of a fact, such as an eye witness. "Circumstantial evidence" is proof of a chain of facts and circumstances indicating that the Defendant is either guilty or not guilty. The law makes no distinction between the weight you may give to either direct or circumstantial evidence.

Now, in saying that you must *consider* all of the evidence, I do not mean that you must *accept* all of the evidence as true or accurate. You should decide whether you believe what each witness had to say, and how important that testimony was. In making that decision you may believe or disbelieve any witness, in whole or in part. Also, the number of witnesses testifying concerning any particular dispute is not controlling. You may decide that the testimony of a smaller number of witnesses concerning any fact in dispute is more believable than the testimony of a larger number of witnesses to the contrary.

In deciding whether you believe or do not believe any witness, I suggest that you ask yourself a few questions: Did the person impress you as one who was telling the truth? Did he or she have a special interest in the outcome of the case? Did the witness seem to have a good memory? Did the witness have the opportunity and ability to observe accurately the things he or she testified about? Did he or she appear to understand the questions clearly and answer them directly? Did the witness's testimony differ from the testimony of other witnesses?

You should also ask yourself whether there was evidence tending to prove that the witness testified falsely concerning some important fact; or whether there was evidence that at some other time the witness said or did something, or failed to say or do something, which was different from the testimony he or she gave before you during the trial.

You should keep in mind, of course, that a simple mistake by a witness does not necessarily mean that the witness was not telling the truth as he or she remembers it, because people naturally tend to forget some things or remember other things inaccurately. So, if a witness has made a misstatement, you need to consider whether that misstatement was simply an innocent lapse of memory or an intentional falsehood; and that may depend on whether it has to do with an important fact or with only an unimportant detail.

When the Government offers testimony or evidence that a Defendant made a statement or admission to someone, after being arrested or detained, the jury should consider the evidence concerning such a statement with caution and great care.

It is for you to decide (1) whether the Defendant made the statement and (2) if so, how much weight to give to it. In making those decisions you should consider all of the evidence about the statement, including the circumstances under which the Defendant may have made it.

Of course, any such statement should not be considered in any way whatever as evidence with respect to any other Defendant on trial.

The indictment charges that the defendants, willfully, knowingly and with intent to convert to their own use, conspired to embezzle, steal and unlawfully take and carry away goods of a value in excess of $100.00, and to receive such stolen goods, that is Magnavox television sets and video recorders (VCR'S), which were moving as an interstate or foreign shipment of freight, all in violation of Title 18, United States Code, Section 371.

Title 18, United States Code, Section 371, makes it a separate Federal crime or offense for anyone to conspire or agree with someone else to do something which, if actually carried out, would amount to another Federal crime or offense. So, under this law, a "conspiracy" is an agreement or a kind of "partnership" in criminal purposes in which each member becomes the agent or partner of every other member.

In order to establish a conspiracy offense it is not necessary for the Government to prove that all of the people named in the indictment were members of the scheme; or that those who were members had entered into any formal type of agreement; or that the members had planned together all of the details of the scheme or the "overt acts" that the indictment charges would be carried out in an effort to commit the intended crime.

Also, because the essence of a conspiracy offense is the making of the agreement itself (followed by the commission of any overt act), it is not necessary for the Government to prove that the conspirators actually succeeded in accomplishing their unlawful plan.

What the evidence in the case must show beyond a reasonable doubt is:

First: That two or more persons, in some way or manner, came to a mutual understanding to try to accomplish a common and unlawful plan, as charged in the indictment;

Second: That the Defendant willfully became a member of such conspiracy;

Third: That one of the conspirators during the existence of the conspiracy knowingly committed at least one of the methods (or "over acts") described in the indictment; and

Fourth: That such "overt act" was knowingly committed at or about the time alleged in an effort to carry out or accomplish some object of the conspiracy.

An "overt act" is any transaction or event, even one which may be entirely innocent when considered alone, but which is knowingly committed by a conspirator in an effort to accomplish some object of the conspiracy.

An "interstate shipment" means goods or property which is moving as a part of interstate commerce; and interstate commerce simply means the movement or transportation of goods from one state into another state.

A person may become a member of a conspiracy without knowing all of the details of the unlawful scheme, and without knowing who all of the other members are. So, if a Defendant has an understanding of the unlawful nature of a plan and knowingly and willfully joins in that plan on one occasion, that is sufficient to convict him for conspiracy even though he did not participate before, and even though he played only a minor part.

Of course, mere presence at the scene of a transaction or event, or the mere fact that certain persons may have associated with each other, and may have assembled together and discussed common aims and interests, does not necessarily establish proof of a conspiracy. Also, a person who has no knowledge of a conspiracy, but who happens to act in a way which advances some purpose of one, does not thereby become a conspirator.

In your consideration of the conspiracy offense as alleged in the indictment you should first determine, from all of the testimony and evidence in the case, whether or not the conspiracy existed as charged. If you conclude that a conspiracy did exist as alleged, you should next determine whether or not the defendant under consideration willfully became a member of such conspiracy.

In determining whether a defendant was a member of an alleged conspiracy, however, the jury should consider only that evidence, if any, pertaining to his own acts and statements. He is not responsible for the acts or declarations of other alleged participants until it is established beyond a reasonable doubt, first, that a conspiracy existed, and second, from evidence of his own acts and statements, that the defendant was one of its members.

On the other hand, if and when it does appear beyond a reasonable doubt from the evidence in the case that a conspiracy did exist as charged, and that the defendant under consideration was one of its members, then the statements and acts knowingly made and done during such conspiracy and in furtherance of its objects, by any other proven member of the conspiracy, may be considered by the jury as evidence against the defendant under consideration even though he was not present to hear the statement made or see the act done.

This is true because, as stated earlier, a conspiracy is a kind of "partnership" so that under the law each member is an agent or partner of every other member, and each member is bound by or responsible for the acts and statements of every other member made in pursuance of their unlawful scheme.

As I instructed you, proof of conspiracy requires proof that the plan of the conspirators had an unlawful purpose or object. I instruct you that both of the purposes alleged in the indictment, that is, theft of goods from interstate commerce and receipt of such stolen goods, are unlawful under federal law. It is not necessary that the defendants know that the relevant goods have traveled in interstate commerce, nor is it required that the goods received be actually stolen, so long as the conspirators believed them to be stolen. If the proof establishes beyond a reasonable doubt that a particular defendant joined a plan to steal or receive goods he believed to be stolen, and the goods in fact were valued at more than $100.00 and were part of an interstate shipment, then that defendant would be guilty. If, however, the evidence fails to establish this as to a particular defendant, then that defendant would not be guilty.

On the question of interstate shipment, I charge you that a shipment from one state to another remains an interstate shipment in the destination state until it arrives at its final destination and is there delivered. Delays en route do not remove shipments from interstate commerce so long as the goods have not reached their final destination.

In this case, the indictment charges that the Defendants conspired to steal goods worth more than $100.00 from an interstate or foreign shipment of goods, and to receive and possess such stolen goods. It is charged, in other words, that the defendants conspired to commit two separate crimes.

I instruct you that it is not necessary for the Government to prove that the Defendant under consideration willfully conspired to commit both of these substantive offenses. It would be sufficient if the Government proves, beyond a reasonable doubt, that the defendant willfully conspired with someone to commit either one of the charged crimes; but, in that event, to return a verdict of guilty, you must unanimously agree upon which of the two offenses the Defendant conspired to commit. If you cannot agree in that manner on either purpose, you must find the Defendant not guilty.

You will note that the indictment charges that the offenses was committed "on or about" a certain date. The Government does not have to prove with certainty the exact date of the alleged offense. It is sufficient if the Government proves beyond a reasonable doubt that the offense was committed on a date reasonably near the date alleged.

The word "knowingly", as that term has been used from time to time in these instructions, means that the act was done voluntarily and intentionally and not because of mistake or accident.

The word "willfully" as that term has been used from time to time in these instructions, means that the act was committed voluntarily and purposely, with the specific intent to do something the law forbids; that is with bad purpose either to disobey or disregard the law.

The case of each Defendant and the evidence pertaining to him should be considered separately and individually. The fact that you may find any one of the Defendants guilty or not guilty should not affect your verdict as to any other Defendant.

I caution you, members of the Jury, that you are here to determine from the evidence in this case whether the Defendant is guilty or not guilty. The Defendant is on trial only for the specific offense alleged in the indictment.

Also, the question of punishment should never be considered by the jury in any way in deciding the case. If the Defendant is convicted the matter of punishment is for the Judge to determine.

Any verdict you reach in the jury room, whether guilty or not guilty, must be unanimous. In other words, to return a verdict you must all agree. Your deliberations will be secret; you will never have to explain your verdict to anyone.

It is your duty as jurors to discuss the case with one another in an effort to reach agreement if you can do so. Each of you must decide the case for yourself, but only after full consideration of the evidence with the other members of the jury. While you are discussing the case, do not hesitate to re-examine your own opinion and change your mind if you become convinced that you were wrong. But do not give up your honest beliefs solely because the others think differently or merely to get the case over with.

Remember that in a very real way, you are judges — judges of the facts. Your only interest is to seek the truth from the evidence in the case.

When you go to the jury room you should first select one of your members to act as your foreperson. The foreperson will preside over your deliberations and will speak for you here in court.

A form of verdict has been prepared for your convenience.

You will take the verdict form to the jury room and when you have reached unanimous agreement you will have your foreperson fill in the verdict form, date and sign it, and then return to the courtroom.

If you should desire to communicate with me at any time, please write down your message or question and pass the note to the marshal who will bring it to my attention. I will then respond as promptly as possible, either in writing or by having you returned to the courtroom so that I can address you orally. I caution you, however, with regard to any message or question you might send, that you should not tell me your numerical division at the time.

APPENDIX 1

COURT INTERPRETER ETHICS AND PROTOCOL

Code of Professional Responsibility

Certified court interpreters are highly skilled professionals who fulfill an essential role in the administration of justice and in the protection of the 4th and 6th Amendment rights for non-English speaking defendants. In their capacity as officers of the court, court interpreters are bound to a professional code of ethics. The Federal Court Interpreters Advisory Board developed a Code of Ethics and Professional Responsibility for all federal court interpreters. The Board adopted the following Canons:

Canon 1 Official court interpreters act strictly in the interest of the court they serve.

Canon 2 Official court interpreters reflect proper court decorum and act with dignity and respect to the officials and staff of the court.

Canon 3 Official interpreters avoid professional or personal conduct which could discredit the court.

Canon 4 Official court interpreters, except upon court order, shall not disclose any information of a confidential nature about court cases obtained while performing interpreting duties.

Canon 5 Official court interpreters respect the restraints imposed by the need for confidentiality and secrecy as protected under applicable federal and state law. Interpreters shall disclose to the court, and to the parties in a case, any prior involvement with that case, or private involvement with the parties or others significantly involved in the case.

Canon 6 Official court interpreters undertake to inform the court of any impediment in the observance of this Code or of any effort by another to cause this Code to be violated.

Canon 7 Official court interpreters work unobtrusively with full awareness of the nature of the proceedings.

Canon 8 Official court interpreters fulfill a special duty to interpret accurately and faithfully without indicating any personal bias, avoiding even the appearance of partiality.

Canon 9 Official court interpreters maintain impartiality by avoiding undue contact with witnesses, attorneys, defendants and their families, and any contact with jurors. This should not limit, however, those appropriate contacts necessary to prepare adequately for their assignment.

Canon 10 Official court interpreters refrain from giving advice of any kind to any party or individual and from expressing personal opinion in a matter before the court.

Canon 11 Official court interpreters perform to the best of their ability to assure due process for the parties; they accurately state their professional qualifications and refuse any assignment for which they are not qualified or under conditions which substantially impair their effectiveness. They preserve the level of language used, and the ambiguities and nuances of the speaker, without any editing. Implicit in the knowledge of their limitations is the duty to correct any error of interpretation, and demonstrate their professionalism by requesting clarification of ambiguous statements or unfamiliar vocabulary and to analyze objectively any challenge to their performance. Interpreters have the duty to call to the attention of the court any factors or conditions which adversely affect their ability to perform adequately.

Canon 12 Official court interpreters accept no remuneration, gifts, gratuities, or valuable consideration in excess of their authorized compensation in the performance of their official interpreting duties. Additionally, they avoid conflict of interest or even the appearance thereof.

Canon 13 Official court interpreters support other official court interpreters by sharing knowledge and expertise with them to the extent practicable in the interests of the court, and by never taking advantage of knowledge obtained in the performance of official duties, or by their access to court records, facilities, or privileges, for their own or another's personal gain.

Canon 14 Official court interpreters of the United States Courts willingly accept and agree to be bound by this code, and understand that appropriate sanctions may be imposed by the court for willful violation.

This interpreter ethics code is part of a proposed interpreters manual to be issued by the Administrative Office, yet to receive final approval.

Source: Administrative Office of the United States Courts, 1991.

APPENDIX 2

PROFESSIONAL RESPONSIBILITY AND ETHICS FOR COURT INTERPRETERS

Ethics And Practice

I. Professional Ethics

A) Accuracy

The court interpreter should always thoroughly and exactly interpret what is said, omitting nothing and stating precisely what has been said, given the exigencies of grammar and syntax in both languages. This complete accuracy applies to all modes of interpreting: simultaneous, consecutive and summary.

B) Confidentiality

The interpreter must protect the confidentiality of all knowledge gained during the course of his/her duties, as he/she is the verbal link between the client and attorney during legal proceedings. Attorney-client privilege pertains to documents, police records, medical files, etc. Consequently, he/she must remember that he/she has an absolute responsibility to keep all oral and written information gained completely confidential. He/She should also not derive personal profit or advantage from any confidential information acquired while acting in a professional capacity.

C) Impartiality

The interpreter should maintain an impartial attitude with defendants, witnesses, attorneys and families. He/She should neither conceive of him/herself nor permit him/herself to be used as an investigator for any party to a case. The interpreter should not "take sides" or consider him/herself aligned with the prosecution or defense.

D) Proficiency

An interpreter should only provide his/her professional services in a matter in which he/she is confident of his/her capacity to perform accurately. He/She should feel no compunction about withdrawing from a case in which he/she feels will be unable to function effectively, due to a lack of proficiency, preparation of difficulty in understanding a witness or defendant. The interpreter should continually improve his/her language skills and increase his/her knowledge of vocabulary in the various areas which might be encountered in court interpreting.

II. Professional Practice

A) Modes of Interpreting

1. Simultaneous Interpretation

This mode of interpreting requires giving an exact rendition of everything being said at the same time it is being spoken in the original language. This is the mode used when relating proceedings to defendants. The interpreter should speak in a soft voice, for the benefit of the defendant only, and should neither summarize, simplify nor explain the proceedings.

2. Consecutive Interpretation

This mode of interpreting is utilized with witnesses and in any situation in which the speaker must first finish his/her statement before the interpreter begins to speak. When interpreting in this mode at the witness stand, the interpreter should make every attempt to permit the speaker to finish his/her statement. To this end, he/she may wish to take notes. The interpreter should interrupt a speaker only if it becomes absolutely necessary to do so in a very lengthy statement. If there is a word or phrase which the interpreter does not hear or understand, he/she should not invent a translation; rather he/she should ask the judge for permission to request that the witness repeat or rephrase the statement and then continue with the interpretation.

3. Summary Interpretation

The summary mode, which is the least preferred technique for legal proceedings, is an accurate simultaneous resume of fragmented statements that may occur in three-way exchanges between the court and attorneys. It differs from the simultaneous mode in that it is not a verbatim rendition of all that is being said because the interpreter is relating the statements of persons who may be interrupting one another. Thus, a mere jumble of words, which may confuse the defendant because he/she cannot identify the speaker, is avoided.

B) First Person

The court interpreter should always utilize the first person singular when interpreting for a witness or in any situation in which a conversation between two or more parties occurs in the courtroom or similar setting.

C) Awareness

The court interpreter should be attentive to all that is taking place around him/her, given the rapidity with which events take place in a courtroom.

D) Low Profile

The interpreter must maintain a low profile, remembering that he/she is not testifying but merely communicating the testimony of another. He/She should not draw attention to his/her interpretation, since the judge and jury must focus only upon the individual requiring interpretation. The interpreter should control overt expressions of opinion, such as surprise, sympathy or disgust, while interpreting for defendants or witnesses. He/She should position himself in such a way so as not to obscure the view of the litigants, judge and jury from the individual who is testifying. The overall aim of the interpreter should be to assure a natural atmosphere in the courtroom such as there would be if no language barrier existed.

E) Language Level

The interpreter should utilize the same level of language used by the speaker. This means that he/she will interpret colloquial, slang, obscene or crude language, as well as sophisticated and erudite language, in accordance with the exact usage of the speaker. It is not the interpreter's task to tone down, improve or edit phrases.

Further, the interpreter should not assume that it is his/her duty to simplify statements for a witness or defendant whom he/she believes cannot understand the speaker's statements. The person requiring an interpreter should request an explanation or simplification, if necessary.

F) Characterizing Testimony

An interpreter should never characterize nor give a gratuitous explanation of testimony. The court or attorney will request clarification from the speaker, if necessary. Except in the case of certain languages in which a gesture or grimace has a particular significance, the interpreter should not offer an explanation or repeat a witness's gesture or grimace.

G) Questions Answered with Questions

The interpreter must translate the exact response of the witness or speaker even if the answer to a question is another question due to the witness not hearing or understanding the initial question.

H) Interpreting Mixed-Language Responses

If a witness testifying in a foreign language suddenly interjects a complete English response, the interpreter should not ask the witness to speak in his/her native language. He/She should stand back so that all parties are aware of the English response and await the court's direction.

I) Conversations During Witness's Testimony

The interpreter should not engage in colloquy with the witness testifying under oath. There should be a simple exchange of questions and answers between the questioner and the witness as if there were no language barrier. During pauses in testimony, such as side-bar conferences or recesses, the interpreter should not converse with the witness.

Source: National Association of Judiciary Interpreters and Translators.

APPENDIX 3

PROFESSIONAL INTERPRETER AND TRANSLATOR ORGANIZATIONS

In the United States, more and more attention is being paid to the need for translators and interpreters, as documented in journals, magazines, and newspapers such as *Hispania*, *Time*, the *Wall Street Journal*, and the *New York Daily News*. Another manifestation of the increase in recognition for these professions is evidenced by the growth of a number of professional associations devoted to translators and interpreters.

Major organizations of foreign language teachers in the United States, such as the American Association of Teachers of Spanish and Portuguese (AATSP), regularly offer one or two sessions and workshops on interpretation and translation at their annual meetings. According to Deanna L. Hammond, translator and interpreter organizations fill a special need for foreign language teachers such as those that comprise the AATSP membership because: 1) the number of introductory, certificate and degree programs in translation and interpretation being offered by universities in the United States is increasing steadily; 2) many professors find that they must provide students with additional information regarding new opportunities in interpretation and translation, as well as apprise them of the status of the profession; 3) many foreign language teachers are interested in part-time, if not full-time work as interpreters and translators, upon retirement from the teaching profession; and 4) conferences sponsored by translator and interpreter associations hold in-depth sessions on the numerous aspects of the profession.[6]

There are numerous local translator and interpreter groups and chapters around the world. The following list offers a selection of several of the largest groups in the United States and abroad:

AMERICAN ASSOCIATION OF LANGUAGE SPECIALISTS (TAALS)
Suite 9
1000 Connecticut Avenue, NW
Washington, D.C. 20036

AMERICAN LITERARY TRANSLATORS ASSOCIATION (ALTA)
University of Texas at Dallas
Box 830688
Richardson, Texas 75083-0688

AMERICAN SOCIETY OF INTERPRETERS (ASI)
P.O. Box 5558
Washington, D.C. 20016

AMERICAN TRANSLATORS ASSOCIATION (ATA)
109 Croton Avenue
Ossining, NY 10562

ASSOCIATION INTERNATIONALE DES INTERPRETES DE CONFERENCE (AIIC)
10 Avenue de Sécheron CH-1202
Switzerland

ASSOCIATION INTERNATIONALE DES TRADUCTEURS DE CONFERENCE
Palais Wilson
Case Postale 31
CH-1211 Geneva 14
Switzerland

ASOCIACION PROFESIONAL DE TRADUCTORES E INTERPRETES (APETI)

Biblioteca Nacional
Paseo de Calvo Sotelo 20
Madrid
Spain

CONFERENCE OF UNIVERSITY STUDIES FOR THE TRAINING OF TRANSLATORS AND INTERPRETERS (CUITI)

Antwerp University
Institute for Translators and Interpreters
Schilderstraat 41
B-2000 Antwerp
Belgium

NATIONAL ASSOCIATION OF JUDICIARY INTERPRETERS AND TRANSLATORS (NAJIT) [formerly C.I.T.A.]

Janice Palma, President
Calle 27, Pt278
Urb. Ponce de León
Guaynabo, Puerto Rico 00657
and
Sara García-Rangel
Treasurer
99 Harrison Avenue
Montclair, New Jersey 07042-2018

APPENDIX 4

SELECTED PERIODICALS

Numerous specialized journals and newsletters discuss theoretical and practical issues of interest to professional translators and interpreters. Several academic journals which have traditionally been devoted to linguistics, language pedagogy, and literature, have begun to publish articles devoted to translation and interpretation. The following entries combine both types of periodicals. I have listed the principal journals, however, the *MLA Directory of Periodicals* and *Ulrich's International Periodicals Directory* should be consulted for additional references.

ATA CHRONICLE

Official Journal of the American Translators Association
109 Croton Avenue 1
Ossining, NY 10562

ATArishi

Newsletter of the Japanese Language Division of the American Translators Association
Japanese Language Services
186 Lincoln Street
Boston, MA 02111

BABEL

International Journal of Translation.
Official Organ of the International Federation of Translators (FIT)
Heiveldstraat 245, B-9110
Gent, Belgium

BILINGUAL REVIEW/REVISTA BILINGÜE

Hispanic Research Center
Arizona State University
Tempe, Arizona 85287

CALIDOSCOPIO

Official Journal of the Argentine Translators
and Interpreters Association (AATI)
Victor Magno Boyé
Lavalle 1569, 8vo, of. 819
Buenos Aires, Argentina

CAPITAL TRANSLATOR

Newsletter of the National Capital (Washington, DC)
Chapter of the American Translators Association
1309 N. Danville Street
Arlington, VA 22201

CIRCUIT

Journal of the Société des Traducteurs de Québec
1010 rue Sainte-Catherine Ouest
Bureau 540
Montréal (Québec)
H3B 1G4 Canada

CUADERNOS DE TRADUCCION E INTERPRETACION

Escuela Universitaria de Traductores e Intérpretes
Universidad Autónoma de Barcelona
08193 Barcelona, Spain

FOREIGN LANGUAGE ANNALS
The American Council on the Teaching of Foreign Languages (ACTFL)
P.O. Box 408
Hastings on Hudson
NY 10706

HISPANIA
Journal of the American Association of Teachers of Spanish & Portuguese (AATSP)
Department of Spanish and Portuguese
University of Southern California
Los Angeles, CA 90089-0358

JEROME QUARTERLY
National Resource Center for Translation & Interpretation
Georgetown University
225 Intercultural Center
Washington, D.C. 20057

LANGUAGE INTERNATIONAL
Geoffrey Kingscott
5 East Circus St.
Nottingham NGI 5 AH
Great Britain

LANGAGE ET L'HOMME
Institut Libre Marie Haps
rue d'Arlon 11
1040 Bruxelles, Belgium

LANGUAGE PROBLEMS AND LANGUAGE PLANNING
University of Texas Press
P.O. Box 7819
Austin, Texas 78713

META
Presses de l'Université de Montréal
Department de Linguistique et Philologie
Université de Montréal
C.P. 6128, Succursale "A"
Montréal (Québec)
H3C 3J7 Canada

MODERN LANGUAGE JOURNAL
University of Wisconsin Press
114 North Murray St.
Madison, WI 53715

MULTILINGUA
Journal of Cross-Cultural and Interlanguage Communication
Walter de Gruyter, Inc.
200 San Mill River Rd.
Hawthorn, New York 10532

PARALLELES. "Cahiers"
Ecole de Traduction et d'Interprétation
Université de Genève
19 Place des Augustins
CH-1211 Genève 4
Switzerland

POLYLINGUA
Department of Humanities
Michigan Technological University
Houghton, MI 49931

TRADUIRE
Official Journal of the French Translators Association (SFT)
BP 295/09
75425 Paris Cedex 09
France

APPENDIX 5

REFERENCE TOOLS: SELECTED LIST OF DICTIONARIES AND GLOSSARIES

The basic tools of the interpreter include fluency in two or more languages, knowledge of the source and target language cultures, the ability to interpret in the consecutive and simultaneous modes and to sight translate, and an extensive vocabulary in the source and target languages. Interpreters and translators alike generally rely on reference tools such as dictionaries, glossaries, terminological data banks or computerized dictionaries, and consultation with colleagues and other language professionals. In court, the interpreter's linguistic proficiency must include jargon, slang, regionalisms and colloquial usage as well as technical language and the formal language of legal codes.

The following list of monolingual and bilingual dictionaries and glossaries is intended to serve as a guide to some of the basic references available to court interpreters. The English references (general and legal) will be useful to interpreters of all languages, whereas the bilingual references target Spanish/English court interpreters and legal translators.

ENGLISH GENERAL REFERENCES

American Heritage Dictionary of the English Language. Boston: Houghton Mifflin, 1981.

Random House College Dictionary. Revised ed. New York: Random House, 1982.

Roget's Thesaurus of Words and Phrases. New edition revised and enlarged by Samuel Romilly Roget. New York: Perigee Books, 1989.

Roget's International Thesaurus. 4th ed. Revised by Robert L. Chapman. New York: Harper & Row, 1977.

Webster's New World Dictionary of American English. Third College Edition. Cleveland & New York: Simon & Schuster, 1988.

Webster's Third New International Dictionary. Philip Babcock Gove, Editor in chief. Springfield, Mass: Merriam-Webster, Inc., 1981.

LEGAL REFERENCES (ENGLISH)

Adams, Dorothy. *Legal Terminology and Transcription*. New York: Gregg Division, McGraw-Hill, 1981.

Black, Henry Campbell. *Black's Law Dictionary*. 6th ed. St. Paul, Minnesota: West Publishing Co., 1990.

Brown, Gordon W. *Legal Terminology*. Englewood Cliffs, New Jersey: Prentice Hall, 1990.

D'Auria, Michael M. *Legal Terms and Concepts in Criminal Justice*. Wayne, New Jersey: Avery Publishing Group, 1983.

Garrett, David K. *Legal Terminology Handbook*. Eau Claire, Wisconsin: Professional Educational Systems, 1986.

Gifis, Steven H. *Dictionary of Legal Terms*. Woodbury, New York: Barron's Educational Series, Inc., 1983.

Knapp, Mary H. *Legal Terminology*. Skokie, Illinois: Stenograph, 1987.

Oran, Daniel. *Oran's Dictionary of the Law*. St. Paul, Minnesota: West, 1983.

Shapiro, Irving. *Dictionary of Legal Terms*. New York: Gould Publications, 1969.

SPANISH
GENERAL REFERENCES

Casares y Sánchez, Julio. *Diccionario ideológico de la lengua española: desde la idea a la palabra, desde la palabra a la idea.* 2a ed. Barcelona: Gustavo Gili, 1973.

Gili Gaya, Samuel, ed. *Vox compacto diccionario de la lengua Española.* 1a ed. Barcelona: Bibliograf, 1982.

Larousse, Pierre. *Pequeño Larousse ilustrado.* Paris: Ediciones Larousse, 1978.

García-Pelayo y Gross, Ramón. *Pequeño Larousse en color.* Paris: Librairie Larousse, 1972.

Moliner, María. *Diccionario del uso del español.* 2 vols. Madrid: Gredos, 1979.

Real Academia Española, *Diccionario de la lengua española.* Madrid: Talleres Espasa-Calpe, 1984.

Roluy Poudevila, Antonio. *Diccionario Porrúa de la lengua española.* Mexico: Editorial Porrúa, 1976.

Seco, Manuel. *Diccionario de dudas y dificultades de la lengua española.* Madrid: Aguilar, 1973.

LEGAL REFERENCES (SPANISH)

Pina, Rafael de and Rafael de Pina Vara. *Diccionario de derecho.* 15th ed. Mexico: Editorial Porrúa, S.A., 1988.

Ribo Durán, Luis M. *Diccionario de derecho.* Barcelona: Bosch, 1987.

Palomar de Miguel, Juan, et al. *Diccionario para juristas.* 1a ed. Mexico: Mayo Ediciones, 1981.

Ramírez Gronda, Juan D. *Diccionario jurídico.* Buenos Aires: Editorial Claridad, 1988.

Rivera García, Ignacio. *Diccionario de términos jurídicos.* Oxford, New Hampshire: Equity Publishing Co., 1985.

GENERAL REFERENCES (ENGLISH-SPANISH)

Cuyas, Arturo. *Appleton's New Cuyas English-Spanish and Spanish-English Dictionary*. New York: Appleton-Century-Crofts, 1972.

Cassell's Spanish-English, English-Spanish Dictionary. London: Cassell New York, 1978.

Diccionario Inglés for Spanish-Speakers. Boston: Houghton Mifflin, 1982.

Gómez de Parada, Alejandro. *Diccionario Porrúa Inglés-Español/Español-Inglés*. 2a ed. Mexico: Editorial Porrúa, 1974.

Merino, José. *Diccionario de dudas inglés-español*. Madrid: Paraninfo, 1971.

Simon & Schuster's International Dictionary. Spanish-English/English-Spanish. Tana de Gamez, ed. New York: Simon & Schuster Publishers. 1973.

University of Chicago Spanish Dictionary. Revised by D. Lincoln Canfield. New York: Pocket Books, 1975.

Vox Modern Spanish/English Dictionary. Lincolnwood, Illinois: National Textbook Company, 1984.

LEGAL REFERENCES (ENGLISH-SPANISH)

Benmaman, Virginia, Norma Connolly, and Scott Loos. *Bilingual Dictionary of Criminal Justice Terms (English/Spanish)*. New York: Gould, 1991.

Festinger, Nancy. *Key Verbs for Court Interpreters*. New York: Court Interpreters and Translators Association, 1986.

Lacasa Navarro, Ramón & Díaz de Bustamante. *Diccionario de derecho, economía y política*. 2a ed. Madrid: EDERSA, 1986.

Meilij de Romero, Gabriela. *Vocabulario legal y empresario (Legal and Business Terms)*. Buenos Aires: Ediciones Depalma, 1987.

Mikkelson, Holly. *The Interpreter's Companion*. Spreckels, CA: Acebo, 1991.

Palma, Janis. *Glossary of Federal Court Terminology*. New York: Court Interpreters and Translators Association, 1986.

Introduction to Judiciary Interpreting. New York: Court Interpreters and Translators Association, 1987.

Robb, Louis A. *Diccionario de términos legales*. Mexico: Editorial Limusa, 1982.

Trabing, Eta M. *Manual for Judiciary Interpreters (Spanish-English)*. Houston, Texas: Agri-Search International, 1979.

Vanson, George N. and Marilyn Frankenthaler. *Spanish-English Legal Terminology*. Cincinnati: South-Western Publishing Co., 1982.

REGIONAL VARIETIES AND SLANG

Alfaro, Ricardo J. *Diccionario de anglicismos*. Madrid: Gredos, 1970.

Carbajo, Antonio. *Cuban Slang. Tesauro de Cubanismos*. Miami Springs, Florida: Language Research Press, 1968.

del Rosario, Rubén. *Vocabulario puertorriqueño*. Sharon, Connecticut: Troutman Press, 1965.

Fuentes, Dagoberto, and José A. López. *Barrio Language Dictionary, First Dictionary of Caló*. Los Angeles: Southland Press, 1974.

Galván, Roberto A., and Richard V. Teschner. *El Diccionario del Español Chicano*. Lincolnwood, Illinois: National Textbook Company, 1991.

Llorens, Washington. *El habla popular de Puerto Rico*. Río Piedras, Puerto Rico: Editorial Edit, Inc., 1971.

Morinigo, Marcos Augusto. *Diccionario de americanismos*. Barcelona: Muchnik, 1985.

Pierson, Raymond H. *Guide to Spanish Idioms. Guía de modismos españoles*. Skokie, Illinois: National Textbook Company, 1980.

Sanchez-Boudy, José. *Diccionarios de cubanismos más usuales*. Miami: Ediciones Universal, 1990.

Santamaría, Francisco Javier. *Diccionario de mexicanismos*. Mexico: Porrúa, 1974.

Vásquez, Librado Keno and María Enriqueta Vásquez. *Regional Dictionary of Chicano Slang*. Austin: Jenkins Publishing Co., The Pemberton Press, 1975.

TECHNICAL AND SPECIALIZED REFERENCES (ENGLISH-SPANISH)

Bermúdez Paredes, Antonio. *Diccionario inglés-español de finanzas y contabilidad.* Madrid: Ornigraf, 1977.

Blanes Prieto, Joaquín. *Diccionario de términos contables inglés-español/español-inglés.* 14th ed. México: Compañía Editorial Continental, 1984.

Collazo, Javier C. *Encyclopedic Dictionary of Technical Terms. Diccionario enciclopédico de términos técnicos.* 3 vols. New York: McGraw Hill, 1980.

Gaballi, P. Prat. *Diccionario de términos comerciales.* Barcelona: Editorial Hispano Europea, 1963.

Leal y Leal, Luis. *Diccionario naval.* Madrid: Editorial Naval, Ministerio de Marina, 1980.

Mascaró y Porcar, José M., ed. *Diccionario médico.* 2a ed. Barcelona: Salvat, 1974.

Robb, Louis A. *Diccionario para ingenieros.* México: Editorial Continental, 1983.

Ruz Torres, Francisco. *Diccionario inglés-español de medicina.* 1a ed. Madrid: Alhambra, 1957.

Taylor, Norman Burke, ed. *Stedman's Medical Dictionary.* Baltimore: The Williams & Wilkins Co., 1946.

Villate, José T. *Dictionary of Environmental Engineering and Related Sciences.* Miami: Ediciones Universal, 1979.

APPENDIX 6

PUBLIC LAW 95-539 (OCTOBER 28, 1978) AMENDED PUBLIC LAW 100-702 (NOVEMBER 19, 1988)

1827. Interpreters in courts of the United States

(a) The Director of the Administrative Office of the United States Courts shall establish a program to facilitate the use of certified and otherwise qualified interpreters in judicial proceedings instituted by the United States.

(b)(1) The Director shall prescribe, determine, and certify the qualifications of persons who may serve as certified interpreters, when the Director considers certification of interpreters to be merited, for the hearing impaired (whether or not also speech impaired) and persons who speak only or primarily a language other than the English language, in judicial proceedings instituted by the United States. The Director may certify interpreters for any language if the Director determines that there is a need for certified interpreters in that language. Upon the request of the Judicial Conference of the United States for certified interpreters in a language, the Director shall certify interpreters in that language. Upon such a request from the judicial council of a circuit and the approval of the Judicial Conference, the Director shall certify interpreters for that circuit in the language requested. The judicial council of a circuit shall identify and evaluate the needs of the districts within a circuit. The Director shall certify interpreters based on the results of criterion-referenced performance examinations. The Director shall issue regulations to carry out this paragraph within 1 year after the date of the enactment of the Judicial Improvements and Access to Justice Act.

(2) Only in a case in which no certified interpreter is reasonably available as provided in subsection (d) of this section, including a case in which certification of interpreters is not provided under paragraph (1) in a particular language, may the services of otherwise qualified interpreters be used. The Director shall provide guidelines to the courts for the selection of otherwise qualified interpreters, in order to ensure that the highest standards of accuracy are maintained in all judicial proceedings subject to the provisions of this chapter.

(3) The Director shall maintain a current master list of all certified interpreters and otherwise qualified interpreters and shall report periodically on the use and performance of both certified and otherwise qualified interpreters in judicial proceedings instituted by the United States and on the languages for which interpreters have been certified. The Director shall prescribe, subject to periodic review, a schedule of reasonable fees for services rendered by interpreters, certified or otherwise, used in proceedings instituted by the United States, and in so doing so shall consider the prevailing rate of compensation for comparable service in other governmental entities.

(c)(1) Each United States district court shall maintain on file in the office of the clerk, and each United States attorney shall maintain on file, a list of all persons who have been certified as interpreters by the Director in accordance with subsection (b) of this section. The clerk shall make the list of certified interpreters for judicial proceeding available upon request.

(2) The clerk of the court, or other court employee designated by the chief judge, shall be responsible for securing the services of certified interpreters and otherwise qualified interpreters required for proceedings initiated by the Untied States, except that the United States attorney is responsible for securing the services of such interpreters for governmental witnesses.

(d)(1) The presiding judicial officer, with the assistance of the Director of the Administrative Office of the United States Courts, shall utilize the services of the most available certified interpreters, or when no certified interpreter is reasonably available, as determined by the presiding judicial officer, the services of an otherwise qualified interpreter, in judicial proceedings instituted by the United States, if the presiding judicial officer determines on such officer's own motion or on the motion of a party that such party (including a defendant in a criminal case), or a witness who may present testimony in such judicial proceedings__

(A) speaks only or primarily a language other than the English language; or
(B) suffers from a hearing impairment (whether or not suffering also from a speech impairment)

so as to inhibit such a party's comprehension of the proceedings or communication with counsel or the presiding judicial officer, or so as to inhibit such witness' comprehension of questions and the presentation of such testimony.

(2) Upon the motion of a party, the presiding judicial officer shall determine whether to require the electronic sound recording of a judicial proceeding in which an interpreter is used under this section. In making this determination, the presiding judicial officer shall consider, among other things, the qualifications of the interpreter and prior experience in interpretation of court proceedings; whether the language to be interpreted is not one of the languages for which the Director has certified interpreters, and the complexity or length of the proceeding. In a grand jury proceeding, upon the motion of the accused, the presiding judicial

officer shall require the electronic sound recording of the portion of the proceeding in which an interpreter is used.

(e)(1) If any interpreter is unable to communicate effectively with the presiding judicial officer, the United States attorney, a party (including a defendant in a criminal case), or a witness, the presiding judicial officer shall dismiss such interpreter and obtain the services of another interpreter in accordance with this section.

(2) In any judicial proceedings instituted by the Untied States, if the presiding judicial officer does not appoint an interpreter under subsection (d) of this section, an individual requiring the services of an interpreter may seek assistance of the clerk of court or the Director of the Administrative Office of the United States Courts in obtaining the assistance of a certified interpreter.

(f)(1) Any individual other than a witness who is entitled to interpretation under subsection (d) of this section may waive such interpretation in whole or in part. Such a waiver shall be effective only if approved by the presiding judicial officer and made expressly by such individual on the record after opportunity to consult with counsel and after the presiding judicial officer has explained to such individual utilizing the services of the most available certified interpreter, or when no certified interpreter is reasonably available, as determined by the presiding judicial officer, the services of an otherwise competent interpreter, the nature and effect of the waiver.

(2) An individual who waives under paragraph (1) of this subsection the right to an interpreter may utilize the services of a noncertified interpreter of such individual's choice whose fees, expenses, and costs shall be paid in the manner provided for the payment of such fees, expenses, and costs of an interpreter appointed under subsection (d) of this section.

(g)(1) There are authorized to be appropriated to the Federal judiciary, and to be paid by the Director of the Administrative Office of the United States Courts, such sums as may be necessary to establish a program to facilitate the use of certified and otherwise qualified interpreters, and otherwise fulfill the provisions of this section and the Judicial Improvements and Access to Justice Act, except as provided in paragraph (3).

(2) Implementation of the provisions of this section is contingent upon the availability of appropriated funds to carry out the purposes of this section.

(3) Such salaries, fees, expenses, and costs that are incurred with respect to Government witnesses (including for grand jury proceedings) shall, unless direction is made under paragraph (4), be paid by the Attorney General from sums appropriated to the Department of Justice.

(4) Upon the request of any person in any action for which interpreting services established pursuant to subsection (d) are not otherwise provided, the clerk of the court, or other court employee designated by the chief judge, upon the request of the presiding judicial officer, shall, where possible, make such services available to that person on a cost-reimbursable basis, but the judicial officer may also require the prepayment of the estimated expenses of providing such services.

(5) Any moneys collected under this subsection may be used to reimburse the appropriations obligated and disbursed in payment for such services.

(h) The presiding judicial officer shall approve the compensation and expenses payable to interpreters, pursuant to the schedule of fees prescribed by the Director under subsection (b)(3).

(i) The term "presiding judicial officer" as used in this section refers to any judge of a United States district court, including a bankruptcy judge, a United States magistrate, and in the case of grand jury proceedings conducted under the auspices of the United States attorney, a United States attorney.

(j) The term "judicial proceedings instituted by the United States" as used in this section refers to all proceedings, whether criminal or civil, including pretrial and grand jury proceedings (as well as proceedings upon a petition for a writ of habeas corpus initiated in the name of the United States by a relator) conducted in, or pursuant to the lawful authority and jurisdiction of a United states district court. The term "United States district court" as used in this subsection includes any court which is created by an Act of Congress in a territory and is invested with any jurisdiction of a district court established by chapter 5 of this title.

(k) The interpretation provided by certified or otherwise qualified interpreters pursuant to this section shall be in the simultaneous mode for any party to a judicial proceeding instituted by the United States and in the consecutive mode for witnesses, except that the presiding judicial officer, sua sponte or on the motion of a party, may authorize a simultaneous, or consecutive interpretation when such officer determines after a hearing on the record that such interpretation will aid in the efficient administration of justice. The presiding judicial officer, on such officer's motion or on the motion of a party, may order that special interpretation services as authorized in section 1828 of this title by provided if such officer determines that the provision of such services will aid in the efficient administration of justice.

(Added Pub.L. 95-539, 2(a), Oct. 28, 1978, 92 Stat. 2040, and amended Pub.L. 100-702, Title VII, 702-710. Nov. 19, 1988, 102 Stat. 4654-4657.)

BILINGUAL GLOSSARY OF LEGAL TERMS

This English/Spanish glossary is intended to introduce aspiring court interpreters to the basic legal vocabulary used in court proceedings. It is a compilation of terms and phrases frequently used in proceedings in U.S. courtrooms, and represents the consensus of several federally certified court interpreters.[a] This glossary is offered as an introduction to the language of the court and is not intended as an exhaustive list of legal terms. Foreign language court interpreters must consult bilingual as well as monolingual dictionaries, legal references, glossaries and dictionaries of court terminology, and other reference sources (see Appendix 5).

ENGLISH	SPANISH
abduction	rapto
abetment	complicidad, incitación
abjure (v.)	abjurar, renunciar
accesory before the fact	cómplice instigador
accesory after the fact	cómplice encubridor
accomplice	cómplice
accused	acusado(a)
to bring an accusation against	presentar una acusación contra
acquit	absolver

acquittal	absolución, sentencia absolutoria
acquitted	absuelto
action	causa, pleito, acto, gestión, proceso, acción
adjourn	levantar o aplazar (una sesion)
advance payment	anticipo, pago por adelantado
affidavit	declaración jurada por escrito, "afidávit"
aforementioned	antedicho, precitado, susodicho, antes mencionado
aforethought	con premeditación
aid and abet	incitar y alentar
alibi	coartada
allegation	alegación, alegato
allege (v.)	alegar, afirmar
the alleged	el supuesto(a); el presunto(a)
alternate juror	jurado suplente
ambush (noun)	emboscada
answer (n.)	contestación a la demanda, defensa, réplica, respuesta
answer [a complaint] (v.)	contestar a una demanda (civil) contestar a una denuncia (penal)
appeal (n.)	apelación (fem.), recurso (m.)
appeal (v.)	apelar apelar de (la sentencia) apelar a (un tribunal)
appearance	comparecencia
appellant	apelante, recurrente
apellate court	tribunal de apelación
arraignment	instrucción de cargos, lectura de acusación, vista incoatoria
arrest	arresto, detención
arresting officer	agente que efectuó el arresto

as from	a partir de
as is	tal cual
as of	desde
as to	por lo que se refiere a, en cuanto a
assumed name	nombre ficticio
assigned counsel	abogado designado por el tribunal
assistant U.S. attorney	fiscal adjunto de los EE.UU.
attempt	intento
to attest; to certify	dar fe
attorney	abogado
bail	fianza
bail bond	bono de fianza
on bail	estar en libertad bajo fianza
to bail someone out	sacar (a alguien) en libertad bajo fianza
to jump bail	huir o fugar estando bajo fianza
bailiff	alguacil
bankrupt	quebrado(a)
bankrupcy	bancarrota; quiebra
being duly sworn	habiendo prestado el juramento de rigor
bench	tribunal; el juez
bench warrant	orden de arresto
beyond a reasonable doubt	sin que quepa una duda razonable; fuera de toda duda razonable
bond	fianza
corporate surety bond	fianza con garantía de fiador
cash bond	fianza de dinero efectivo
personal surety bond	fianza de palabra; caución de buena conducta
bondsman	fiador, agente de fianzas
breach of contract	incumplimiento de un contrato
breach of trust	abuso de confianza

bribe (n.)	soborno
brief (n.)	escrito, alegato, memorial, relación
bring a suit	demandar
burden of proof	la carga de la prueba; obligación de comprobar los cargos;
calendar	lista de casos, pleitos
capital punishment	pena de muerte
cartel	organización, cartel
case (noun)	caso
dismiss a case	desechar un caso
rest a case	terminar el alegato
settle a case	transar
state one's case	exponer los hechos
cash (n.)	efectivo
chairman of the board	presidente de la junta directiva
challenge for cause	recusación con causa
change of venue	cambio o traslado de jurisdicción
charges	imputaciones; cargos
charge (v.) [of a crime]	acusar [de un delito]
charge the jury	dar instrucciones al jurado
circumstantial evidence	prueba circunstancial
claim (v.)	reclamar, alegar
clerk of court	secretario(a) de actas del tribunal
closing argumensts	alegatos finales
code	código, clave
to come into force	entrar en vigor
commercial paper	documentos mercantiles; efectos de comercio
competent witness	testigo hábil
complaint	denuncia (penal); demanda, queja
contempt (of court)	desacato al tribunal

continuance	aplazamiento
contest (v.)	impugnar, disputar
contrite	arrepentido(a)
controlled substance	substancia regulada
consent (n.)	consentimiento
conspire	confabular; conspirar
conspiracy	confabulación; conspiración
convict (v.)	condenar
conviction	condena; fallo de culpabilidad
coroner	médico forense
corporation	sociedad anónima
costs and attorneys fees	costos y honorarios
counsel	abogado
count (n.)	cargo, acusación
counterfeit	falsificación
county	condado
court	tribunal, juzgado
courtroom	sala del tribunal
courthouse	el juzgado, palacio de justicia, edificio de los tribunales
cover-up	encubrimiento
crime	delito
criminal	delincuente
criminal law	derecho penal
criminal proceedings	causa penal
criminal record	antecedentes penales
cross-examination	contra-interrogatorio; repreguntas
damages	daños y perjuicios
death penalty	pena capital, pena de muerte

deed	escritura; hecho
default	incumplimiento
defendant	acusado(a)
defense	defensa
defense counsel	abogado defensor
defraud	defraudar, estafar
deliberations	deliberaciones
deny	negar; denegar
deposition	declaración jurada
detrimental	perjudicial
direct examination	examen o interrogatorio directo
disavow	repudiar
disclaim	negar
discovery	divulgación de pruebas; obtención de pruebas; exhibición
discovery order	orden de divulgación de pruebas
discretion	discreción
dismiss [charges]	sobreseer, desestimar, dar por terminado(a), declarar sin lugar
district attorney	fiscal estatal, fiscal de distrito
docket	lista de causas
docket number	número del acta, número de presentación
documentary proof	prueba documental, constancia
double-dealing	duplicidad; traicion
downpayment	pago inicial, cuota inicial, entrada
due process of law	debido y adecuado proceso legal
due proof	prueba debida
DUI	manejar (conducir) en estado de embriaguez
drop charges	retirar los cargos

Drug Enforcement Administration (DEA)	Agencia Contra las Drogas (DEA), Dirección Federal Antinarcóticos
drunkeness, to be drunk	ebriedad; estar ebrio, borracho
duress (under duress)	bajo coacción
to entrap	tender una trampa
entrapment	inducción al delito
equity	valor acumulado, patrimonio neto, plusvalía (Mex); capital
estoppel	impedimento
estreat the bond	revocar la fianza, cobrar la fianza
evidence	prueba
evidenciary hearing	audiencia probatoria
ex-convict	ex-presidiario, reo
executor	albacea
exemption	exención
exhibit	artículo de prueba, documento de prueba, prueba instrumental
expenses	gastos
expert witness	perito, testigo pericial
expert witness testimony	testimonio pericial
extenuating circumstances	circunstancias atenuantes
extradition	extradición
eye witness	testigo presencial, ocular
fact	hecho
facts in issue	hechos litigiosos
false arrest	arresto ilegal
false statements	declaraciones falsas
Federal Bureau of Investigations (FBI)	Buró Federal de Investigaciones (FBI)
fee	honorarios (pl.)

felony	delito mayor
file a motion	radicar un pedimento; presentar una petición
Fifth Amendment	la quinta enmienda constitucional
file (v.)	archivar, presentar, radicar
fine (n.)	multa
foreclosure	ejecución de hipoteca
forfeit (v.) (property)	perder un derecho (decomisar)
forge	falsificar
forgery	falsificación
foreman, foreperson	presidente del jurado
forthwith	inmediatamente
fraud	fraude (m.)
full pardon	perdón
false imprisonment	detención ilegal
forgiveness	indulto, perdón
good behavior	buena conducta
government witness	testigo de cargo
grand jury	gran jurado, jurado acusatorio jurado de acusación
graft	soborno, peculado
grand larceny	hurto mayor
grievance	agravio
grounds	causal (fem.); motivos
guilt	culpa
guilty verdict	veredicto o fallo de culpabilidad
at gunpoint	a punta de pistola encañonada
handwriting comparison	comparación grafológica
handwriting expert	perito grafólogo
harass	hostigar, acosar

hearing	audiencia, vista
hearsay evidence	prueba o evidencia por referencia, testimonio de oídas
hereafter	en lo sucesivo, en adelante, a continuación
herein	aquí, en este
hereinbelow	a continuación
hereby	por este medio, por el presente
hereunder	conforme a este documento
hereunto	aquí
herewith	adjunto, anexo, con el presente
hit and run	causar un accidente y fugarse
hitman	asesino profesional, sicario
hold court	sesionar (el tribunal), estar en sesión
hold for trial	prisión preventiva
hold in contempt	declarar en desacato
hold-up	salteo, asalto, atraco
homicide	homicidio (en sentido amplio)
justifiable homicide	inculpable
hostile witness	testigo hostil, desfavorable
hot tip	confidencia fidedigna, informe seguro
hung jury	jurado indeciso, en desacuerdo, sin veredicto
identification card	carnet o cédula de identidad
ill-gotten	mal adquirido, malhabido
impeach	desacreditar, impugnar, refutar, tachar
impounded	decomisado, confiscado, embargado
income	ingresos
income tax	impuestos sobre la renta
inconclusive	no concluyente, poco convincente
incriminating evidence	pruebas incriminatorias

to indict	procesar, acusar formalmente
indictment	acta de acusación de gran jurado, documento incoatorio
information	acusación de la fiscalía
inheritance	herencia
initial appearance	comparecencia inicial
injunction	interdicto, prohibición judicial, requerimiento, mandato judicial
insanity	locura, insania [término forense], demencia
inspection	inspección
inspect	inspeccionar
inspector	inspector
intent	intención
interrogatories	posiciones
to propound interrogatories	articular posiciones
to answer interrogatories	absolver posiciones
intestacy	morir intestado (sin testamento)
invoice	factura
irrelevant	inaplicable, no pertinente
IRS: Internal Revenue Service	el Servicio de Rentas Internas
job	trabajo, empleo
judge (n.)	juez (el juez o la juez) [la palabra juez es género común de dos DRAE, 1984]
judge (v.)	juzgar
judgment	sentencia, fallo, decisión, dictamen, disposición
judiciary	poder judicial
jump bail	fugar o huir estando bajo fianza
jurisdiction	jurisdicción, competencia
juror	jurado, miembro del jurado
jury	jurado

jury box	banca del jurado, palco del jurado
jury instructions	instrucciones al jurado
kickback	comisión ilícita, mordida (Mex.) coima (Chile)
knowledge	conocimiento
to the best of my knowledge	Según mi buen saber y conocimiento, A mi leal saber y entender, A mi buen y leal saber
knowingly and willfully	a sabiendas y voluntariamente
law	el derecho; la ley
law enforcement agent	agente de la autoridad, agente encargado del cumplimiento de la ley, agente del orden público
to bring a lawsuit	entablar una demanda
law in force	ley vigente
lawyer	abogado
leading question	pregunta insinuante, que insinúa la respuesta
lease (noun)	contrato de arrendamiento
legal costs	costas procesales
legal fees	honorarios
legal stamps	sellos legales
let the record stand	que quede establecido en las actas
let the record show	que conste en acta
letterhead	membrete
liability	obligación, responsabilidad legal
lie detector	detector de mentiras
literally	al pie de la letra
litigant	litigante, pleiteador
litigation	litigio
loan agreement	acuerdo o contrato de préstamo
loiter	callejear, vagabundear

lookout (n.)	vigía
loot (n.)	botín
loot (v.)	saquear
magistrate judge	juez de instrucción
malice	malicia
malice aforethought	premeditación y alevosía; malicia premeditada
manager	gerente
mandatory jail sentence	condena mandatoria
manslaughter	homicidio no premeditado
material	esencial, material
marshal	alguacil, oficial de los tribunales, márshal
material witness	testigo esencial
mental disability	incapacidad mental
mercy	compasión
at the mercy of	a la merced de
Miranda Warnings	Advertencia Miranda; derechos constitucionales
misappropriation	malversación de fondos
misdemeanor	delito menor, infracción penal
mistrial	juicio nulo
money order	giro postal
motion	pedimento, petición, moción (P.R.; EE.UU.)
motion for directed verdict	pedimento de veredicto absolutorio mandado por el juez
motion granted	pedimento admitido, concedido
motion to dismiss	pedimento para declarar sin lugar, retirar
motion to sever	pedimento de separación de las las partes
motion to suppress	pedimento para excluir pruebas
name	nombre

first name	de pila
last name	apellido
nickname	apodo
negligence	descuido, negligencia
negligible	insignificante
no bill	fallo no acusatorio del gran jurado
not guilty	no culpable
notice	aviso, notificación
objection	objeción, oposición
to obstruct	obstruir
off-the-record	extraoficial, oficioso
offense	delito
on the grounds of	por causa de
on your behalf	en su nombre
open-and-shut case	caso obvio
in open court	en audiencia pública
opening statement	declaración inaugural, exposición inicial del caso, exposición de apertura
order	orden, decreto, auto
ordinance	estatuto, ordenanza
outcome	resultado
out of order	improcedente
to overrule	desestimar, denegar, no aceptar
parole	libertad condicional
parties	las partes
parties to the suit	litigantes
payment	pago
penalty	castigo
peremptory challenge	recusación sin causa
perjury	perjurio, falso testimonio

perjurer	perjuro
personal property	propriedad personal, bienes muebles
petit jury	jurado [del juicio]
plaintiff	demandante, querellante, parte actora
plea	alegato, alegación; súplica
plead (guilty) change of plea	declararse (culpable) cambio de declaración
plea bargain	negociación de declaración de culpabilidad
plea bargain agreement	convenio de declaración de culpabilidad
pleadings	declaraciones, alegaciones
police record	antecedentes penales
policy insurance policy	política póliza de seguro
postpone	posponer, aplazar
postponement	aplazamiento
power of attorney	poder
prejudice	prejuicio
preliminary hearing	preliminares; vista preliminar
presentence investigation report (PSI)	informe de investigación previa a la condena
press charges	formular cargos
preliminary examination	preliminares
pre-trial services	servicios previos al juicio
pre-trial detention	detención previa al juicio, prisión preventiva
printed	impreso
probable cause	motivo fundado, causa presunta, motivo de procesamiento
probation	libertad vigilada
probation officer	agente de libertad vigilada
probate (v.)	correr testamentaria; legalizar un testamento

procedure	procedimiento, diligencia, tramitación
proceedings	diligencia, proceso
proffer (n.)	exposición
pronounce sentence	fallar, dictar una sentencia
proof	evidencia
prosecute	procesar
prosecutor	fiscal, abogado acusador
prosecuting attorney	fiscal
provisions	disposiciones
public defender	abogado de oficio, defensor público
pursuant to	conforme a
question (v.)	interrogar, preguntar, examinar
real estate	bienes raíces
real property	bienes inmuebles
reasonable doubt	duda razonable
rebuttal	refutación
receipt	recibo
record (n.)	las actas; constancia
record (v.)	registrar; hacer constar; grabar
records	registros
registration	matrícula, inscripción
rehabilitation	rehabilitación
reimburse	reembolsar
release (v.)	liberar, soltar, poner en libertad
relevant	pertinente
remand	devolver; reencarcelar; entregar
removal hearing	audiencia para traslado a otra jurisdicción
rent (n.)	alquiler
rent (v.)	alquilar

repeal (v.)	abrogar, anular
reprieve to grant a reprieve	suspensión temporal, indulto conceder una conmutación
reputed	supuesto(a)
restraining order	interdicto, orden judicial inhibitoria
retain counsel	contratar a un abogado
retainer	anticipo sobre honorarios del abogado
revoke	revocar
rider	claúsula adicional
robbery	robo
search and seizure	registro y embargo
search warrant	orden de registro, de allanamiento, orden de cateo (Mex.)
search (v.)	registrar
self-defense	defensa propia
seize	confiscar, decomisar, ocupar
sentence (n.)	condena, sentencia
sentence (v.)	imponer una condena
sentencing	imposición de la pena
serve a sentence	cumplir una condena
set (v.)	fijar
sever	separar
silencers	silenciadores
speedy trial	juicio expedito, sin demora
Social Security Administration	Administración del Seguro Social
standing (n.)	personería, fundamento o base legal
standing discovery order	orden pendiente de obtención de pruebas
state (v.)	exponer, declarar
statement	declaración, dictamen

statement of earnings	estado de cuentas
status conference	vista para determinar el estado del caso
stay (v.), to suspend	suspender
steal	robar, hurtar
statute	estatuto, reglamento
stipulation	estipulación, acuerdo
subpoena (n.)	citación, comparendo
subscribed and sworn to	suscrito y juramentado
to sue	demandar, poner pleito
suit (n.)	pleito
summation	resumen, conclusión, alegato final
suppress	excluir, suprimir
Supreme Court	Tribunal Supremo
surveillance	vigilancia
sustain an injury	sufrir una lesión
sustain an objection	sostener una objeción
strike from the record	eliminar de las actas
swear	jurar, prestar el debido juramento
sworn statement	declaración bajo juramento
take an oath	prestar juramento
take the stand	pasar al estrado (banquillo) de testigos
taxes	impuestos
taxpayer	contribuyente
technicality	detalle técnico, tecnicismo
tenant	inquilino(a)
testify	declarar, testificar, atestiguar
testimony	declaración, testimonio
in testimony whereof	en fe de lo cual
throw out (a case)	desestimar, rechazar

ties	vínculos, lazos
tort	agravio, acto dañoso
transcript	transcripción
trial	juicio
stand trial	ser procesado, ir a juicio
true bill	acusación de gran jurado o jurado acusatorio
trust (n.)	fideicomiso
undercover	encubierto
under oath	bajo juramento
undersigned	suscrito(a)
unemployed	desempleado(a)
United States attorney	fiscal
unlawful	ilegal
uphold	sostener, apoyar
venue	jurisdicción
change of venue	cambio de jurisdicción
verdict	veredicto, decisión
return a verdict	pronunciar un veredicto
verdict form	planilla de veredicto
victimless crime	delito sin víctima
violation	infracción
voir dire (Fr.)	voir dire
vouch for	responder por, garantizar
under the influence	bajo los efectos
waive	renunciar, desistir
warning	advertencia, aviso
weigh the evidence	sopesar las pruebas
whereas	por cuanto
whereby	en virtud del cual
will (n.)	voluntad (fem.); testamento

wiretap	intervención de las líneas telefónicas
with prejudice	sin posibilidad de volver a radicar la demanda o denuncia
withdraw	retirar
witness (n.)	testigo
witness for the defense	testigo de descargo, de la defensa
witness for the prosecution	testigo de cargo, de la fiscalía
writ	auto, decreto, mandamiento, orden judicial

[a] I wish to acknowledge the collaboration of several federally certified court interpreters who reviewed a preliminary draft of this glossary and contributed to its present form. I am particularly indebted to María Juana Cazabon, Nelson Durán, and Anthony Rivas.

NOTES

Introduction

1. Victoria Fromkin and Robert Rodman, *An Introduction to Language* (New York: Holt, Rinehart and Winston, Inc., 1988), 326.

2. Ibid.

3. G. Van Slype, et al., *Better Translation for Better Communication* (Oxford: Pergamon Press, 1983), 19.

4. Ruth L. Bennett, ed. *AATSP Career Handbook* (New York: AATSP Career Education Service, 1987), 3.

5. Frank Greve, "U.S. Pays Dearly for its Scarcity of Translators," *Miami Herald*, 9 June 1986.

6. Mildred Larson, *Meaning-Based Translation: A Guide to Cross-Language Equivalence* (Lanham, MD: University Press of America, Inc, 1984), ix.

PART I

Chapter 1

A Brief History of Court Interpreting in U.S. Courts

1. Jean Herbert, "How Conference Interpretation Grew," in *Language Interpretation and Communication*, ed. David Gerber and H. Wallace Sinaiko (New York: Plenum, 1978), 5.

2. Etilvia Arjona, "Translator and Interpreter Training in Europe and the USA" (unpublished ms., n.d.) cited in Benmaman, "Legal Interpretation: A New

Profession Coming of Age" (Paper delivered at the Annual Meeting of the American Association of Teachers of Spanish & Portuguese, Denver, Colorado, 21 August 1988), 3-5.

3. David and Margareta Bowen, *Steps to Consecutive Interpretation* (Washington, D.C.: Pen and Booth, 1984), 2. The modes of interpretation are defined, and their use in court proceedings is discussed in chapter 3.

4. Jack Kaufman (writer and director). *Trial at Nuremberg*. United Artists Television. Wolper Productions, Inc. Film documentary, 1964.

5. For additional information on the federal and state systems, see Henry J. Abraham, *The Judicial Process*, 5th ed. (New York: Oxford University Press, 1986), 142-176. I discuss the role of the interpreter in immigration proceedings in chapter 6.

6. Abraham, *Judicial Process*, 143.

7. Henry C. Black, *Black's Law Dictionary* (St. Paul, Minnesota: West Publishing Co., 1990), 1407-1408.

8. Stephen H. Gifis, *Dictionary of Legal Terms* (Woodbury, N. Y.: Barron's Educational Series, Inc., 1983), 305.

9. *See* Black, *Black's Law Dictionary*, 350.

10. Abraham, *Judicial Process*, 162.

11. David Lawrence, Jr., "Mr. President, We *Need* Those Judges." *Miami Herald*, Sunday, 28 April 1991.

12. Alicia Pousada, "Interpreting for Language Minorities in the Courts," in *Language and Public Life*, ed. James E. Alatis and G. Richard Tucker (Washington, D.C.: Georgetown University Press, 1979), 191.

13. Nancy Schweda-Nicholson, "Court Interpreter Training: A Growing Need," in *Proceedings of the 1985 Eastern Michigan University Conference on Languages for Business and the Professions*, ed. Geoffrey M. Voght (Washington, D.C.: ERIC Microfiche, 1986), 940.

14. Schweda-Nicholson, "Court Interpreter Training," 938.

15. United States v. Tapia, 631 F.2d 1207 (1980), 1210. See Susan Berk-Seligson, *The Bilingual Courtroom* (Chicago: Chicago University Press), 198-214, for her discussion of appeals based on interpreting issues.

16. Monte v. State of Florida, 443 S.2d 339 (1983), 342.

17. Schweda-Nicholson, "Court Interpreter Training," 940-41.

18. U.S. Congress. Senate Hearings. Committee on the Judiciary. S. 1724, *Bilingual Courts Act*, 93rd Congress, second session, 1973-74.

19. Public Law 95-539, 18 U.S.C., Section 1827, 1978.

20. Edward Baca, telephone conversation with author, 27 September 1990.

21. U.S. Congress, Senate Committee on the Judiciary, *Court Interpreters Improvement Act of 1985*, 99th Congress 1st Session, S. 1853, 2.

22. *Court Interpreters Improvement Act*, 4-5. This bill, introduced by Senator Hatch and others, was referred to the Senate Committee on the Judiciary. The bill did not become law.

23. U.S. Congress, Congressional Committee on the Judiciary, Report 100-590, 1988, 2.

24. Ibid, 3.

25. Public Law 100-702, 28 U.S.C., Section 1828, 1988.

26. Administrative Office of the United States Courts. Interim Regulations of the Director of the Administrative Office of the United States Courts Implementing the Court Interpreters Amendments Act of 1988. Washington, D.C., November 16, 1989.

27. Ibid.

28. *Elusive Decade of Hispanics* (Miami: Cuban American Policy Center, Cuban American National Council, Fall 1989), 6-7.

29. "U.S. Hispanic Population at All-Time High," *Miami Herald*, 12 October 1989, 8A.

30. Alain L. Sanders, "*Libertad* and *Justicia* for All," *Time*, 29 May 1989, 65.

31. Ann Green, letter to the author, 23 August 1990.

32. Schweda-Nicholson, "Court Interpreter Training," 949.

33. See Berk-Seligson, *The Bilingual Courtroom*, 26-33, for a discussion of state provisions and state and federal case law regarding the right to court-appointed interpreters.

Chapter 2

The Interpreting Process

1. David Gerver's essay, "Empirical Studies of Simultaneous Interpretation: A Review and a Model," in *Translation. Applications and Research*, ed. Richard W. Brislin (New York: Gardner, 1976), 165-203, offers a thorough review of research in the field from its inception until the mid 1970s. He discusses the reasons for lack of knowledge about simultaneous interpretation (166-67) and the complex processes involved in simultaneous interpretation within the context of theory and research in human information processing (191-94). See also Josiane F. Hamers and Michel H.A. Blanc, *Bilinguality and Bilingualism* (Cambridge: Cambridge U

Press, 1990), 144-58, for an up-to-date survey of research on translation and interpretation. The authors, who point out that research is extremely scarse in the field, present an excellent discussion of some of the relevant problems concerning language processing in interpretation and translation.

2. Cf. Danica Seleskovitch, "Interpretation, A Psychological Approach to Translating," in *Translation. Applications and Research*, ed. Richard W. Brislin (New York: Gardner, 1976), 97-99.

3. Ibid, 98-99.

4. Seleskovitch, 99.

5. Gerald F. Seib, "Pardonnez-Moi, Mr. Bush: In French You Make No Sense," *Wall Street Journal*, 21 June 1989, 1-A7.

6. David Bowen and Margareta Bowen, *Steps to Consecutive Interpretation* (Washington, D.C.: Pen and Booth, 1984), 18-19.

7. See also D. Seleskovitch, *Language, Langues et Mémoire, étude de la prise de notes en interprétation consécutive*. (Paris: Minard, 1975) and D. Seleskovitch, *Interpreting for International Conferences*.

8. See Geoffrey R. Loftus and Elizabeth F. Loftus, *Human Memory. The Processing of Information*. (Hillsdale, New Jersey: Lawrence Erlbaum Associates, 1976), 43-47.

Chapter 3

Defining the Terms

1. Danica Seleskovitch, *Interpreting for International Conferences* (Washington, D.C.: Pen & Booth, 1978), 2.

2. Wilhelm K. Weber, *Training Translators and Conference Interpreters* (Orlando: Harcourt Brace Jovanovich, 1984), 27, states that the most difficult aspect of interpreting is the speed with which it must be accomplished. The sequence of instruction: sight translation, consecutive interpretation, and simultaneous interpretation, leads students gradually to a point where they are able to cope with this problem.

3. Ibid.

4. Susan Berk-Seligson, *The Bilingual Courtroom* (Chicago: University of Chicago Press, 1990), 271.

5. Berk-Seligson, *The Bilingual Courtroom*, 194-96.

6. Stephen Capaldo, "An Apology for Consecutive Interpretation," *Meta* 25,

no. 2 (June 1980): 245.

7. See J.-F. Rozan, *La prise de notes en interprétation consécutive* (Geneva: Georg, 1956).

8. María Juana Cazabon, "Memory and Note-Taking in Consecutive Interpretation" (Lecture delivered at the Workshop on Consecutive Interpretation for Interpreters of the Executive Office for Immigration Review, Miami, FL), May 1990.

9. Geoffrey R. Loftus and Elizabeth F. Loftus, *Human Memory. The Processing of Information* (Hillsdale, New Jersey: Lawrence Erlbaum Associates, 1976), 45.

10. John A. Henderson, "Note-Taking for Consecutive Interpreting," *Babel* 22, no. 3 (1976): 107-16.

11. Cf. Sylvie Lambert, "Information Processing among Conference Interpreters: A Test of the Depth-of-Processing Hypothesis," *Meta* 33,3 (1988): 378.

12. Glemet, qtd. in Gerver, "Empirical Studies of Simultaneous Interpretation: A Review and a Model," in Brislin, *Translation. Applications and Research*, 168.

13. Seleskovitch, *Interpreting for International Conferences*, 32.

14. F. Goldman-Eisler, "Segementation of Input in Simultaneous Interpretation," *Journal of Psycholinguistic Research* 1 (1972): 127-40.

15. Ibid. See also Henri Barik, "Summary of a Study on Simultaneous Interpretation." *L'Interprète* 4 (1972): 8-10.

16. Public Law 95-539 (Amended Public Law 100-702), 28 U.S.C., Section 1828, 1988.

17. David Gerver, "The Effects of Noise on the Performance of Simultaneous Interpreters: Accuracy of Performance," *Acta Psychologica* 38 (1974): 159-67.

18. "Use of Two Interpreters to Cover a Trial When Necessary." *Court Administration Bulletin* (March 1991), 2-3.

19. Alicia Betsy Edwards, "Ethical Conduct for the Court Interpreter," *Court Manager* (Spring 1988), 24.

Chapter 4

Language and Culture

1. Many of the ideas expressed in this chapter were developed in my article,

"Foreign Language Interpreters in the Courtroom: The Case for Linguistic and Cultural Proficiency," *Modern Language Journal* 75 (c 1991 by the Board of Regents of the University of Wisconsin System), pp. 285-95; used by permission of The University of Wisconsin Press.

2. Eugene A. Nida, "Science of Translation," *Language* 45 (1969): 484. Nida uses the term "receptor" to emphasize that the message must be decoded by those who receive it.

3. Susan Bassnett-McGuire. *Translation Studies* (New York: Methuen, 1980), 16-18.

4. Eugene A. Nida and William Reyburn. *Meaning Across Cultures* (New York: Orbis, 1981), 30.

5. Cf. Danica Seleskovitch, *Interpreting for International Conferences* (Washington, D.C.: Pen & Booth, 1978), 9.

6. Alice Edwards, "Avoiding Foreign Faux Pas," *AAA World* July-August 1989, 15.

7. Nancy Ross-Hanigan, "Good Gestures Aid Understanding, Studies Find," *Miami Herald*, March 6, 1988, 7G.

8. Edward Sapir. *Culture, Language, and Personality* (Los Angeles: U of California Press, 1956), 69.

9. Benjamin Lee Whorf, "The Relation of Habitual Thought and Behavior to Language." *Language, Thought, and Reality*. John B. Carroll, ed. (Cambridge, MA: M.I.T. Press, 1978), 158.

10. Gail L. Nemetz Robinson. *Crosscultural Understanding. Processes and Approaches to Foreign Language, English as a Second Language and Bilingual Education* (New York: Pergamon, 1985), 14-15.

11. Bassnett-McGuire, *Translation Studies*, 13-14.

12. François Grosjean, *Life with Two Languages* (Cambridge: Harvard University Press, 1982), 157.

13. R. Bruce W. Anderson, "Perspectives on the Role of Interpreter," in Richard W. Brislin, ed. *Translation. Applications and Research* (New York: Gardner, 1976), 215.

14. See Einar Haugen, *Bilingualism in the Americas: A Bibliography and Research Guide* (University, AL: Univ of Alabama Press), 1956.

15. "Voulez-vous devenir interpr0te de conférence?" Geneva: AIIC [Journal of the International Association of Conference Interpreters], 1979, 11.

16. Jean A. Perkins, "The Value of Foreign Language Study," *ADFL Bulletin* 20 (1988): 25.

17. Storer H. Rowley, "There Must Be 30 Ways to Say Snow in

Inuktitut, Anyway," *Chicago Tribune*, 4 December 1990. In "The Melting of a Mighty Myth," *Newsweek*, 22 July 1991, 63, Jerry Adler and Niko Price discuss research which refutes the claim that Eskimos have more words for "snow" than anyone else. Anthropologist Laura Martin, for instance, has found that references to the number of Eskimo snow words vary widely (one casually referred to "100"), and that the "story" has become increasingly incredible.

18. Perkins, "The Value of Foreign Language Study," 25.

19. Ibid.

20. Fujiko Hara, "Understanding the Silent Culture of the Japanese." *Meta* 33, no. 1 (1988): 22.

21. *Civil Law* is the law handed down from the Romans. It is law that is based on one elaborate document or "code," rather than a combination of many laws and judicial opinions. See Daniel Oran, *Oran's Dictionary of the Law* (St. Paul: West, 1983), 78.

22. Antoine Georges, "Haiti: Language and Culture." (Lecture delivered at the Workshop for Immigration Interpreters, Executive Office for Immigration Review, Miami, FL, May 1990); Marilyn Tayler, "Interpreting/Translating Assistance in Immigration Proceedings." *Immigration and Nationality Law*, vol. 11, Edwin R. Rubin and Robert E. Jucean, eds. San Diego: American Immigration Lawyers Association, 1988, 9.

23. Josiane F. Hamers and Michel H.A. Blanc, *Bilinguality & Bilingualism* (New York: Cambridge U Press, 1990, 245.

24. François Grosjean, *Life with Two Languages*, 230.

25. Christopher Thiéry, "True Bilingualism and Second Language Learning." *Language Interpretation and Communication*. Ed. David Gerver & H. Sinaiko (New York: Plenum, 1978), 146.

26. R. Bruce W. Anderson, "Perspectives on the Role of Interpreter," 212-213.

27. Grosjean, "The Bilingual as a Competent but Specific Speaker-Hearer." (Paper presented at the Symposium on Bilingualism, Ninth Annual Boston University Conference on Language Development, October 1984), 8-9.

28. For excellent discussions of bilingualism see, for example, Grosjean, *Life with Two Languages* (note 12, above) and Hamers and Blanc, *Bilinguality and Bilingualism* (note 23, above).

Chapter 5

Interpreting Nonstandard Language

1. Many of the ideas expressed in this chapter were developed in two of my articles. I gratefully acknowledge *Hispania* and the SUNY Research Foundation for permission to incorporate and adapt portions of those articles: "Interpreting in Miami's Federal Courts: Code-Switching and Spanglish," *Hispania* 73 (March 1990): 272-78, and "The Challenge for the Court Interpreter in Southern Florida," in American Translators Association Scholarly Monograph *Series*, volume 4, *Interpreting: Yesterday, Today, and Tomorrow*, David Bowen and Margareta Bowen, eds. (Binghamton, New York: State University of New York (SUNY) at Binghamton, 1990): 91-95.

2. Victoria Fromkin and Robert Rodman, *An Introduction to Language* (New York: Holt, Rinehart and Winston, 1988), 254.

3. Fromkin and Rodman, 253.

4. See Elena M. de Jongh and Ana Roca, "The Preparation of Court Interpreters in Southern Florida," in *Sociolinguistics of the Spanish Speaking-World: Iberia, Latin America, United States*, Carol Klee and Luis A. Ramos-García, eds. Tempe, Arizona: Bilingual Press/Editorial Bilingüe, 1991, 349-58.

5. The term *language-switching* is preferred to "code-switching" by prominent scholars of T/I because theoreticians such as Seleskovitch refer to interpretation as a code-switching operation (Margareta Bowen, personal communication, 5 October 1989).

6. Lucía Elías-Olivares, "Language Use in a Chicano Community: A Sociolinguistic Approach," in *Spanish in the U.S. Setting*, Lucía Elías-Olivares, ed. (Rosslyn, Va: National Clearinghouse for Bilingual Education, 1983), 125.

7. Metro-Dade Planning Department, Research Division.

8. Figures compiled from Carlos Harrison, "Region Becoming More Latin, Less Cuban." *Miami Herald*, 12 September 1988, 1 & 3B, and *Ethnic Block Voting and Polarization in Miami* (Miami, FL: Cuban American National Council, Summer 1991), 7-8.

9. "Minority gains doubled pace in the 1980s." *Miami Herald*, 11 March 1991, 10A.

10. "Hispanic Population at All-Time High." *Miami Herald* 12 October 1989, 8A.

11. Elías-Olivares, "Language Use in a Chicano Community," 123.

12. Elías-Olivares, 125.

13. Ibid.

14. María Juana Cazabon, Personal communication.

15. Grosjean, *Life with Two Languages*, 145.

16. Sylvia Gonzales, *La Chicana Piensa—The Social-Cultural Conscious of a Mexican American Woman.* Reprinted by permission of MacMillan Publishing Company from *¿Qué me cuenta?* by M. Kasey Hellerman. Copyright 1977 by M. Kasey Hellerman. Italics added.

17. I am grateful to federally certified interpreter Elisa Cabal, who transcribed the taperecorded conversation from which these excerpts are taken.

18. Adapted from an example given at the Federal Court Interpreters Workshop, Miami, FL, 1988.

19. As explained by Benmaman, Connolly, and Loos, the word "*delito* can be used for all felonies. *Falta* is the term used for misdemeanors. *Crimen* is a term applied only to violent felonies." See Virginia Benmaman, Norma Connolly, and Scott Loos, *Bilingual Dictionary of Criminal Justice Terms (English/Spanish)* (New York: Gould, 1991), 47.

20. Irene Tomassini, Personal communication.

21. Pier Paolo Giglioli, ed. *Language and Social Context* (New York: Penguin Books, 1986, 15.

22. Giglioli, 13-16.

23. According to Jorge Guitart the connection between the label of *gusano* 'worm' given to Cubans who left the island after Castro's revolution, and the Cuban slang term for duffel bag is coincidental. Reference to duffel bag as *gusano* is a consequence of the shape of the object (Personal communication, 10 December 1988). Note that Cuban Spanish is usually regarded as part of Caribbean Spanish, a grouping that for Zamora Munne and Guitart includes the three Antillean islands as well as the coastal areas of Mexico, Panama, Colombia, and Venezuela. See J.C. Zamora Munne and Jorge M. Guitart, *Dialectología hispanoamericana* (Salamanca: Almar, 1982).

Chapter 6

Interpreting in Court

1. See Appendix 5 for a list of selected glossaries and dictionaries.

2. Abraham, Henry J. *The Judicial Process.* 5th ed. (New York: Oxford

University Press, 1986, 8.

3. Abraham, *The Judicial Process*, 139.

4. Abraham, *The Judicial Process*, 107.

5. Abraham, *The Judicial Process*, 106.

6. *Handbook for Federal Grand Jurors*. Foreword by The Honorable C. Clyde Atkins, U.S. District Court for the Southern District of Florida. n.p., May 1980, p. 6.

7. Virginia Benmaman, Norma Connolly, and Scott Loos, *Bilingual Dictionary of Criminal Justice Terms (English/Spanish)*. (New York: Gould, 1991), 91.

8. Joseph J. Senna and Larry J. Siegel, *Introduction to Criminal Justice* (St. Paul: West, 1987), 575.

9. Abraham, *The Judicial Process*, 139.

10. Daniel Oran, *Oran's Dictionary of the Law* (St. Paul, Minnesota: West, 1983), 325.

11. Faith Mesnekoff, Esq., Personal communication, 12 August 1991.

12. Senna and Siegel, *Introduction to Criminal Justice*, 576.

13. There are cases in which a defendant may waive his right to a trial by jury and agree to be tried by the judge alone, as sole trier of fact.

14. See Abraham, *The Judicial Process*, 138-9.

15. Suzanne M. Carroll, Personnel Liaison Officer, EOIR, Personal communication, November 1990 and February 1991. In November 1990 the Executive Office for Immigration Review anticipated hiring approximately forty Language Specialists for positions in twenty-one cities throughout the United States. Minimum qualifications for employment are a four year degree from an accredited college, majoring in Spanish language studies or experience in progressively responsible positions in which translating and interpreting have been the major function of that position.

As stated by Marilyn Tayler, immigration proceedings are "deemed to be civil in nature. Thus, the full panoply of rights inherent in the criminal process, such as Sixth Amendment rights, are not available to respondents or applicants in immigration proceedings . . . since immigration hearings are administrative proceedings, the requirements for interpreter qualifications under the 1978 Court Interpreters Act do not apply . . ." (p. 59). See "Interpretation/Translation Assistance in Immigration Proceedings." *Immigration Journal* 11, no. 3 (July-Sept. 1988): 45, 57-62.

16. The information provided in this section draws heavily from the *Interpreter's Handbook* drafted by the Interpreter Advisory Committee, Office of the Chief Immigration Judge. The handbook is designed to serve interpreters who

work in the Executive Office for Immigration Review as a resource document.

17. *Interpreter's Handbook*, Office of the Chief Immigration Judge (Washington, D.C.: U.S. Department of Justice, n.p., n.d.), 174.

Chapter 7

Court Interpreting as a Profession

1. I.A. Richards, "Toward a Science of Translating," in *Studies in Chinese Thought*, 55, Memorir 75 (Chicago: University of Chicago Press, 1953), 250.

2. Richard Brislin, introduction to *Translation. Applications and Research* (New York: Gardner Press, 1976), 1.

3. Nancy Festinger, "Court Interpreting: Maintaining Linguistic Fidelity in the Crossfire of Legal Battles." Lecture delivered at the Annual Dinner of the Court Interpreters and Translators Association (C.I.T.A.), New York City, December 7, 1985, 3.

4. Elaine Chaika, *Language. The Social Mirror*. 2d ed. (Cambridge: Newbury House, 1989), 183.

5. Veda R. and Robert P. Charrow, "Characteristics of the Language of Jury Instructions." In *Language in Public Life*. J. Alatis and G. R. Tucker, eds. (Washington, D.C.: Georgetown University Press, 1979), 164.

6. Roseanne Dueñas González, "The Design and Validation of an Evaluation Procedure to Diagnose the English Aural-Oral Competency of a Spanish Speaking Person in the Justice System." (Ph.D. diss., University of Arizona, 1977), 68.

7. Dueñas González, 69.

8. William O'Barr, *Linguistic Evidence. Language, Power, and Strategy in the Courtroom* (New York: Academic Press, 1982), 21.

9. O'Barr, 25. See pp. 16-26 for a thorough discussion of the nature of legal language. See also Susan Berk-Seligson, *The Bilingual Courtroom* (Chicago: University of Chicago Press, 1990), 12-25.

10. Virginia Benmaman, Norma Connolly, and Scott Loos, *Bilingual Dictionary of Criminal Justice Terms (English/Spanish)* (New York: Gould, 1991), 16.

11. Benmaman, Connolly, and Loos, *Bilingual Dictionary*, vii.

12. Rosalind Resnick, "Crackdown on *Notarios*." *Business/Monday*, 17 April 1989.

13. Ibid.

14. Rosalind Resnick, "New Law Aims to Rein in State's *Notarios Públicos*." *Miami Herald Business/Monday*, 8 July 1991, 15.

15. Successful completion of an internship is required at Florida International University for the Certificate in Court Interpreting and Legal Translation.

16. Nancy Schweda-Nicholson, 1987, 285.

17. *Ballad of Gregorio Cortez*. Film. Moctesuma Esparza Productions, Inc., 1982.

18. Alain L. Sanders, "*Libertad* and *Justicia* for All." *Time* (29 May 1989), 65.

19. Henry C. Black, *Black's Law Dictionary*. 6th ed. St. Paul, Minnesota: West, 1990, 1210.

20. Virginia Benmaman, "Legal Interpreting: A New Profession Coming of Age." Paper presented at the Annual Convention of the American Association of Teachers of Spanish and Portuguese, Denver, August 20-22, 1988, 15.

21. Benmaman, "Legal Interpretation," 17.

22. Benmaman, "Legal Interpretation," 18-19.

23. Benmaman, "Legal Interpretation," 19.

24. Schweda-Nicholson, "Language Planning and Policy Development for Court Interpretation in the United States," in *Language Problems and Language Planning* 10 (Summer 1986): 153-54.

25. Benmaman, "Legal Interpretation," 6.

26. Alicia Pousada, "Interpreting for Language Minorities in the Courts." In *Language and Public Life*, James E. Alatis and G. Richard Tucker, eds. (Washington, D.C.: Georgetown U Press, 1979), 193.

27. The Florida Court Interpreters Act, to which the author is consultant, will be considered by the Florida legislature in 1992.

28. Etilvia Arjona, Personal communication, August 1991.

29. Arjona, "The Court Interpreters Certification Test Design." In *Spanish Language and Public Life in the United States*. Lucía Elías-Olivares, ed. (Berlin: Mouton, 1985), 183.

30. *The Federal Court Interpreter Certification Manual. Haitian-Creole 1990-1993*. Tucson, Arizona: University of Arizona Federal Court Interpreter Certification Project, 1990, 34.

31. Arjona, "The Court Interpreters Certification," 197.

32. Ed Baca, Personal communication.

33. Arjona, "The Court Interpreters Certification," 197.

34. Embodied in the due process concept are "the basic rights of a defendant in criminal proceedings and the requisite for a fair trial." (*Black's Law Dictionary*, 501).

Part II

1. Courtesy Linda Haughton.

2. Courtesy Linda Haughton.

3. Courtesy Linda Haughton.

4. Courtesy John "Jack" C. Webb.

5. To incorporate sight translation and consecutive interpretation practice, use the transcript in the following manner: students who play the role of English-speaking witnesses sight translate their testimony into Spanish (or another foreign language). The "interpreter" then interprets all foreign language utterances into English and all English utterances into the foreign language. The testimony of these witnesses is then rendered in English in the consecutive mode.

6. Deanna L. Hammond, "Translator and Interpreter Associations in the United States," *Hispania* 73 (September 1990): 689-91.

BIBLIOGRAPHY

Abraham, Henry J. *The Judicial Process.* 5th ed. New York: Oxford University Press, 1986.

Adelo, Samuel A. "Interpreting in Court is an Exacting Task." *Citations* 5, no. 1 (1988): 6.

Adler, Jerry, and Niko Price, "The Melting of a Mighty Myth." *Newsweek* (22 July 1991): 63.

Almeida, Frank, and Sophia Zahler, eds. *Los Angeles Superior Court Interpreters Manual.* Los Angeles, CA: Los Angeles Superior Court, 1981.

Altano, W. Brian. "The Intricate Witness-Interpreter Relationship." In *Interpreting: Yesterday, Today, and Tomorrow*, edited by David and Margareta Bowen, 96-100. American Translators Association Scholarly Monograph *Series*, vol. 4. Binghamton, New York: State University of New York at Binghamton, 1990.

Amastae, John, and Lucía Elías-Olivares, eds. *Spanish in the United States. Sociolinguistic Aspects.* Cambridge: Cambridge University Press, 1982.

Anderson, R. Bruce W. "Interpreter Roles and Interpretation Situations: Cross-cutting Typologies." In *Language Interpretation and Communication*, edited by David Gerver and H. Wallace Sinaiko, 217-30. New York: Plenum Press, 1978.

—. "Perspectives on the Role of Interpreter." *Translation: Applications and Research*, edited by Richard Brislin, 208-28. New York: Gardner Press, 1976.

Argyle, Michael. "Inter-Cultural Communication." In *Cultures in Contact*, edited by Stephen Bochner, 61-79. Oxford: Pergamon, 1982.

Arjona, Etilvia. "Institutional Factors Affecting the Design of Translation/Interpretation Programs." Paper presented at the annual meeting of Spanish in the U.S./El Español en los Estados Unidos Conference, Miami, FL, 1988.

—. "Intercultural Communication and the Training of Interpreters at the Monterey Institute of Foreign Studies." In *Language Interpretation and Communication*, edited by David Gerver and H. Wallace Sinaiko, 35-44. New York: Plenum Press, 1978.

—. "The Court Interpreters Certification Test Design." In *Spanish Language Use and Public Life in the United States*, edited by Lucía Elías-Olivares, Elizabeth A. Leone, Rene Cisneros, and John R. Gutiérrez, 181-200. Berlin: Mouton, 1985.

Ballad of Gregorio Cortez. Film. Robert M. Young (director). Moctesuma Esparza Productions, Inc., 1982.

Barik, Henri. "Interpreters Talk a Lot, Among Other Things." *Babel* 18, no. 1 (1972): 3-10.

—. "Simultaneous Interpretation: Qualitative and Linguistic Data." *Language and Speech* 18 (July-Sept. 1975): 272-96.

—. "Simultaneous Interpretation: Temporal and Quantitative Data." *Language and Speech* 16 (1973): 237-70.

—. "Summary of a Study on Simultaneous Interpretation." *L'Interprète* 4 (1972): 8-10.

Barkin-Riegelhaupt, Florence. "Testing Bilingual Language Proficiency: An Applied Approach." In *Spanish Language Use and Public Life in the USA*, edited by Lucía Elías-Olivares, 166-80. Berlin: Mouton, 1985.

Bassnett-McGuire, Susan. *Translation Studies*. London and New York: Methuen, 1980.

Benmaman, Virginia. "Legal Interpretation: A New Profession Coming of Age." Paper presented at the annual meeting of the American Association of Teachers of Spanish and Portuguese, Denver, 1988.

Benmaman, Virginia, Norma Connolly, and Scott Loos. *Bilingual Dictionary of Criminal Justice Terms (English/Spanish)*. New York: Gould, 1991.

Bennett, Ruth L., ed. *AATSP Career Handbook*. Flushing, New York: AATSP Career Education Service, 1987.

Berk-Seligson, Susan. "A Sociolinguistic View of the Mex-American Speech Community: A Review of the Literature." *Latin American Research Review* 15, no. 2 (1980): 65-110.

—. *The Bilingual Courtroom. Court Interpreters in the Judicial Process*. Chicago: University of Chicago Press, 1990.

—. "The Impact of Politeness in Witness Testimony: The Influence of the Court

Interpreter." *Multilingua* 7, no. 4 (1988): 412-39.

—. "The Role of Register in the Bilingual Courtroom: Evaluative Reactions to Interpreted Testimony." *International Journal of the Sociology of Language* 79 (1989): 79-91.

Beslisle, Estelle, and Margareta Bowen. "Final Testing of Interpreting Students." National Resource Center for Translation and Interpretation. Washington, D.C.: Georgetown University, n.d.

Bickely, Verner C. "Language as the Bridge." In *Cultures in Contact. Studies in Cross-Cultural Interaction*, edited by Stephen Bochner, 99-125. Oxford: Pergamon, 1982.

Black, Henry C. *Black's Law Dictionary*. 6th ed. St. Paul, Minnesota: West Publishing Co., 1990.

Bochner, Stephen, ed. *Cultures in Contact*. Oxford: Pergamon Press, 1982.

—. *The Mediating Person: Bridges Between Cultures*. Boston: G.K. Hall & Co., 1981.

Bowen, David, and Margareta Bowen. "Diplomacy and Communication across Cultures: Degrees of Cultural Barriers." *Journal of the Washington Academy of Sciences* 77, no. 1 (March 1987): 36-39.

—, eds. *Interpreting: Yesterday, Today and Tommorow*. American Translators Association Scholarly Monograph *Series*, vol. 4. Binghamton, New York: State University of New York at Binghamton, 1990.

—. *Steps to Consecutive Interpretation*. Washington, D.C.: Pen and Booth, 1984.

—. "The Results to be Expected from a Stay Abroad." In *Translation Theory and its Implementation in the Teaching of Translating and Interpreting*. Akten des Internationalen Kolloquiums der Association Internationale de Linguistique Appliquée (AILA), Saarbrucken, 25-30 Juli 1983. Wolfram Wilss/Gisela Thome (Hrsg.), 279-88. Tubingen: Gunter Narr Verlag, 1983.

Brislin, Richard, ed. *Translation. Applications and Research*. New York: Gardner Press, 1976.

—. "Translation and Content Analysis of Oral and Written Materials." In *Handbook of Cross-Cultural Psychology: Methodology*. vol. 2. Edited by Harry C. Triandis and John W. Berry, 389-444. Boston: Allyn and Bacon, Inc., 1980.

Brooks, Nelson. *Language and Language Learning*. New Haven: Yale University Press, 1970.

Buhler, Hildegund, Ingrid Kurz, and Margareta Bowen. "Report of the Georgetown University Roundtable—Interpretation and Nonverbal

Communication." National Resource Center for Translation and Interpretation. Washington, D.C.: Georgetown University, n.d.

Bundy, Nancy L. "Semiotics and Language Teaching." Paper presented at the annual meeting of the American Association of Teachers of Spanish and Portuguese, Denver, 1988.

Buskirk, Cheryl, and David Bowen. "Final Testing of Translation Students." National Resource Center for Translation and Interpretation. Washington, D.C.: Georgetown University, n.d.

Capaldo, Stephen. "An Apology for Consecutive Interpretation." *Meta* 25, no. 2 (June 1980): 244-48.

Cassidy, John R. "Never Ask a Uruguayan Waitress for a Little Box: She Might Apply her Foot to your Eyelet." *Language Quarterly* 10, no. 1 (Summer 1983): 1-3.

Cazabon, María Juana. "Memory and Note-Taking in Consecutive Interpretation." Lecture delivered at the Workshop for Interpreters, Executive Office for Immigration Review, Miami, FL, May 1990.

Chaika, Elaine. *Language. The Social Mirror*. 2nd ed. Cambridge: Newbury House, 1989.

Charles, Rae Bernal. "Conference Interpreting." *The Incorporated Linguist* 7, no. 4 (October 1968): 77-82.

Charrow, John, and Veda Charrow. "Characteristics of the Language of Jury Instructions." *Language in Public Life*. edited by James E. Alatis and G. Richard Tucker, 163-84. Washington, D.C.: Georgetown University Press, 1979.

Chernov, G.V. "Linguistic Problems in the Compression of Speech in Simultaneous Interpretation." *Tetradi Perevodchika* 6 (1969): 52-65.

—. "Towards a Psycholinguistic Model of Simultaneous Interpretation." *Linguistische Arbeitsberichte* 7 (1973): 225-60.

Collet, Peter. "Meetings and Misunderstandings." In *Cultures in Contact*, edited by Stephen Bochner, 81-98. Oxford: Pergamon, 1982.

Comment. "The Right to an Interpreter." *Rutgers Law Review* 25 (1970): 145-71.

Congrat-Butler, Stephan. *Translation and Translators: an International Directory and Guide*. New York: R.R. Bowker Co., 1979.

Conway, Harry. "Breaking the Language Barrier." *Meetings & Conventions* 20 (December 1985): 81-87.

"Court Interpreters Improvement Act of 1985." 99th Congress, 1st Session, S.1853, November 14 (legislative day, November 12) 1985.

Federal Court Interpreters Manual. Washington, D.C.: Administrative Office of the United States Courts, forthcoming.

Crouch, Alan. "Barriers to Understanding in the Legal Situation." *Law Institute Journal* 53, no.9 (September 1979): 505-8.

—-. "Interpreters, Translators and Legal Services: Towards a Better Understanding." *Law Institute Journal* 55 (May 1981): 264-9.

Cruse, D.A. *Lexical Semantics*. Cambridge: Cambridge University Press, 1986.

Curry, Richard A., *et al. Carreras: Leyes*. Boston: Houghton Mifflin, 1985.

de Jongh, Elena M. "A Brief Glossary of Drug-Related Language." *Jerome Quarterly* 5, no. 1 (Nov.-Dec. 1989): 6-7.

—. "Court Interpreting: The Anatomy of a Profession." *Resources in Education*. Washington, D.C.: ERIC Clearinghouse on Languages and Linguistics, 1990. (Microfiche No. ED 314 935)

—. "Interpreting in Miami's Federal Courts: Code-Switching and Spanglish." *Hispania* 73 (March 1990): 274-8.

—. "Foreign Language Interpreters in the Courtroom: The Case for Linguistic and Cultural Proficiency." *Modern Language Journal* 75 (Autumn 1991): 285-95.

—."Cultural Proficiency and Nonverbal Communication in Court Interpreting." *Confluencia*, in press.

—-. "The Challenge for the Court Interpreter in Southern Florida." In *Interpreting: Yesterday, Today and Tomorrow*, edited by David and Margareta Bowen, 91-95. Binghamton, New York: State University of New York (SUNY) at Binghamton, 1990.

de Jongh, Elena M., and Ana Roca. "Interpreting Spanish Codes in Southern Florida: The Preparation of Court Interpreters." In *Sociolinguistics of the Spanish-Speaking World: Iberia, Latin America, and the United States*, edited by Carol Klee and Luis Ramos-García, 349-58. Tempe, Arizona: Bilingual Press/Editorial Bilingüe, 1991.

de la Cuesta, Leonel A. *Lecciones Preliminares de Traductología*. Costa Rica: Ediciones Guayacán, 1987.

Del Valle, Manuel. "Hispanics' Language Rights and Due Process." *New York Law Journal* 186, no. 21 (July 30, 1981): 1-2.

Delisle, Jean, ed. *L'Enseignement de l'Interprétation et de la Traduction. De la Théorie a la Pédagogie*. Cahiers de Traductologie, No. 4. Ottawa: University of Ottawa Press, 1981.

Duff, Alan. *The Third Language*. Elmsford, New York: Pergamon Press, 1983.

Edwards, Alice. "Avoiding Foreign Faux Pas." *AAA World* (July-August 1989): 14-15.

Edwards, Alicia Betsy. "Ethical Conduct for the Court Interpreter." *The Court Manager* (Spring 1988): 22-25.

Edwards, Jane, and Humphrey Tonkin, eds. *Language Behavior in International Organizations*. New York: Center for Research and Documentation on World Language Problems, 1984.

Ekvall, Robert E. *Faithful Echo*. New York: Twayne, 1960.

Elías-Olivares, Lucía. "Language Use in a Chicano Community: A Sociolinguistic Approach." In *Spanish in the U.S. Setting: Beyond the Southwest*, edited by Lucía Elías-Olivares, 120-28. Rosslyn, Va: National Clearinghouse for Bilingual Education, 1983.

Elías-Olivares, Lucía, and Elizabeth A. Leone, Rene Cisneros, and John R. Gutierrez, eds. *Spanish Language Use and Public Life in the USA*. Contributions to the Sociology of Language, 35. Berlin: Mouton, 1985.

Elusive Decade of Hispanics. Miami: Cuban American Policy Center, Cuban American National Council, Fall 1989.

Escobar, Javier, Max Daggett, and Berta Savariego. *Bilingual Skills for Commerce and Industry*. Cincinnati: South-Western Publishing Co., 1984.

Ethnic Block Voting and Polarization in Miami. Miami, FL: Cuban American National Council, Summer 1991.

Ewell, Miranda, and David Schrieberf. "How Court Interpreters Distort Justice." *San Jose Mercury News* (17 Dec., 1989): 1 & 17A. (Pt. 1 of a three-part series).

Fawcett, Peter. "Teaching Translation Theory." *Meta* 26 2 (June 1981): 141-47.

Federal Court Interpreters Advisory Board. *Report to the Director*. Washington, D.C.: Administrative Office of the United States Courts, 1987.

Ferenczy, Gyula. "Postgraduate Short-Term Training of Interpreters and Translators at the Faculty of Liberal Arts, Budapest University. *Babel* 23, no. 4 (1977): 181-82.

Festinger, Nancy. "Court Interpreting: Maintaining Linguistic Fidelity in the Crossfire of Legal Battles." Lecture given at the annual C.I.T.A. dinner, New York City, December 7, 1985.

Frankenthaler, Marilyn R. "How to Work with Court Interpreters." *New Jersey Lawyer* 95 (Spring 1981): 24-30.

—. *Skills for Bilingual Legal Personnel. Técnicas para el personal bilingue en el área legal*. Cincinnati: South-Western Publishing Co., 1982.

—. "Spanish Translation in the Courtroom." *Social Action and the Law* 6, no. 4 (1980): 51-62.

Frankenthaler, Marilyn R., and L. McCarter. "A Call for Legislative Action: The Case for a New Jersey Court Interpreters Act." *Seton Hall Legislative Journal* 3, no. 2 (Summer 1978): 125-65.

Fromkin, Victoria, and Robert Rodman. *An Introduction to Language*. New York: Holt, Rinehart and Winston, Inc., 1988.

Gaddis Rose, Marilyn. *Translation Spectrum, Essays in Theory and Practice*. Albany, New York: State University of New York Press, 1981.

García Yebra, Valentín. *En torno a la traducción*. Madrid: Gredos, 1983.

—. *Teoría y práctica de la traducción*. 2 vols. Madrid: Gredos, 1982.

Garretson, Deborah A. "A Psychological Approach to Consecutive Interpretation." *Meta* 26, no. 3 (Sept 1981): 244-53.

Georges, Antoine. "Haiti: Language and Culture." Lecture given at the Workshop on Consecutive Interpretation, Executive Office for Immigration Review, Miami, FL, May 1990.

Gerver, David. "The Effects of Source Language Presentation Rate on the Performance of Simultaneous Conference Interpreters." In *Proceedings of the 2nd Louisville Conference on Rate and/or Frequency Controlled Speech*, edited by E. Foulke, 162-84. University of Louisville, 1969.

—. "Empirical Studies of Simultaneous Interpretation: A Review and a Model." In *Translation. Applications and Research*, edited by Richard Brislin, 165-203. New York: Gardner, 1976.

—. "The Effects of Noise on the Performance of Simultaneous Interpreters: Accuracy of Performance." *Acta Psychologica* 38 (1974): 159-67.

—. "Simultanoeus Listening and Speaking and Retention of Prose." *Quarterly Journal of Experimental Psychology* 24 (1974): 337-41.

Gerver, David, and H.Wallace Sinaiko, eds. *Language Interpretation and Communication*. New York and London: Plenum Press, 1978.

Gifis, Stephen H. *Law Dictionary*. New York: Barron's, 1984.

Giglioli, Pier Paolo, ed. *Language and Social Context*. New York: Viking Penguin, 1986.

Glemet, R. in R. Brower, ed. *On Translation*. Cambridge: Harvard University Press, 1958.

Glossary of Terms Used in the Federal Court. Washington, D.C.: Administrative Office of the United States Courts, 1980.

Goddard, K.A. "Translation and Bilingualism." *Babel* 18, no. 2 (1972): 18-23.

Gode, A. "Language as Culture." *Babel* 10, no. 1 (1964): 23-25.

Gold, David L. "On Quality Interpretation: II." *Babel* 22, No. 3 (1976): 117-19.

—. "Planning a School for Translators and Interpreters." *Babel* 21, no. 3 (1975): 107-8.

Goldman-Eisler, F. "Segmentation of Input in Simultaneous Interpretation." *Journal of Psycholinguistic Research* 1 (1972): 127-40.

González, Roseanne Dueñas. *The Design and Validation of an Evaluative Procedure to Diagnose the English Aural-Oral Competency of a Spanish Speaking Person in the Justice System.* Ann Arbor, Michigan: University Microfilms, 1977.

Greve, Frank. "U.S. Pays Dearly for its Scarcity of Translators." *Miami Herald* (Sunday, 9 June 1986): 20A.

Grosjean, François. *Life with Two Languages.* Cambridge: Harvard University Press, 1982.

—. "The Bilingual as a Competent but Specific Speaker-Hearer." Paper delivered at the Symposium on Bilingualism, Ninth Annual Boston University Conference on Language Development, October 1984.

Grusky, Lenne. "Using a New Technique for Witness Stand Interpreting." *ATA Chronicle* 18, no. 10 (October 1989): 12-13.

Guenthner, F. and M. Guenthner-Reutter, eds. *Meaning and Translation.* New York: New York University Press, 1978.

Hamers, Josiane F., and Michel H.A. Blanc. *Bilinguality and Bilingualism.* Cambridge: Cambridge University Press, 1990.

Hammond, Deanna L. "Translator and Interpreter Associations in the United States." *Hispania* 73 (September 1990): 689-91.

Handbook for Federal Grand Jurors. Foreword by The Honorable C. Clyde Atkins, U.S. District Court for the Southern District of Florida, 1980.

Hanna, B.T. "The Training of Conference Interpreters." *Meta* 3, no. 1 (1958): 12-17.

Hara, Fujiko. "Understanding the Silent Culture of the Japanese." *Meta* 33, no. 1 (1988): 22-24.

Haugen, Einar. *Bilingualism in the Americas: A Bibliography and Research Guide.* University, AL: University of Alabama Press, 1956.

Haughton, Linda. "Court Interpreting." Lecture given at the Mini Seminar on the Teaching of Legal Translation and Court Interpreting. Florida International University, 7 June 1986.

Henderson, John A. "Note-taking for Consecutive Interpreting." *Babel* 22, no. 3 (1976): 107-16.

—. "Some Psychological Aspects of Simultaneous Interpreting." *Incorporated Linguist* 21, no. 4 (1982): 149-52.

Hendrickx, Paul. "Enseignement de l'interprétation simultanée." *Babel* 15, no. 4 (1969): 216-20.

Herbert, Jean. "How Conference Interpretation Grew." In *Language Interpretation and Communication*, edited by David Gerber and H. Wallace

Sinaiko, 5-10. New York: Plenum, 1978.

—. *Manuel de l'interpréte*. Geneva: Georg, 1952.

Horn, Pierre L. "The Methodology of a College Course in Interpreting." *Modern Language Journal* 59 (1975): 25-28.

"How our Government Works." *U.S. News & World Report* (28 January 1985): 37-52.

Howe, Joseph, and Walker J. Blakely, eds. *Assignment in Trial Practice*. 4th ed. Boston: Little Brown and Company, 1975.

Ingram, Robert M. "Sign Language Interpretation and Public Policy in the United States." In *Languages in the International Perspective*, edited by Nancy Schweda-Nicholson, 213-22. Norwood, New Jersey: Ablex Publishing Corp., 1986.

"Interpreters' Job Action Halts Meetings at United Nations, New York." *L'Interprète* 2 (July 1974): 8-9.

Interpreter's Handbook. Office of the Chief Immigration Judge, Executive Office for Immigration Review, U.S. Department of Justice, n.d.

Joos, Martin. *The Five Clocks*. New York: Harcourt, Brace & World, 1967.

Kade, Otto, and Claus Cartellieri, "Some Methodological Aspects of Simultaneous Interpreting." *Babel* 17, no. 2 (1971): 12-16.

Kelly, Louis G. *The True Interpreter. A History of Translation Theory and Practice in the West*. New York: St. Martin's Press, 1979.

Knapp, Mark L. *Nonverbal Communication in Human Interaction*. 2nd ed. New York: Holt, 1978.

Kolers, Paul A. "Bilingualism and Information Processing." *Scientific American* 220 (1973): 78-86.

—. "It Loses Something in the Translation." *Psychology Today* (May 1969): 32-35.

Kordic, Mara. "A propos de l'interprétation consécutive — Traduction orale." *Babel* 16, no. 2 (1970): 80.

Kouindjy, Louis J. "Note on the Development of the Simultaneous Interpretation System." *L'Interpr0te* 2 (June 1972): 2-3.

Lado, Robert. "Language and Thought: Effect of Translation vs. Interpretation." *TESOL Quarterly* 13, no. 4 (December 1979): 565-71.

Lambert, Sylvie. "Information Processing among Conference Interpreters: A Test of the Depth-of-Processing Hypothesis." *Meta* 33, no. 3 (1988): 377-84.

Larson, Mildred. *Meaning-based Translation: A Guide to Cross-language Equivalence*. Lanham, MD: University Press of America, 1984.

Lawrence, David, Jr. "Mr. President, We *Need* Those Judges." *Miami Herald*

(Sunday, 28 April 1991): 3C.

Lawson, E.A. "Attention and Simultaneous Translation." *Language and Speech* 10 (1967): 29-35.

Leeth, John. "The Court Interpreter Examination." Office of Court Reporting and Interpreting Services. Washington: Administrative Office of the United States Courts, n.d.

Lipski, John M. "Spanish-English Language Switching in Speech and Literature: Theories and Models." *The Bilingual Review* (Sept-Dec. 1982): 191-212.

Loftus, Geoffrey, and Elizabeth F. Loftus. *Human Memory. The Processing of Information.* Hillsdale, New Jersey: Lawrence Erlbaum Associates, Inc., 1976.

Macías, Reynaldo F. "Language Choice and Human Rights in the United States." In *Language in Public Life*, edited by James Alatis and R. Tucker, 86-191. Washington, D.C.: Georgetown University Press, 1979.

McElhaney, James W. "Cross-Examination." *ABA Journal* (1 March 1988): 117.

Merril Valdés, Joyce, ed. *Culture Bound: Bridging the Culture Gap in Language Teaching*. Cambridge: Cambridge University Press, 1986.

Morawitz, Christiane de. "Sur l'enseignement de l'interprétation de conférence." *Babel* 12, no. 3 (1966): 39.

Neubert, Albrecht. "Semiotic Aspect of the Training of Interpreters and Translators." *Linguistische Arbeits Berichte* (Leipzig) 2 (1970): 10-18.

New Jersey Supreme Court Task Force on Translation and Interpretation Services. Background Report #21: *Interpreting and Translating as Professions.* Trenton, New Jersey. January 20, 1984.

Newmark, Peter. *Approaches to Translation.* Elmsford, NY: Pergamon Press, 1981.

—. *A Textbook of Translation.* London: Janus Book Publishers, Inc., 1986.

—. "The Theory and Craft of Translation." *Language Teaching & Linguistic Abstracts* 9, no. 1 (1976): 5-26.

Nida, Eugene. "Science of Translation." *Language* 45, no. 3 (1969): 483-98.

—. *Language Structure and Translation.* Stanford: Stanford University Press, 1975.

—. *Toward a Science of Translating*. Leiten, Netherlands: E. J. Brill, 1964.

Nida, Eugene, and Charles Taber. *The Theory and Practice of Translation.* Leiden: E.J. Brill, 1969.

Nida, Eugene, and William D. Rayburn. *Meaning Across Cultures.* Maryknoll, New York: Orbis Books, 1981.

Nostrand, Howard Lee. "Culture in Language Teaching: The Next Phase." *ADFL Bulletin* 20, no. 1 (September 1988): 29-34.

—. "Authentic Texts and Cultural Authenticity: An Editorial." *Modern Language Journal* 73 (1989): 49-52.

O'Barr, William M. "The Language of the Law." *Language in the USA*, edited by Charles A. Ferguson and Shirley Brice Heath, 386-406. Cambridge: Cambridge University Press, 1981.

—. *Linguistic Evidence. Language, Power, and Strategy in the Courtroom.* New York: Academic Press, 1982.

Olerón, P., and H. Nanpon. "Recherche sur la traduction simultanée." *Journal de Psychologie Normale et Pathologique* 62, no. 1 (1964): 73-94.

Oran, Daniel. *Oran's Dictionary of the Law*. St. Paul, Minn: West, 1983.

Palma, Janis. *Handbook for the Legal Profession: Working with Interpreters.* NAJIT, 1989.

Paneth., Eva, "The Interpreter's Task and Training." *The Incorporated Linguist* 1, no. 4 (1962): 102-9.

Pattern Jury Instructions. Criminal Cases. U.S. Eleventh District. District Judges Association. 1985 Edition. St. Paul, Minnesota: West Publishing Co., 1985.

Perkins, Jean A. "The Value of Foreign Language Study." *ADFL Bulletin* 20, no. 1 (September 1988): 24-25.

Pilley, A.T. "The Training, Qualifications and Professional Status of Interpreters." *Incorporated Linguist* 1, no. 3 (1962): 69-70.

Poplack, Shana. "Bilingual Competence: Linguistic Interference or Grammatical Integrity?" In *Spanish in the US Setting: Beyond the Southwest*, edited by Lucía Elías-Olivares, 107-29. Rosslyn, Va.: National Clearinghouse for Bilingual Education, 1983.

—. "Bilingualism and the Vernacular." In *Standard Language/Vernacular Relations in Bilingual Education*, edited by B. Hartford, A. Valdman, and C. Foster. New York: Plenum Press, 1980.

Pousada, Alicia. "Interpreting for Language Minorities in the Courts." *Language and Public Life*, edited by James E. Alatis and G. Richard Tucker, 186-208. Washington, D.C.: Georgetown University Press, 1979.

Probasco, Denise, and Patricia Pavone McDonald. *Court Interpreter Validation Study and Examination Plan*. Sacramento: State Personnel Board, June 1979.

Repa, J. "A Training Program for Court Interpreters." *Meta* 26, no. 4 (1981): 394-96.

Resnick, Rosalind. "New Law Aims to Rein in State's *Notarios Públicos*." *Miami Herald Business/Monday* (8 July 1991): 15.

—. "Unethical Notaries Prey on Immigrants." *Miami Herald Business/Monday* (13 March 1989): 7.

Richards, I.A. "Toward a Theory of Translation." In *Studies in Chinese Thought*. American Anthropological Association, vol. 5, Memoir 75. Chicago: University of Chicago Press, 1953.

Roberts, Roda P., *L'Interprétation aupres des tribunaux*. Ouvrage collectif. Ottawa: Editions de l'Université d'Ottawa, 1981.

—. "The Role and Teaching of Theory in Translator Training Programmes." *Meta* 23, no. 2 (1988): 164-73.

Robinson, Gail L. Nemetz. *Crosscultural Understanding. Processes and Approaches to Foreign Language, English as a Second Language and Bilingual Education*. New York: Pergamon, 1985.

Roditi, Edouard. "Interpreting: Its History in a Nutshell." Washington, D.C.: National Resource Center for Translation and Interpretation, Georgetown University, n.d.

Roy, John D. "The Difficulties of Limited-English-Proficient Individuals in the Legal Setting." In *The Language Scientist as Expert in the Legal Setting*, edited by Robert W. Rieber and William A. Stewart, 73-84. New York: *Annals of the New York Academy of Sciences*, vol. 606, 19 November 1990.

Rozan, J.F. *La Prise de Notes en Interprétation Consécutive*. Ecole d'Interpr0tes. Geneve: Georg, 1959.

Sánchez, Rosaura. "Spanish Codes in the Southwest." In *Modern Chicano Writers*, edited by Joseph Sommers and Tomás Ybarra-Franjo, 41-53. Englewood Cliffs: Prentice-Hall, 1977.

Sanders, Alain L. "*Libertad* and *Justicia* for All." *Time* (29 May 1989): 65.

Sapir, Edward. *Culture, Language and Personality*. Los Angeles: University of California Press, 1956.

Saville-Troike, Muriel, ed. *Linguistics and Anthropology*. Washington: Georgetown University Press, 1977.

Schmitt, C. "Translating and Interpreting, Present and Future." *Incorporated Linguist* 21, no. 3 (1982): 96-102.

Schweda-Nicholson, Nancy. "**Ad hoc** Interpreters in the American Judicial System: Equality, Inequality ... Quality?" *Meta*, forthcoming.

—. "Beyond the Court Interpreters Act of 1978: The Federal Court Interpreters Advisory Board." *Proceedings of the 1987 American Translators Association Annual Meeting*, edited by Karl Kummer, 281-86. Medford, NJ: Learned Information, Inc., 1987.

—. "Court Interpreter Training: A Growing Need." In *Proceedings of the 1985 Eastern Michigan University Conference on Languages for Business and the Professions*, edited by Geoffrey M. Voght. Washington, D.C.: ERIC Microfiche, 1986.

—. "Language Planning and Policy Development for Court Interpretation Services in the United States." *Language Problems and Language Planning* 10, no. 2 (Summer 1986): 140-57.

Seib, Gerald F. "Pardonnez-Moi, Mr. Bush: In French You Make No Sense." *Wall Street Journal* (21 June 1989): 1-A7.

Seleskovitch, Danica. "Création d'un doctorat de 3e cycle 'Science et techniques de l'interpretation et de la traduction,' délivré par l'Université de Paris III — Sorbonne Nouvelle," *Babel* 22, no. 3 (1976): 120.

—. "Interpretation, a Psychological Approach to Translation." In *Translation. Applications and Research*, edited by Richard W. Brislin, 92-115. New York: Gardner Press, 1976.

—. *Interpreting for International Conferences*. Washington, D.C.: Pen & Booth, 1978.

—. *Langage, Langues et Mémoire. Etude de la Prise de Notes en Interprétation Consécutive*. Paris: Letters Modernes Minard, 1975.

Seleskovitch, Danica, and Marianne Lederer. *Pédagogie Raisonnée de L'Interprétation*. Bruxelles-Luxembourg: Didier +rudition, 1989.

Senna, Joseph J., and Larry J. Siegel. *Introduction to Criminal Justice*. St. Paul, Minnesota: West Publishing Co., 1987.

Simon, Paul. *The Tongue-Tied American*. New York: Continuum Press, 1980.

Smith, Marjorie. "A Matter of Interpretation." *Newsweek* (December 14, 1987): 9.

Szuki, Atsuko. "Aptitudes of Translators and Interpreters." *Meta* 33, no. 1 (1988): 108-14.

Taber, Charles. "Sociolinguistic Obstacles to Communication Through Translation." *Meta* 25, no. 4 (1980): 421-29.

Taber, Charles R., and Euguene A. Nida. *La traduction: théorie et méthode*. London: Alliance Biblique Universelle, 1971.

Tayler, Marilyn R. "Interpretation/Translation Assistance in Immigration Proceedings." *Immigration Journal* 11, no. 3 (July-Sept. 1988): 45, 57-62.

—. "Interpretation/Translation Assistance in Immigration Proceedings." *Immigration and Nationality Law*, edited by Edwin R. Rubin and Robert E Juceam, 9-25. San Diego: American Immigration Lawyers Association, vol II, June 1988.

Thiéry, Christopher. "True Bilingualism and Second Language Learning." In *Language Interpretation and Communication*, edited by Ed. David Gerver and H. W. Sinaiko, 145-54. New York: Plenum, 1978.

Trial at Nuremberg. Jack Kaufman (writer and director). United Artists Television. Wolper Productions, Inc. Film documentary, 1964.

Ullmann, Stephen. "Why Words Change their Meaning." *Incorporated Linguist* 8, no. 1 (1968): 2-6.

18 United States Code. Section 1827, 1978.

28 United States Code. Section 1828, 1988.

"U.S. Hispanic Population at All-time High." *Miami Herald* (12 October 1989): 8A.

United States Congress. Senate Committee on the Judiciary. Report 100-590 (1988).

United States Senate. The Bilingual Courts Act. Hearings before the Subcommittee on Improvements in Judicial Machinery of the Committee on the Judiciary, Ninety-third Congress, Second Session on S. 1724. Washington, D.C.: U.S. Government Printing Office, 1974.

"Use of Two Interpreters to Cover a Trial When Necessary." *Court Administration Bulletin* (March 1991): 2-3.

Valdés, Guadalupe. "When Does a Witness Need an Interpreter? Preliminary Guidelines for Establishing Language Competence and Incompetence." *La Raza Law Journal* 3 (Spring 1991): 1-27.

Van Slype, G., *et al. Better Translation for Better Communication.* Oxford: Pergamon Press, 1983.

Vázquez-Ayora, Gerardo. *Introducción a la Traductología.* Washington, D.C.: Georgetown University Press, 1977.

Viereck, Wolfgang. "Drug Lingo." *Idioma* (Munich) 5-6 (1968): 193-198.

"Voulez-Vous Devenir Interpr0te de Conférence?" Geneva: *AIIC* (Journal of the International Association of Conference Interpreters) 1979: 11pp.

Wallace, Richard. "Some Notaries Prey on Aliens, INS Says." *Miami Herald* (24 September 1988): 1B & 2B.

Warden, J.G. "Suggestions for a Course in Oral Translation." *Incorporated Linguist* 5, no. 3 (1966): 70-76.

Weber, Wilhelm K. *Training Translators and Conference Interpreters.* ERIC Clearinghouse on Languages and Linguistics Language in Education: Theory and Practice, 58. Orlando: Harcourt Brace Jovanovich, 1984.

Weis, Erich. "Translation — a Profession." *Babel* 13, no. 1 (1967): 14-22.

Welcome to the Federal Court. Washington, D.C.: Federal Judicial Center, Dolley Madison House, n.d.

Westman, Donald, and Craig Chapman. "Applications of the Language Laboratory to Training in Simultaneous Interpretation." *Meta* 22, no. 4 (1977): 264-9.

Whorf, Benjamin Lee. "The Retention of Habitual Thought and Behavior to Language." In *Language, Thought, and Reality*, edited by John B. Carroll, 134-59. Cambridge, MA: M.I.T. Press, 1978.

INDEX